The Concise Dictionary
of Medical-Legal Terms

The Concise Dictionary of Medical-Legal Terms

A general guide to interpretation and usage

Joseph A. Bailey, II, MD, FACS

Orthopaedic Surgery and Orthopaedic Genetics
Independent Medical Examiner and Qualified Medical Examiner for
State of California Worker's Compensation Division

Instructor at California State University, San Bernadino
Division of Undergraduate Studies

Instructor at University of California, Riverside
Division of Biomedical Sciences

The Parthenon Publishing Group

International Publishers in Medicine, Science & Technology

NEW YORK   LONDON

36430920

Library of Congress Cataloging-in-Publication Data
Bailey, Joseph A., 1935–
    A concise dictionary of medical-legal terms: a general
    guide to interpretation and usage / Joseph A. Bailey II.
        p. cm.
    ISBN 1-85070-680-8
    1. Medical jurisprudence--Dictionaries. I. Title.
    [DNLM: 1. Jurisprudence--United States--dictionaries.
    2. Forensic Medicine--dictionaries. W 13 B154c 1998]
RA1017. B35 1998
614'.1'03--dc21
DNLM/DLC
for Library of Congress.   97–8985
                                                      CIP

British Library Cataloguing in Publication Data
Bailey, Joseph A.
    A concise dictionary of medical-legal terms: a general
    guide to interpretation and usage
    I. Medical jurisprudence - Terminology - Dictionaries
    I. Title
    614. 1'014

    ISBN 1-85070-680-8

Published in the USA by
The Parthenon Publishing Group Inc.
One Blue Hill Plaza,
PO Box 1564, Pearl River
New York 10965, USA

Published in the UK and Europe by
The Parthenon Publishing Group Ltd.
Casterton Hall, Carnforth
Lancs. LA6 2LA, UK.

Copyright © 1998 Parthenon Publishing Group.

Printed and bound by
Bookcraft (Bath) Ltd., Midsomer Norton, UK

Foreword

I recommend this book to all who are interested in an easy-to-use reference work. I found this book to be an excellent general explanation of the history of words I use every day and an explanation of their background. Over my years as a judge, I have read many professional books, articles and medical reports. At times, there are terms which need definition to make sense of what I am asked to digest. This practical book gives the reader a quick means of defining terms and also a philosophical basis for them. The style of presentation in this work is more than a pro-forma dictionary presentation.

In my early years as a judge, I was introduced to Dr Bailey through his skill at writing medical reports submitted in a large number of my cases. I have also observed him during cross-examination in the courtroom. His knowledge is excellent and his means of explaining medical conditions is easily understood. At a time when other physicians wrote long medical reports, Dr Bailey kept his concise and straightforward.

I have read this book and find it very useful as a reference tool both for my professional work and at home. This work reflects Dr Bailey's time, care and dedication to terminology. Communication is the key in any field based on words. It is an art form premised on language. I compliment Joseph Bailey on setting forth an excellent working tool which I can use every day.

Robert E. Welch
Presiding Workers Compensation Judge

What is medical-legal?

Medical-legal is an umbrella term for the dynamic interaction of law and medicine. It has two major subdivisions — the *regulation of medicine by law* and the *utilization of medicine by law*. The value of the regulations and utilizations is dependent on who is assessing it.

The *regulation of medicine* is performed by the legal system which is overwhelmingly comprised of attorneys. Methods of thinking in law and medicine are as different as oil and water. They do not mix well together in general and regarding the regulation of medicine in particular. Certain regulations are double-edged swords, for example, from one medical perspective of the sword, those regulations likely to be considered appropriate include the licensing procedures, many of the public reporting requirements (e.g. specific infectious diseases), certain restrictions on practice, and certain redresses for wronged patients. From the opposing edge of the sword, the latter three are viewed medically as inappropriate or even morally wrong, as with issues pertaining to abortion, termination of treatment, informed consent, confidentiality, duty to warn, legal and patient rights contrary to sound medical judgment.

The *utilization of medicine by law* is very broad within the public and private fields of law. *Criminal law* is a large component of public law. It requires not only *forensic medicine* but also the *forensic sciences*. Forensic medicine is the medical specialty that assists in the detection of crime. Forensic scientists are quasi-medical or non-medical persons who do the same. Members of forensic science and medicine tend to work harmoniously with the law. Such members include;

- Forensic pathologists — using postmortem examination as a major tool, they determine the cause of sudden and unexpected deaths. They are also involved in occupational injury, negligent injury, motor vehicle accidents, paternity suits, child custody conflicts, etc.

- Forensic toxicologists — arising into prominence in the nineteenth century, they began by giving evidence on such topics as intentional poisonings and drug use. Subsequently, they have been involved in industrial and environmental poisoning situations.

- Forensic anthropologists — they identify bones and skeletal remains using comparative body and bone measurements and morphology.

- Forensic odontologists — they identify human remains through dental evidence (e.g. bite-mark impressions).

- Forensic chemists and biologists — they use DNA 'fingerprinting' and other measures to determine the content, type, authenticity, and so on of pertinent evidence.

- Criminalists — those who retrieve and analyze physical evidence related to the crime. This might include drugs, hair, fibers, soil, blood, paint chips, firearms or other weapons, fingerprints, documents. The largest crime laboratory in the world is operated by the US Federal Bureau of Investigation.

- Jurists — their basis of the classification of disease is concerned with the legal circumstances in which (sudden) death occurs, the cause of which is not clearly evident. Thus, some deaths and diseases are classified as medical-legal and fall within the jurisdiction of coroners and medical examiners.

- Forensic psychiatrists — as early as the nineteenth century they determined the mental health of an individual to stand trial and thus, his blame worthiness. Later, this was expanded to include testimony involving injuries related to crimes, assault, rape, the necessity for involuntary commitment, and whether or not ones criminal behaviour was the product of mental illness (with an inability to distinguish right from wrong).

Utilization of medicine in private law is very prominent in certain subdivisions of torts. From a doctor's perspective, torts relate primarily to personal injury or in any issue involving significant mind/body negligence.

Whether there is utilization of medicine in private or public law, the term medical jurisprudence seems most appropriate. Some consider *medical jurisprudence* to be synonymous with *legal medicine*. However, the term legal medicine seems to be more broad and more in the realm of 'medical-legal' or 'the legal aspects of medicine.' Somewhere within all of these confusing synonyms the term *health law* is used. Health law would seem to apply more to the public reportings and resultant actions pertaining to communicable diseases overseen by public health officials. Nevertheless, jurisprudence is the science of law or a system of laws scientifically considered, classed, and interpreted. Examples of 'medical jurisprudence' include (1) those of sex relations — rape, pregnancy, delivery, legitimacy; (2) inflicted injuries — wounds, poisoning, infanticide, homicide; (3) disqualifying diseases — mental alienation; (4) deceptive practices (e.g. feigned diseases); (5) questions of identity, age, and life insurance.

As used in this dictionary the term medical-legal means

the science that deals with the relation and application of medical facts to legal problems. Those medical or non-medical personnel giving legal evidence may appear before courts of law, administrative tribunals, inquests, licensing agencies, boards of inquiry or certification, or other investigative bodies. No matter how it is defined, doctors cannot avoid medical-legal involvement. Doctors' participation in the medical-legal field may be at a mild, slight, moderate, or extreme level as follows:

- Mild medical-legal involvement: doctors certify persons for national insurance plans or Workers' Compensation; certify the occurrence of a birth; certify the cause of death; notify the authorities of any cases of specified infectious diseases, or other public reporting requirements.

- Slight medical-legal involvement: in personal injury or Workers' Compensation cases doctors primarily provide treatment. They can serve as percipient witnesses by relating facts they have observed and without making interpretations of their observations. Also, they may determine when mentally disturbed persons need to be detained to protect themselves or others.

- Moderate medical-legal involvement: this includes those doctors who not only diagnose and treat patients in litigation but use special words in addressing disputed issues. For example, in the Workers' Compensation arena, the 'Big 5' involvements are the determinations

for and the resultant degree to which there should be provisions for: (i) therapy; (ii) temporary disability; (iii) personal disability benefits, (iv) rehabilitation; and (v) death benefits, if applicable. Otherwise, doctors here serve as expert witnesses — interpreting facts they have observed using special medical knowledge.

- Extreme medical-legal involvement: this is the performance of those activities that can be classified as forensic. It may encompass dramatic activities like determining the size and sex of a body by examining just a few bones, identifying a corpse from its dental pattern, or detecting evidence of rape or of unsuspected murder. Much less dramatic, but perhaps more common, are disease and death caused by exposure of the individual to some unrecognized danger to health in her working or living condition. Could the illness or disease be attributable to fumes or dusts in a factory?

In summary, the term *medical-legal* covers the regulation and utilization of medicine by the legal profession. The utilization of medicine can be in public law or private law. It is with criminal law (public law) that forensic medicine or forensic sciences applies. There seems to be no generally accepted term for the doctors' involvement in torts (private law) beyond that of a *personal injury doctor* or a *Workers' Compensation doctor*. Medical jurisprudence covers the employment of medical knowledge for the clarification and settlement of certain problems arising in law courts. In short,

Preface

If wisdom can be defined as knowledge of the truth, used in the correct way, in the right system, and at the appropriate time, then the goal of higher thinking is to have knowledge that leads to wisdom. Expertise in theory, training and experience make for reliable judgments. Reliable judgments are fundamental for the correct application of knowledge to realistic situations and both make one superior in one's field. And that is the purpose of this dictionary.

This dictionary brings together many of those philosophies, principles, causes and effects, approaches, and other fundamentals that seem to be relatively stable in medical-legal spheres. Such a determination has been made based on those repeating terms and concepts noted throughout my 25 years of professional experience in all sorts of medical-legal arenas — particularly in the California Workers' Compensation System. In fact, this dictionary has at its core those word concepts used in putting together *The Handbook for Workers Compensation Doctors* (Institute of Continuing Education, PO Box 1662, Orange, California 92668).

Surprisingly, there remain in medical-legal circles many terms and concepts that are still undefined (e.g. repeated), hazily defined (e.g. substantial), confusingly defined (e.g. proximate cause) or defined with a significant 'double meaning' (e.g. speculate). Then there are those commonly used but unnamed methods that are clumsy to explain. For these I have coined terms such as *sub rosa* observations and palpitations. Otherwise every attempt has been made to stay with established tradition.

One of the problems in trying to understand medical and legal language is that experts use terms in the context of the topic at hand. Such an approach allows for adequate 'bits and pieces' discussions. However, for the purpose of seeing similarities and differences in a broader perspective, this dictionary stresses the 'big picture'. Hence, many skeletal frameworks have been offered as a spring-board for analytical and synthesis thinking. Examples include a classification of law, a classification of medical patients, and the scope of pathological lesions.

A fun addiction for me is to track down fascinating stories of words. Excerpts are presented in this dictionary for several reasons. First, to carry the reader back to ancient thought as to what premier words meant. Often ancient thought has many advantages.

Second, to show broader meanings of words that have been confiscated by medicine or law. To know both the special and broader meanings enables one to select, explain and apply appropriate words and their definitions for the fashioning of 'common ground'. This helps one either avoid trouble or get out of trouble in report writing, depositions and/or as a witness in court.

Third, to show that medicine and law use different words for the same concept. For example, in the Anglo-Saxon, Norman-French and Latin-Greek collocation, one trio of the legal system is that of ask/question/interrogate. Similarly, a medical trio pertaining to the same concept is leech/doctor/physician. Becoming aware of such trios helps make medical and legal terminology less overwhelming.

Fourth, learning stories behind words gives useful 'memory hooks' for otherwise drab and hard to remember terms (e.g. syndrome). In putting together these stories, it was necessary to shape 'bits and pieces' of information. I believe that in abstract matters something does not have to be absolutely true for it to get the job done. This is how the fun type of the Scientific Method works (see entry in text).

The information in this dictionary is particularly designed to help those just entering the medical-legal field. For more detailed or specific knowledge the reader should consult more comprehensive references that are specific to his or her local legal system. No two systems have exactly the same constitution, statutes or rules for civil law, common law or court procedures. In the USA, for example, there are 51 court systems – 50 states plus the federal court system. Thus, it is prudent to consult experts in the medical-legal field for refinements peculiar to one's locale.

Whether out of my unending curiosity or my intense desire for the truth I have unintentionally put many friends and acquaintances on the spot with my questions about the meanings of words we use every day. To all of them I offer my apologies and extend my appreciation, especially to Jabbour Semaan, who has given excellent treatment to my patients over the last 15 years; Attorney Dick Zeigler for his support in supplying me with reference material; Fred Williams for our heated but friendly discussions about concepts; to my highly skilled typists and office staff, Kim Kirchoff, Marilyn Jackson, Kay Ruffolo, Opal Eshelman and Vickie O'Brien; to my sons Brian and Joey; and Adelita Castro who has been consistent over the last 18 years in supplying me with thought-shaping information as well as diplomatic criticisms.

Joseph A. Bailey, II
San Bernardino,
California
1998

A priori As a way of thinking, this begins the story of reasoning. Earliest man associated ideas on the basis of cause and effect relations. By inferring certain effects (e.g. smoke) from a given cause (e.g. fire) or by working from a general principle towards a necessary conclusion based on them, they were engaged in a priori (i.e. deductive) thinking. By contrast, working back from effect to cause (e.g. from death to disease – from particular instances towards a general law), they were using a posteriori (i.e. inductive) thinking. As a method of thinking, a priori was in the hub of knowledge. With traditional subjects of metaphysical (i.e. concerning things outside sense experience) inquiry – namely God, freedom of the will, and the immortality of the soul or with the classical philosophical problems concerning the nature of truth, goodness and beauty, a priori judgments would be reached by reference to axioms. For example, in mathematics and logic, theorems were deduced from given axioms by individual introspection – investigating a concept independently of what a person might discover through the occurrence. Because theorems are not verifiable by observation or experiment, they were continually attacked philosophically by Empiricists who believed knowledge came only from experience, not theory. Today, a priori truths are considered true no matter what happens in the world of experience. Example: all female horses are female, or parallel lines do not meet. These 'truths' are dependent upon assuming the correctness of the axioms of the traditional systems of which they are a part. In short, a priori thinking is knowledge by reflection and their conclusions are true by authoritative agreement. To accuse others of having assumed a fact or conclusion a priori is often to disparage them for having failed to support a judgment through evidence or analysis. Compare with Analogy reasoning, A posteriori (i.e. after the fact). See also Axiom, Deductive reasoning, Disease, Speculate.

Abet see Incite

Ability see Rehabilitation

Abnormal A real definition is a set of necessary and sufficient conditions that exactly delimit a concept. However, abnormal, normal and normal variant cannot be adequately defined because they are words of focus. *Words of focus* pick out *the* ballpark where the game is played in order to distinguish it from similar ballparks where different games are played. This is called 'pigeonholing' or compartmentalizing a concept. From a Gaussian distribution curve comes the concept of abnormal and normal. This may be illustrated by a study of the distribution of a large number of shots on a target (which has been ruled with parallel, equidistant, vertical lines) by a marksman or woman. A line that bisects the middle compartment represents the 'bull's-eye' or the aim point of the target. Distributions of the shots may be tabulated by counting the shots and recording the percentages corresponding to the numbers found in each of the vertical compartments. There is a tendency to have the maximum number of shots at the centre with a progressive decrease in frequency as the distance increases from the center. The symmetry is also in the distribution of the shots either side of the center compartment. In other words, *normal* would be the central portion of a distribution curve and the extreme portions of the curve would be abnormal. Between normal and abnormal would be *normal variant*. On the extreme left of this curve is 'negative abnormal' and on the extreme right 'positive abnormal'. Both must be considered in relation to something. For example, if negative abnormal is considered destructive, then negative abnormal people are those who break rules so as to significantly harm themselves and/or others. By contrast, positive abnormal people break rules constructively and create new patterns or standards. In medicine, manifestations of a disease would be considered as negative abnormal while *adaptation* is positive abnormal. Typically, abnormal attracts the most attention. See also Adaptation, Normal, Normal Variants.

Absolute certainty see Beyond reasonable doubt, Scientific method

Absolute end see Death, End

Absolute facts see Evidence, Facts

Abuse of process see Malicious

Acceleration In medicine it is when a lesion undergoes adverse progression with increased rapidity. Compare with Precipitated disease or injury. See also Reoccurrence of an injury.

Accumulative microtrauma Minor successive injuries to the same part of the body or normal activities which alone are insufficient to cause disability but whose total effects result in a condition causing disability or injury. See also Continuing trauma, Date of injury.

Accuse see Appeal

Acquired medical conditions These are of a non-genetic nature. These can be: (a) *congenitally acquired* lesions (those external factors that affect the developing fetus *in utero*); (b) *tarda conditions* (those congenital/developmental lesions present before or at birth; but not manifest until sometime after birth); or (c) *Post natal acquired* injuries or diseases, which may be of a psychological and/or medical nature. Compare with Congenital conditions, Heritable, Inherited, Tarda.

Act That process of power that can be within a person or external to the person. Compare with Action. See also Event, Trust.

Act of God An event that happens purely through the operation of nature independent of, and uninfluenced by, human agency or human negligence.

Action That process of power that is external to a person. Compare with Act.

Activities of daily living (ADL) This denotes the basic activities that are needed for daily life. It includes self-care (e.g. preparing food, eating, cleaning up and personal hygiene); performing daily home activities (e.g. caring for the home and personal finances); social, hobby and recreational activities; means of getting to and from different places, stores or work; communication activities; and work activities, etc. How ADLs are related to the particular environment of the individual patient is an important aspect of rehabilitation. See also Non-work activities.

Activity terms see Box 1 Activity terms, Vocational rehabilitation terms

Actual notice see Notice

Actual restrictions These are activities a person cannot do because of physical inability or because the activity produces severe pain. For example, a patient with a frozen right shoulder cannot do overhead work with the right upper limb.

Acute From the Latin *acutus*, meaning sharp, pointed, needle. This is a concept that began with Hippocrates. It referred to a sharp, sudden or severe type of disease that tends to lead quickly to a crisis (e.g. acute appendicitis). Acute specific injuries are those that result from mechanical traumas which induce rupture of cells. *Immediate operative* treatments are between 4 and 14 days. Otherwise, in medicine, acute often refers to an arbitrary time period of 3 weeks, or sometimes 6 weeks. Compare with Chronic, Injury, Specific injury, Subacute.

Acute specific injuries see Acute

Adaptation These are advantageous changes of behavior, physiology or structure by which a person modifies him or herself into a particular environment. Adaptation is a beneficial mental or physical response to stress. Compare with Cumulative trauma, injury, normal, specific injury. See also Abnormal, Health, Stress.

Adaptive responses see Normal

Adjective law Deals with rules of practice or procedure. It provides a method to enforce or maintain rights and to obtain redress if they are violated.

Adjudicate To hear and render a final judgment in a legal proceeding. See also Adjudication.

Adjudication Is the determination of a controversy and a pronouncement of a judgment based upon the available evidence. It implies a final judgment of the court. See also Adjudicate, Disposition.

Adjusters Investigate, set right, arrange and settle litigated claims regarding personal injury or property damage. See also Claims examiners.

Box I Activity terms

Balancing	Maintaining body equilibrium to prevent falling when walking, standing, crouching or running on narrow, slippery or erratically moving surfaces; or maintaining body equilibrium when performing gymnastic feats
Bending	Angulation from neutral-straight position about joint (e.g. elbow) or spine (forwards or lateral spine flexion)
Carrying	Transporting an object, usually holding it in the hands or arms or on the shoulder
Climbing	Ascending or descending ladders, stairs, scaffolding, ramps, poles and the like, using feet and legs and/or hands or arms. For climbing the emphasis is placed on body agility; for balancing, it is placed on body equilibrium
Crawling	Moving about on hands and knees or hands and feet
Crouching	Bending body downward and forward by bending legs and spine
Feeling	Perceiving attributes of objects such as size, shape, temperature or texture by means of receptors in skin, particularly those of finger tips
Fingering	Picking, pinching or otherwise working with fingers primarily (rather than with whole hand or arm as in handling)
Handling	Seizing, holding, grasping, turning or otherwise working with hand or hand (fingering not involved)
Kneeling	Bending legs at knees to come to rest on knee or knees
Lifting	Raising or lowering an object from one level to another (includes upward pulling)
Pushing	Exerting force on an object so that the object moves away from the force (includes slapping, striking, kicking and treadle actions)
Pulling	Exerting force on an object so that it moves towards the force (includes jerking)
Reaching	Extending the arms in any direction
Sitting	Remaining in the normal seated position
Standing	Remaining on ones feet in an upright position at a work station without moving about
Stooping	Bending body downward and forward by bending spine and waist

Terms that describe intensity of pain

A *severe* pain would preclude the activity precipitating the pain

A *moderate* pain could be tolerated, but would cause marked handicap in the performance of the activity precipitating the pain

A *slight* pain could be tolerated, but would cause some handicap in the performance of the activity precipitating the pain

A *minimal* (mild) pain would constitute an annoyance, but would cause no handicap in the performance of the particular activity (and would be considered a non-ratable permanent disability)

Terms that describe frequency of occurrence of symptoms

Occassional	Approximately 25% of the time
Intermittent	Approximately 50% of the time
Frequent	Approximately 75% of the time
Constant	Approximately 90–100% of the time

Administrative law Deals with the operation of the various executive and legislative agencies of government and prescribes what they are supposed to do and how they are supposed to execute it.

Administrative vision see Disability

Admiralty law Deals with maritime affairs, both criminal and civil. It is the law of the sea and is handled by the federal courts. See also Maritime law.

Admissible evidence Information that may be introduced in court to aid the judge or jury in deciding the merits of a case. Judges first determine if its value is outweighed by such factors as undue consumption of time, prejudice, confusion of issues or there is a danger that the jury will be misled. Such information is likely to be excluded if there are other ways to prove the necessary facts. See also Evidence.

Admission The voluntary acknowledgement that certain facts are true. It is a statement by the accused or by the adverse party that tends to support the charge or claim against her or him, but is not necessarily sufficient to establish guilt or liability. In a civil procedure, an admission is a pre-trial discovery device by which one party asks another for a positive affirmation or denial of a material fact or allegation at issue. See also Discovery, Stipulation.

Adrenaline high see Date of injury

Adversary system In an adversary system, the parties to a legal dispute are opponents, each producing in the trial evidence that supports his or her own position. As each side can present its opinion for impartial consideration, the adversary proceeding is the foundation of our system of justice. See also Litigants, Pain and suffering, Procedural law, Trial.

Adverse parties Are those antagonistic to some other. Two opposing lawyers may be strenuous antagonists during a trial but warm friends outside the court. Accordingly, adverse carries no idea of feeling and in this it differs from hostile. See also Adversary system, Litigants, Trial.

Adverse progression A downhill destructive course which can relate to health, tendencies, influences, facts and opinions. For prevention see Prophylactic, Relative rest, work restrictions. See also Future medical treatment, Homeostasis, Interim permanent disability

Advocate A person who pleads his or her client's case in a court of law. See Adversary system, Art of Medicine.

Afferent see Efferent

Affiant A person who makes a sworn statement for legal purposes. Affidavits and depositions denote testimony reduced to writing. Affidavits generally are not associated with cross-examination. Compare with Witness. See also Affidavit, Deposition, Evidence, Proof, Testimony.

Affidavit A written statement made under oath before an officer of the court, a notary public or someone legally authorised to certify the statement. See also Affiant, Oath.

Affirmative defense Although the charge is not denied, the defendant raises extenuating or mitigating circumstances (e.g. self-defense or entrapment) to avoid civil or criminal responsibility. This is a 'yes but' situation where the initial affirmative 'yes' is followed by the concealed, contradictory 'but'. See also Answer, Assumption of risks, Declaration, Defense, Duress, Extenuating circumstances, Foreseeable risk, mitigating circumstances, Negligence, Proximate cause.

Aggravate see Reoccurrence

Aggravated assault see Assault

Aggravation Is to make worse, more serious or more severe. This means that an injury can 'light up' pre-existing and presently dormant lesions (*reoccurrence*). Aggravation can also worsen a high or low-grade ongoing disease or injury condition regardless as to whether it is or is not causing a disability. According to California Labor Code Section 4663, aggravation of a pre-existing disease or condition may constitute an injury. However, under the California Labor Code Section 4750, the employer is liable only for that portion of disability reasonably attributed to the aggravation which makes apportionment proper. If the subsequent condition was caused by a new industrial incident, such as lifting, and this leads to a deterioration in the earlier condition it may be treated as an aggravation. Aggravation is particularly important in cumulative trauma where some work activity has speeded up the pathological process of slow cell death. Proper assessment of this considers the tissue structure most likely to be involved. Compare with Exacerbation. See also Apportionment terms, Injury,

Lighting up, Precipitated disease, Reoccurrence of an injury.

Aging Is an intrinsic irreversible and deleterious process resulting in a certain kind of progressive change in living systems coincidental with the passage of time. There is a decrease in viability and increase in vulnerability. These changes of bodily faculties, sensibility and energies render the person progressively more likely to die from an accidental cause of random incidence. In normal aging there is a 'reserve' reduction in the *seven factors of function* (i.e. *quickness of action, co-ordination of movement, strength, security, endurance, safety and prestige of physique*).

Agony see Pain

Agreed medical examiners see Referee, Universal witness

Agreement see Compromise settlement

Allegations of fact This is a statement of what the contributing party expects to prove, whether for the plaintiff or the defense. For example, in the plaintiff's statement of facts, contained in his complaint, he or she alleges crimes against the defendant. See also Answer, Defendant's complaint.

Allowed medical condition A condition that has been legally recognized or accepted as caused by an industrial incident. Even though this may be *medical fiction* doctors must still provide an opinion based on stated acceptance of the legally allowed condition. For example, the doctor might say, 'condition x' cannot be medically ascribed to the patient's industrial injury. However, since it has been recognized and accepted legally, in my opinion, the patient has a 5% impairment. The rating system used should then be stated (e.g. American Medical Association Guide I, II, III, IV, etc.). See also Medical Fiction.

Almost constant Continually recurring. See Chronic.

Alternative work see Americans with Disabilities Act

Ambiguous This carries the etymological notion of wandering around uncertainty. It is from '*Ambi*', meaning around, and 'ago' meaning go, thus producing 'going around' (i.e. to go round and round, shilly shally). *Limbo* is chaos in the choice of solutions because of multiple variables. This causes a person's mental processes to go round and round.

Ambulance chaser Lawyer or lawyer's agent who follows an ambulance to the scene of an automobile accident or other disaster to offer professional services to the injured and tries to persuade them to institute lawsuits for damages. This is considered unethical. Contrast with Ethics, Honesty, Integrity.

Amendment Comes from Latin *admendare*, to remove faults, correct. It is the act of altering or modifying a law, bill, resolution or motion, usually because of an error, defect or incompleteness of prior works. See also Expungement.

American Medical Association disability see Disability, Impairment.

Americans with Disabilities Act (ADA) Title I of 1990 ADA legislation prohibits discrimination in present or future employment against any *qualified individual with a disability* (QID). This includes health insurance and other fringe benefits. It also requires employers to provide 'reasonable accommodation' where feasible that will enable a QID to function in the job through modified or alternative work. A QID is a person with a physical or mental impairment that substantially limits one or more major life activities. In this respect a *substantial impairment limitation* is one that restricts the QIDs ability to perform either a class of jobs or a broad range of jobs in various classes when compared to the average person having comparable training, skills and abilities. The inability to perform a single, particular job does not constitute a substantial limitation. For example, if company X has only one job requiring lifting more that 75 lbs, the inability of the injured worker to lift 75 lbs would preclude that job, but would not qualify as a disability under ADA. A requirement of a QID is that he or she has the ability to perform the *essential functions* (i.e. the fundamental job duties) of the employment position with or without reasonable accomodation. It does not include incidental duties or functions. For example, the essential functions of a clerk include the ability to read, write, hear, walk, sit, type and operate any special type of machinery. If a clerk were unable to walk, a reasonable accommodation might be to assign mail distribution to another staff member and to increase the typing load of the injured clerk. However, the essential functions of a data entry position include the ability to read, write, sit and key in data. If the clerk was no longer able to key in data because of a carpal tunnel syndrome, the data entry firm would not be expected to try to accommodate this worker. Although the determination of a QID status is an administrative decision without legally requiring direct doctor involvement, employers will need to determine at an early stage not only if the person can do the whole job, but whether he is capable of performing the essential functions of the position. Employers should provide information on *how* a function is currently performed as well as describing *what* it involves. It would then be wise to obtain a doctor's opinion on the critical demands, risk factors and functional capabilities, or lack of functional capabilities, so the employer can determine if modified or alternate work is available. Appropriate and accurate medical information is needed by the employer in order to make these decisions, or doctors' reports are likely to be introduced in court as evidence regarding whether an individual has a disability as defined in the ADA and whether he or she can perform the essential functions of the position. The more specific, the more objective, and the more depth of medical information related to functional work capability that is in the doctors' reports, the more useful the reports. The published text of the ADA is available from the Equal Employment Opportunities Commission (EEOC), The Bureau Of National Affairs Inc., Washington, DC 20037. This will be an area of major importance in the future. See also Essential functions, Disability, Discrimination, Job tasks, Modified work.

Amicus curiae 'A friend of the court.' This is a bystander, usually an attorney, who gives information on some matter of law in regard to which the judge is doubtful or mistaken.

Analogy reasoning Is the simplest and most popular form of reasoning. It is based upon the general principle that 'if two things resemble each other in many points, they will probably resemble each other in more points.' This can lead to a large degree of error. For example, it might be said that because mushrooms are edible, then toadstools (which resemble them) must also be fit to eat. Prejudiced people sometimes use this form of reasoning to infer, for instance, that because James Smith has a red nose and is a drunkard, then Sam Jones who also happens to have a red nose is also a drunkard. It can lead to a dangerous act of lazy reasoning. Unfortunately, many do believe these false analogies. Compare with Deductive reasoning, Inductive reasoning.

Analysis To think in a reasoning manner involves three processes: analysis, comparison and classification. Analysis is taking apart the quality of things for the

purpose of examination. It is 'splitting hairs' as opposed to 'lumping hairs'. See also Classification.

Anasarca see Edema

Anatomical abnormality The part is present but subnormal (e.g. weakened quadriceps muscle) or supernormal (over-strengthened quadriceps muscle relative to the hamstrings). In other words, there is 'too much or too little.' The law considers these as 'objective', but medically they may be anywhere on the 'objective/subjective scale.' Compare with Anatomical loss, Functional abnormality, Functional loss, Objective minus. See also Facts, Objective, Objective/subjective scale.

Anatomical loss Is an actual loss of a body part. This is objective. Compare with Anatomical abnormality, Functional abnormality, Functional loss. See also Facts, Objective.

Anatomical position This is the starting point for the measurements of joints. The patient is erect with the upper limbs hanging at the sides of the body and the palms turned forward so that the ulnar boarder of the little fingers touch the outer side of the thighs. In this position the anatomical references can be discussed or measured in a standard manner. See Figure 1.

Anatomical references These are the terms used when referring to the body. The two chief planes of the body are the *sagittal plane* (dividing the body into right and left halves) and the *coronal plane* (dividing the body into front and back). When the body is divided into top and bottom, this is the *horizontal or transverse plane*. There are two surfaces of the body, the *front* (anterior, ventral) and the *back* (posterior, dorsal). The head end of the body is called *Cephalad* (superior, upper), while the opposite end is called *Caudad* (inferior, lower). *Medial* (mesial, ulnar) describes parts nearest to the sagittal plane, while *lateral* (radial, fibular) describes those that are farthest. In *supination* the palms and soles of the feet are directed to the face but in *pronation* the palms and feet look away from the face. *Internal* defines inner relationships of the body (e.g. heart, lungs, liver); *external* defines outside relationships (e.g. hair). *Proximal* (or central) is the beginning of a part such as the arm or thigh. This contrasts with distal (or peripheral) which designates distance from the source (e.g. a hand or foot). Orthopaedists describe any limb problem with respect to what happens to the distal portion (e.g. valgus or varus position of the legs). See Figures 1, 5 (page 57).

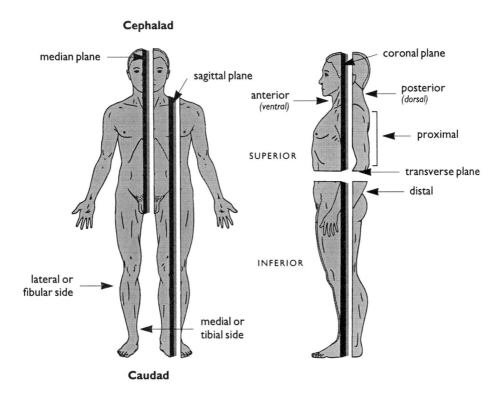

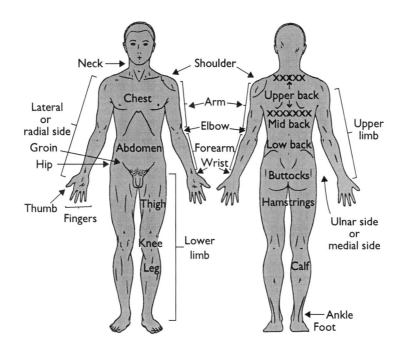

Figure 1 The 'anatomical reference' terms

Anesthesia dolorosa Pain in an area or region that is anesthetized or anesthetic

Anger Ancient Indo-Europeans thought that this negative emotion related to a constriction, squeezing, strangling or choking, similar to that of anxiety. It contained a notion of trouble, sorrow, distress or affliction. This gave rise to 'grief'. By the thirteenth century anger was still part of the concept of 'rage'. The meaning of rage then moved towards 'mad' (as with a rabid dog) and on to 'insane' (disordered intellect). Anger bifurcated in the direction of 'indignant', 'inflamed' and 'wrathful'. Anger is now considered a psychologically inflamed mind. See also Anxiety, Suffer.

Anglo-American law see Procedural law

Anguish Anger that causes suffering. See Anxiety, Anger

Answer Is the defendant's response to the plaintiff's allegations as stated in a complaint. It contains a denial of all the allegations the defendant wishes to dispute, as well as any affirmative defenses by the defendant and any counterclaims against the plaintiff. If a defendant fails to answer a summons or complaint, he may be liable for default for damage claimed in it. In a relevant answer, the person admits those allegations believed to be true but denies the rest. Compare with Brief, Declaration, Pleadings, Reply. See also Contested claim, Defendant, Defense.

Anterior An anatomical reference term used when observing and discussing the patient. It is the front, ventral or face-side surface of the patient's body. Compare with Posterior. See also Anatomical references and Figure 1.

Anxiety As a concept it originates from the Indo-European base of *angg*, meaning narrow as in breathing. Anything interfering with breathing meant a loss of self-control. The ancients thought that when the central breathing rhythm was broken, it would be necessary to struggle to catch your breath; this was called *worry*. The resulting choking or suffering, would be hard to keep to yourself. During the middle ages deliberate choking was used by the law as part of its trial by ordeal methods. If the accused was innocent, the angel Gabriel would intervene. *Anguish*, in fourteenth century England, had distress or suffering as its central notion. By the sixteenth century the meaning of anguish plus anxiety had reverted to the Latin *angere*, to choke or to strangle. Both implied mental or physical pain, but intensely so in the case of anguish. Both were caused by self-torturing (*distress*). See also Anger, Suffer.

Apocrine see Sweat

Appeal Initially, it seems to have been used in the nautical context of 'directing a ship towards a particular landing.' Its use was then extended metaphorically to mean 'address' or 'accost', from which came two legal applications – 'accuse' and 'call for the reversal of judgment'. Appeal had both these meanings when it was first adopted into English from old French *apeler*. 'Accuse' died out in the nineteenth century, but the latter meaning has flourished and led to the more general sense 'to make an earnest request.' Anciently, a person, who felt himself wronged would try and seize an opportunity to call out to the king for redress and thereby secure reversal of the judgment. From this derives the modern legal sense, a request by the losing party in a lawsuit or criminal trial that the judgment be reviewed by a higher court. The *appellant* (the one first named in published decisions) is the party to a lawsuit who appealed, while the *appelle* is the party prevailing in the lower court who argues, on appeal, against setting aside the lower courts' judgment. Appellees may also be called *respondents*. The superior court is said to have appellate jurisdiction. An appeal is usually based on a claimed error of law by the lower court judge. In a civil case either party can appeal; in a criminal case only the convicted defendant can appeal. See also Appellate judges, Court, Judicial reviews, Litigants, Respondent.

Appearance of the human body see Ectomorph, Endomorph, Mesomorph, Smoke screen

Appearance Literally means to make visible. A plaintiff or defendant (the litigants), or the attorney of either, makes the attendance required in court as a voluntary submission to the jurisdiction of the court. See also Litigants, Medical probability.

Appellant see Appeal

Appellate judges Such judges decide the outcome of appeals in judicial reviews. They sit in groups of between three and nine or more, depending on the court, to cancel out any bias. Their decision is published as a written opinion to provide a means of checking the outcome. See Appeals, Judicial reviews.

Appellee see Appeal

Appliance Is some device, apparatus, machine, contraption, contrivance, implement, equipment, gear or tool accessory designed specially for a particular use. Proper fitting and making of the appliances are as important as knowing which appliance to prescribe. If appliances are not reasonably comfortable or do not function properly, they are a hindrance to the patient rather than a help. In addition, appliances must accomplish the treatment required and not add an extra hazard in case management. California Labor Code Section 4600 allows for all medical, dental, surgical and hospital treatment reasonably necessary to cure or relieve from the effects of the injury. This includes nursing care, medications, medical and surgical supplies, artificial members, eyeglasses, hearing aids, crutches, braces of all types, corsets, supports, trusses, canes and other medical aids (California Labor Code Section 3208, 3209.5). This may include a Jacuzzi spa (44 California Compensation Case 748) or a van for paraplegics (41 CCC 344). See also Physical mobility aids.

Applicant Is the party who initiates the complaint in an action or proceeding. Related terms include petitioner, plaintiff and complainant. See also Litigants.

Application see Application for Adjudication of Claim

Application for Adjudication of Claim Original proceedings for the adjudication of compensation rights and liabilities start when an application is filed. The official title of the application for normal workers' compensation benefits is an Application for the Adjudication of Claim (simply called *application*). Applications are completed in longhand or by typewriter. The party applying for benefits is termed the *applicant* and the adverse party is termed the *defendant*. Supplementary proceedings are commenced by the filing of a petition setting forth the general nature of the controversy and the specific relief requested.

Apportionment Is a division of responsibility for permanent disability. It separates the slices of the '*disability pie*' relating to industrial exposure (e.g. the various specific and cumulative trauma episodes) and ratable factors of impairment that are independent of 'and uninfluenced by' industrial exposure. An employer is liable for that slice of the disability pie due solely to its industrial exposure. In California, it is not acceptable to apportion to lifestyle, hobbies, activities of daily living, or pre-existing non-disabling pathological lesions or aging. See also Apportionment terms, Average, Comparative negligence, Exacerbation, Preexisting, Pre-injury capacity.

Apportionment terms These include acceleration, aggravation, concurrent, exacerbation, the natural history of a disease, natural progression of disease or injury, a new injury or disease, occurrence, precipitated disease or injury, recurrent disease, reoccurence and superimposed condition. See also the individual entries for these terms.

Apprentice professional Are those just learning the system. Apprentice comes from old French *aprendre*, meaning to learn as in acquiring a skill. Compare with Journeyman doctors, Master professional.

Arbiter From the Latin *arbiter*, meaning judge. It refers to a non-judicial officer appointed by the court to decide a controversy according to the law. The arbiter unlike an arbitrator, can act arbitrarily, but he or she needs the court's confirmation on his or her decision for it to be final. Compare with Arbitrator. See also Fair play, Fair hearing.

Arbitration Is the submission of a dispute to an impartial person for a final decision (award). It can be either *compulsory arbitration* mandated by law (agreed to by the parties), *voluntary arbitration* (agreed by the parties) or *binding arbitration* (where the parties agree to be bound by the decision). In the case of binding arbitration there is no appeal. Compare with Proceedings. See also Award.

Arbitrator Is one who acts as an appointed judge or referee in a dispute referred to him or her by the parties. Arbitrators must remain aloof from the disputing parties. They may not act arbitrarily but, because they are accountable, must abide by the rules of procedure and act judiciously. Decisions usually cannot be appealed. Compare with Arbiter. See also Fair play, Fair hearing.

Archives see Document

Arising out of employment (AOE) The major aspect of AOE is the *mechanism of injury*; that is, whether and how work activities have led to the pertinent (pilot) injury. Doctors make this *cause and effect* determination that work exposure has, or has not, contributed to 'the injury.' Such conclusions are based upon reasonable medical probability (i.e. more likely than not). Essential clues for specific injuries are found in the medical history, while those for cumulative injuries and occupational diseases derive from risk factors noted in the work history. See also Cause, Mechanism of injury, Pilot injury.

Arithmetical progression see Exponential

Arm of the court see Referee

Arraignment see Preliminary hearing, Prosecution

Art of medicine Constitutes those humanistic qualities contributing to the cure of, or relief from, the effects of a disease or injury. *Humanistic qualities* include integrity, respect, compassion, availability, the expression of sincere concern, the taking of time to explain all pertinent aspects of the patient's illness to the patient, as well as being non-judgmental about lifestyles, attitudes and values of the patients, whatever the doctor's personal opinion. During the days of folk medicine, the art of medicine was at its zenith with suggestion playing a major role — for example, a phrase used frequently was 'this medicine will make you feel better.' Today, the art of medicine is being the patient's advocate as the doctor guides the patient through a disease or injury. Technically, medicine is not a science but a learned profession which is deeply rooted in a variety of sciences, so that the art and the science of medicine are the skillful use of medical knowledge, intuition and judgment. These are used to extract, from a mass of contradictory clinical findings and testing data, the clues that are worth pursuing and those that must be dismissed. This is followed by the selection of the best therapeutic modalities, which includes estimating whether a proposed treatment entails a greater risk than the disease. Medical knowledge, intuition and judgment are important factors in deciding whether to treat a patient or to engage in *masterful inactivity* or *watchful waiting*. See Deceptive patients, Doctor–patient relationship, Empathy, Narcotic, Red flag lesions, Red herring pathological lesions, Trust, Watchful waiting.

Artificial person see Classification of law

Ascites see Edema

Assault An (apparent) attempt to inflict bodily injury upon another by using unlawful force, accompanied by the apparent ability to injure that person if not prevent-ed. An assault need not result in a touching; this would be *battery*. Thus, no physical injury need to be proved to establish an assault. An assault may be either a civil or criminal offence. *Aggravated assault* is an assault with a dangerous or deadly weapon. See also Classification of law.

Assault and battery see Assault, Classification of law

Assertiveness see Behavior methods

Associational intelligence The ability to notice or perceive connections between disparate circumstances, people or things; it improvizes by fabricating from what is available. Compare with Intuitional intelligence, Spacial intelligence.

Assumption of risk This, in torts, is an affirmative defense used by the defendant in a negligence suit. The defendant claims that the plaintiff had knowledge of an obvious dangerous condition or situation and yet voluntarily exposed himself to the hazard, thereby relieving the defendant of legal responsibility for any resulting injury. In contract law, it is the agreement by an employee to assume the risks of ordinary hazards arising out of his or her occupation. See also Affirmative defense, Risk.

Assumptions Are that which is taken for granted on the basis of what is known or felt to be true and, from there, come to a conclusion. In every hypothesis something is allowed to be assumed. This is in the realm of a reasoned opinion, although some assumptions can be irrational. See also Facts, Hypothesis, Legal opinion facts, Presume.

Atrophy see Objective minus

Attachment Legally, this means bringing the property under the custody of the law. Medically, attachments are the establishment of specific and enduring emotional bonds. It is seen earliest between the infant (3 to 6 months old) and the parent(s). The infant and parent(s) must spend a *minimal amount of time interacting*. Once this requirement has been satisfied, it is the *intensity and quality* of the interaction that is the next most important factor. See also Trust.

Attorney–client privilege A confidential communication between the attorney and his or her client that is protected from disclosure to any other party. It can be waived by the client but not by the attorney. See also, *Ex parte*, Privileged communication.

Attractive nuisance see *Sine qua non*

Auscultation see Physical examination

Autacoids Are a heterogeneous group of several hundred chemical mediators that maintain the body's homeostasis. All are employed by the body in the execution of various functions in health, disease or injury. Practically no biological function is without them and autacoids have been detected in almost every tissue and body fluid. Examples are histamine, serotonin, prostaglandin and thromboxane.

Authenticate see Valid

Autonomic nervous system Derived from the Greek words 'autos' or self, plus 'nomos' or law, this term literally means 'a law unto-itself.' Hence, it is self-governing or independent. It was applied in 1898 by the English physiologist John Newport Langley to the cranial, thoracolumbar and sacral out flows. Previously, it had been called the involuntary nervous system by Gaskell. See also Emotions, Rage.

Autopsy From the Greek word *autopsia*, or seeing with your own eyes, this term is composed of *autos*, or self, plus *opsis*, or sight. Originally, the term meant ocular observation or a personal examination. Later it came to refer to an examination of the body. It is now restricted to mean a postmortem examination and was apparently introduced into medical terminology in this sense in 1829. See also Coroner, Postmortem.

Avenging see Negative pleasures, vengeance

Average In ancient times, the king or the lord of a manor apportioned contributions to their tenants. These contributions were required to be given to the sheriff. Contributions were determined by a certain percentage of a day's work as estimated by the number of the tenants' carthorses. Such a proportionate contribution was the average that may or may not have been altered by special circumstances. Furthermore, tenants had to carry a certain amount of provisions in wartime according to their positions. How they carried these provisions could vary. For example, a horse could carry more than a mule. However, the stipulated amount – the average – remained the same. By the sixteenth century the concept was applied to damage. When cargo at sea was damaged or thrown overboard in a storm, compensation money was paid to the losers by those whose cargo was received in good shape in order to 'average' out the loses. Since the eighteenth century, average has taken the current mathematical and general sense of 'mean', the medial sum, the usual or that which is typical of a group. A *mean* is the result obtained by dividing the sum of several different quantities by the number of quantities. For example, the average of 5, 8 and 14 is 9. See Apportionment, Damages, Normal, Pre-injury capacity.

Award Originally, this meant a favorable decision after an examination. Today, in law, it means to grant, concede or adjudge to after careful weighing of evidence. For example, a jury awards damages. Award decisions in arbitration are not subject to judicial review, although courts may review them. See also Arbitration, Damages.

Axioms Come from discovering a basic fact of reality that can not be broken down into smaller facts or parts. Axioms require no proof or explanation because 'it is what it is'. Axioms are seeds of knowledge. See A priori, Inductive reasoning.

Axonotomesis see Nerve injuries, Seddon classification of nerve injuries.

B

Bad days see Future medical treatment

Bad faith One of the meanings of the word *religion* is 'to bind tightly'. Belief in a religion 'binds' the believer to a definite code of morals and ethics, either out of fear of God or the desire to emulate the divine. *Honesty* was a major aspect of early religions. One who was honest acted with careful regard for the rights of others, especially in matters of business or property. *Honorable people* scrupulously observed the dictates of a personal honor that was higher than any demands of mercantile law or public opinion. Honest people did not steal, cheat, defraud or take an unfair advantage that would be allowed them. Thus, honorable people could trust each other. This trust, when combined with their religious belief, was called *faith* – a belief of the heart. Faith in ones peers was good and dishonesty was considered bad. Bad faith came to mean a breech of faith; a willful failure to respond to plain, well-understood statutory or contractual obligations. Bad faith was dishonesty in fact, in conduct or in the transaction concerned. Today, bad faith implies the conscious doing of a wrong because of dishonest intentions or moral transgressions. See also Default, Equity, Fair play, Good Faith, Grievance.

Bad rap To be accused or slandered unjustly.

Bail see Bailiff

Bailiff Is an example of how the French language has influenced English legal terms. For more than a century after the Norman Conquest in 1066, French was England's legal language. Thus, most of the technical terms of the law, especially of private law, are of French (and ultimately Latin) origin. The word bailiff derives originally from *bajulus*, the Latin noun meaning 'one who bears burdens for pay; porter', which gave rise to the French verb *bajulare* (to carry a burden, keep in custody). From this verb the French formed *baillier*, meaning 'to bear, manage, take care of, as well as to hand over and deliver.' In early French, the noun, *bail* (custody, jurisdiction) was

derived from baillier. This led to the noun bailiff meaning a king's officer having jurisdiction in a certain district. In the thirteenth century it developed the English metaphorical meaning of a 'person in charge, administrator.' Today, a bailiff is considered a court attendant or officer who keeps charge of a court session by keeping order, custody of the jury and custody of the prisoners while in court.

Bar The original sense of a 'rail' or 'barrier' has developed various figurative applications over the centuries. In the fourteenth century it applied to the 'rail in court before which a prisoner was arraigned' (as in 'prisoner at the bar'). In the sixteenth century it related to a 'partition separating qualified from non-qualified lawyers in hall' (as in 'call to the bar'). Today, the term 'bar' refers to the whole body of attorneys and counselors, or the members of the legal profession collectively. They are thus distinguished from the '*bench*', denoting the whole body of judges. Bar associations of attorneys may be either national, state or local. Compare with Bench.

Baseball arbitration This is when both qualified medical evaluators disagree on disputes in issue, the judge has to pick one or the other and not compromise between the two. It is an either/or decision. Therefore, unrealistic reports – too highly rated or too lowly rated doctors' report – are thrown out.

Battery see Assault

Beginning The first part of an action. Contributory causes meet at one point to initiate a beginning. Those causes are within the broad category of *origin*. 'Begin' comes from a prehistoric west German common verb *biginnan*. End is the antonym of begin, just as effect is the antonym of cause. In medicine, the beginning is the moment a normal situation or condition becomes abnormal (e.g. the start of a pathological lesion). In the taking of a history from a patient, the doctor focuses on when a problem began and then works back to the cause(s) as contributory to the beginning.

Behavior expressions These are expressions that are overt, tempered, masked or concealed. See the entries for each word.

Behavior methods used in court These are aggressive, passive, passive–aggressive and non-aggressive. Originally, aggression was a mild term of 'approaching somebody' or going after what a person wanted. This is the overall sense that is used here. *Destructive aggression* relates to a violent attack, while *passive* (from the Latin *pati*, to suffer) is the receiving of action. Therefore, passive–aggression behaviors are those which stay with the familiar while going after what a person wants in subtle ways. *Non-aggressive* behaviors include moving into a position of self-defense and self-protection. Once there, a person stays in this position and manages any situation as it occurs. There is no attacking or retreating. Assertiveness is non-aggressive.

Bench It was an old Spartan custom to have seating arrangements on benches that indicated the chain of command, with those of highest rank sitting at the front. In the thirteenth century, the legal profession borrowed this concept and applied it specifically to the seat on which government officials sat. These officials included judges or magistrates in court, bishops in the House of Lords, aldermen in the 'Council Chamber,' etc. By extension, bench signified the dignity of holding such an official status. In the House of Commons the leading members of the government occupy the front bench to the right of the speaker (*the treasury bench*). The opposition leaders occupy the opposite front bench. Those seated in the back benches (called *back-benchers*) were ordinary members of the House of Commons who did not hold office. Today, the bench consists of not only the place where the trial judge sits, but also the judges composing the court collectively and the court itself. 'The court' is to be distinguished from 'the *bar*'. See also Bar.

Bench warrant This is a court order for the arrest of a person guilty of contempt, against whom an indictment has been filed or who has not obeyed a subpoena to make an appearance. See also *Ex parte*, Subpoena.

Beneficial orthopedic work see Therapeutically beneficial

Beneficiary see Trust

Benign In medicine this refers to the slight or mild nature of an illness or the non-aggressive character of a cancer. Contrast with Guilt, Malignant.

Best evidence see Evidence

Beyond a shadow of doubt Occurs with the highest form of proof (e.g. demonstrative direct evidence). See also Certainty.

Beyond reasonable doubt In the past, prudent citizens had strong religious convictions about the divine. These constituted their moral standards and this was based on faith. Since there was no positive proof, their moral certainty was nearly 100%. During medieval times in Saxon England, guilt or innocence was often determined by the 'trial by ordeal' in which the suspect was subjected to a physical test (e.g. walking barefoot over red-hot plow shares). If the suspect passed the test unhurt, the jury was satisfied to a moral certainty that the suspect was innocent. Otherwise, the suspect was condemned as guilty. Charlemagne (AD 771–814), King of the Franks, defeated the Saxons in the ninth century and converted them to Christianity. He instituted the 'sworn inquest,' the forerunner to the grand jury. Sworn witnesses would then come forward to say the accused was innocent or guilty. This has carried over to the present time in as much as the standard in a criminal case requires that the jury be satisfied to a moral certainty that every element of a crime has been proven by the prosecution. This standard of proof does not require that the state establish absolute certainty by eliminating all doubt, but it does require that the evidence is so conclusive that all reasonable doubts are removed from the minds of the prudent person. This is equivalent to a scientific theory. Compare with Medical probability, Preponderance of evidence. See also Certainty, Clear and convincing evidence, Jury, Witness.

Binding arbitration see Arbitration

Biological Law see Scientific method

Biological normal see Normal

Birth see Death, Zygote

Blame Coming from Greek *blasphemein*, to say profane things about, blame, *blaspheme* originally carried the idea of judgment and sentence. Blaspheme retained the meaning of 'profanity' and was absorbed into the English language via religion. Blame became 'to scold,' as chiding often occurs before the real culprit is identified. Eventually, blame developed into the more down-to-earth sense 'reproach, censure.' *Censure* means to criticize adversely for some fault or offense that has not necessarily reached the degree of crime. Blame is to find fault with, as well as place responsibility upon, something or someone for wrongdoing and then to condemn. Blame can either be felt or uttered.

Blaspheme see Blame

Body shapes see Appearance of the human body

Bonafide From a Latin term meaning 'in good faith.' A *bonafide person* is one who is good, virtuous, innocent and without fraud or deceit. For example, a *bonafide purchaser* is one who has bought property in good faith for good consideration. This implies honesty, integrity and probity, which are demanded of professionals by society. Compare with Bad faith. See also Fair play, professionalism.

Bonafide person see Bonafide

Bonafide purchaser see Bonafide

Bone setters see Manipulation

Booking form see X-ray and work sheet

Bow legs see Figure 5 (page 57)

Brain Etymologically, the word 'brain' is of doubtful origin. It may have derived from Greek *bregma*, meaning the upper part of the head, or the Gaelic *breith*, meaning judgment of wit. As Gower (Confessio II) said in 1390, 'The wit and reason... is in the cells of the brain.' Subsequently, 'brain' has been considered as the supervisory centre of the nervous system. If we subscribe to this, then the flatworm has a beginning brain and is able to learn.

Brain death see Death

Brain stem see Death

Branches of the Government See Checks and balances

Brief This is a written argument prepared by one party in a lawsuit to explain to the court its opinions and the applicable laws. It includes only the essential arguments, a statement of the legal questions involved, which law should be applied and the application of that law the lawyer wishes the court to use.

Bruise see Contusion

Burden of persuasion see Burden of proof

Burden of proof The original Indo-European meaning of burden was both the carrying and giving of birth to a load. In the law of evidence, the responsibility of proving a point is called burden of proof (or burden of persuasion). For example, defendants must prove apportionment with a preponderance of the evidence (*Pullman-Kellogg* v. *WCAB*, 45 CCC 170). Injured workers usually have the burden of proof to show that the injury was work-related – the exception is *presumptions*. While in a criminal case the prosecutor has the burden of proving the guilt of a defendant beyond a reasonable doubt and to a moral certainty. In the workers' compensation system the burden of proof is a mere preponderance of the evidence (California Labor Code section 3202.5). This means that the quality of evidence has more convincing force and has the greater probability of truth. If the judge believes it is 'more likely than not' that the applicant is right, then he or she may return a verdict in the injured workers' favor. Similarly, in civil cases, plaintiffs must provide 'clear and convincing evidence' for juries to rule in their favor. Thus, the *standard of proof* is different in criminal cases from that in civil or workers compensation cases. Substantial evidence has as its minimum the fulfilment of all elements of the law (see Proving California Labor Code section 4663 Apportionment) based on reasonable medical probability. If the doctor makes statements based on speculation, guess or surmise, then there is no substantial evidence. A goal for doctors to strive for is the standard of proof of criminal cases – also called 'beyond a reasonable doubt.' See Beyond reasonable doubt, Clear and convincing evidence, Evidence, Pre-ponderance of evidence, Proof, Shifting the Burden of proof.

Buried illness/proof see Concealment in medicine

Burns' bench test see Faker signs

C

Calculated risk see Risk

Call for the reversal of judgment see Appeal

Camille see Euphemisms

Candid see Honesty

Canon law system Dogma decreed by church counsels as well as authoritative lists of books accepted as 'holy scripture'.

Capacity see Metric system

Carbuncle see Sweat

Cardinal virtues see Reasonable

Case An action, cause, writ or controversy at law or in equity. Equity is a method of finding a way to achieve a lawful result when legal procedure is inadequate.

Case self-betrayal These are patients who are so co-operative and so open that they say things that would hurt their litigated case. Often, they do not even have an attorney.

Case conclusion In a *finding and award*, there is a hearing before a trier of facts (e.g. judge). The judge listens to the arguments, makes a judgment and determines the amount of damages. In a *stipulated award*, the adverse parties agree on the facts of the case, present the facts to the judge and the judge settles the case. The judge does not hear testimony. In a *compromise and release*, the adverse parties agree, not to the facts, but to the results and to the disposition of the case. Generally, this does not require the involvement of the judge beyond getting a stamp of approval for legality. See also Arbitration, Conclusion, Judgments *in personam*, Take nothing.

Case law Law based on previous decisions of appellate courts, particularly the supreme court. See also Jurisprudence, Ratio *decidendi*.

Case rests see Rest

Casual worker A person employed by the owner or occupant of a residential dwelling to perform duties that are incidental to the ownership, maintenance or use of the dwelling. This includes the care and supervision of children, as well as duties that may or may not be personal, in the course of the trade, business, profession or occupation of such owner or occupant. Casual workers are mostly paid by the day, while *regular hands* are paid once or twice a week.

Catastrophizing Anticipating or misinterpreting events as particularly severe.

Caudad see Anatomical references, Inferior, Figure 1 (page 7)

Causalgia see Autonomic nervous system, Sensation classification

Causality The doctrine or principle of causes. See Cause.

Causation This is of fundamental importance in the medical-legal arena — did work exposure or personal injury, for example, contribute to a disability? A person has a legal right to sue in order to determine the answer to causation (i.e. a right of action). However, to have a *cause of action* there must be sufficient facts to form the basis of a valid lawsuit and that gives rise to a right of action. See also Disorder, Etiology, Standing before the court.

Causation issues A prime purpose of medical-legal reports is to address medical issues in a format useful for administrative use. For example, one question may be, 'Is the injury directly or proximately related to work exposure?' In which case the answer may well be, 'Based upon the patient's history to me and my physical examination, as well as review of medical records/radiographs, it is my opinion, that the patient's diagnosis is X, Y and Z. Further, it is my opinion that the specific injury of 2/28/93 is the direct or proximate cause of X, Y and Z.' Alternatively, in the case of *claimed aggravation*, it might be said that 'It is not reasonable, based on sound medical judgment, to conclude that A, B and C (i.e. the claimed pre-existing condition) pre-existed the industrial injury/occupational exposure. In addition, it is not reasonable to conclude that the industrial injury/occupational exposure caused an aggravation of conditions A, B and C.' See also Pre-existing, Proximate cause, Report comments.

Cause It has been (and is) accorded a premier status in philosophy, psychology, law, religion, science and blame throughout the ages and in all cultures. Originally, from the Latin *causa*, it refers to a trampled road bed and this concept created the word *effect* (to bring about). Hence, 'cause and effect' constitute the *law of causality* that says 'all actions are caused by entities'. Cause is something that determines any motion or change or produces a phenomenon. Joining of the egg and the sperm causes the developing embryo. *Legal causation* is a legal doctrine requiring the establishment of the fact that an effect, result or condition was caused by a specific, identifiable action or acts. Medically, there are three major categories pertaining to cause. The first is the *primary, immediate or inciting cause*, and this is the trigger factor which initiates the disease (e.g. *Diplococcus pneumoniae* is the cause of this patient's pneumonia) or injury (e.g. a blow on the head is the cause of this patient's skull fracture). Examples of primary cause include genetic, congenital and acquired diseases or injuries. They can be easily remember by remembering the acronym 'MINT', where M is malformation, I is infection or inflammation, N is neoplasms and T is Trauma. Second, *precipitating causes* are those conditioning factors which permit the immediate cause to act, as when a vehicle accident results in the blow on the head. Third, *predisposing causes* are those general circumstances which enable the immediate cause to act, such as a 'drunk driver' in the vehicle accident or malnutrition in the case of pneumonia. Beware of 'red herrings'; for instance, *D. pneumonia* is found in a patient's sputum and yet the patient may either not have pneumonia or the pneumonia may be caused by a virus. Also be wary of 'medical illogic' — every blow on the head is not associated with a skull fracture, or the blow that seemed most obvious may not have been the actual cause. A significant legal application of cause

pertains to incidents which arise out of, or occur in the course of employment, when it is necessary to prove there was a causal connection between employment and the injury or disease. Here, such a connection need not be the sole cause, but rather a *contributory cause is sufficient* (21 CCC 49). See also A priori, Disease, Etiology, Koch's postulates, Pathogenesis, Pathology scope.

Cause and effect Medical evidence can be used as a basis for the identification of a relationship between medical conditions and an identifiable injury/occupational exposure. What the law requires is that medical analysis establishes, within a reasonable degree of medical probability or certainty, the existence or lack of existence for these opinions. Solid reasons must be given for these opinions. This has be discussed extensively in the author's book, *The Handbook for Workers' Compensation Doctors*. For legal acceptance of opinions related to cause and effect, the doctor must make a definite statement of opinion to a reasonable degree of medical probability or certainty that a condition is or is not related to the injury or occupational exposure in question. See also A priori, Arise out of employment, Cause, Etiology.

Cause of action These are the grounds of a lawsuit. The composite of facts alleged would, if proved, enable the complainant to obtain a judgment. See also Allegations of fact, Brief, Causation Claim, Color of law, Complaint, Standing before the court.

Censure see Blame

Centigrade to fahrenheit On these scales, 0°C and 32°F, or 100°C and 212°F, are the same temperature. Between the boiling point and the freezing point on a centigrade thermometer there are 100 gradations (or degrees), while on a fahrenheit thermometer there are 180 degrees. Therefore, 100°C degrees equals 180°F degrees or 1°C degree equals 1.8°F. To change centigrade to fahrenheit, multiply centigrade readings by 1.8 and add 32. A short cut is to add 40 to the centigrade reading, multiply the sum by 1.8 and subtract 40. Conversely, to change fahrenheit readings to centigrade, either subtract 32 from the fahrenheit reading and divide by 1.8, or add 40 to the fahrenheit readings, divide the sum by 1.8 and subtract 40. See also Metric system.

Centimeter see Metric system

Central see Anatomical references, Figure 1 (page 7)

Cephalad see Anatomical references, Figure 1 (page 7)

Cerebrum Part of the brain which includes the corpus callosum, cerebral cortex, thalamus and hypothalamus.

Certain see Classifying information

Certainty From the Latin *certus*, meaning sure, fixed, it is a word with many complexities involved in its conceptualization. Much depends upon who is doing the deciding and what is being decided. Objective or subjective certainty may, or may not, be real. Nevertheless, certainty indicates that the involved persons are absolutely convinced of what has happened, is happening, or is going to happen. Legally, *demonstration*, in the strict and proper sense, is the highest form of proof and is the closest to absolute certainty. When the law transfers this concept into medicine, problems arise. For example, whereas functional losses and anatomical losses are objective factors of impairment, functional abnormalities and anatomical abnormalities may or may not be objective despite the law considering them to be demonstrable. However, the law often does not recognize proof and certainty in medical matters not demonstrable. *Subjective plus* type medical conditions are examples. This has led to doctors being asked such naive questions as, 'Are these patients' problems objective or subjective?' One type of certainty pertains to that which is real (from the Latin *res*, meaning a thing). *Real* signifies having existence, not merely in thought, but in fact; the genuine as opposed to the imitation. Mention has been made of moral certainty in matters beyond a reasonable doubt. See also Beyond a shadow of doubt, Medical certainty, Medical probability, Subjective plus.

Certainty scale of decisions see Classifying information

Cervical spondylosis Though evidence of the clinical manifestations of cervical spondylosis (CS) has been noted for 4000 years, this is a relatively recently described clinical condition. It has been called many different names and confused with many other disease processes. Outdated synonyms include osteoarthritis, hypertrophis arthritis, proliferative arthritis, vertebral osteophytosis and osteoarthritis deformans. Since there is no clear definition or classification in the literature, the author considers CS as that *condition which results when osteophytes compress the spinal cord and nerves.* Short of such neurological involvement, the problem can be considered as a degenerative joint disease. However, as commonly used, CS describes any combined bone and

joint degeneration of significance. In true CS, in addition to myelopathic involvement, there may also be involvement of vasculature, sympathetic nerves and local soft tissue pressure (e.g. on the esophagus). Compare with Diffuse idiopathic skeletal hyperostosis (DISH).

Chambers The ultimate source of chamber is the Greek *kamara*, literally meaning 'something with an arched cover', 'room with a vaulted roof'. In later Latin the word developed the senses of 'vault' and 'room in a dwelling'. Chambers has subsequently come to signify the private offices of judges. A hearing in chambers takes place in the judge's office outside of the presence of the jury and the public. See also In camera.

Change of venue Moving a lawsuit or criminal trial to another place for trial. See also Venue.

Character The sum total of a person's personal qualities in moral, legal and social situations. Character is roughly who the person is. It starts with the individual's belief system and gives rise to the person's attitudes, behaviors and work product. It can be changed by altering the belief system. A person's most noble beliefs are drawn from what they consider to be the best out of any metaphysical system (i.e. transcendent levels of reality). These beliefs become the basis for life-guiding standards, values and power desired. Beliefs qualify as noble when they are enduring, consistent and permanent (i.e. permanent and stationery). See also A priori, Bad faith, Genotype, Reasonable, Record, Respect.

Character disorders see Psychogenic disease

Charge An address given by a judge to a jury at the end of a trial telling them the principles of law they are to apply in reaching a decision. The charge may also include instructions given during the trial for the jury's guidance. In criminal law, charge is a description of the underlying offense in an accusation or indictment. Otherwise, charge may be any burden or encumbrance upon a person, upon public or private property, or upon resources. A property tax is an example. See also Allegations of facts, Brief, Cause of action, Charged, Claim, Complaint.

Charged see Prosecution

Checks and balances The United States constitution guarantees that each *branch of the government* — executive, judicial, legislative, has some measure of influence over the other branches. One authority may choose to block procedures of another branch. Checks and balances prevent any one branch from accumulating too much power. Also, it encourages co-operation between branches as well as comprehensive debate on controversial policy issues. For example, to enact a federal law, the *Senate* and the *House of Representatives* must each vote to pass the law. If they agree, the President must sign the law. Although he can veto it, it can still be enacted if two-thirds of both houses vote to override the veto. Under this arrangement, both Congress and the President can check each other. In addition, the Supreme Court can declare laws and executive acts unconstitutional, but Congress can propose constitutional amendments to overturn judicial decisions, as well as impeach and remove federal judges. The same process operates at lower court levels.

Chief complaints Are those of primary concern to patients. Although those complaints direct medical focus, all of the complaints are often needed for a complete diagnosis. Complaints may be specific, limited and steady; migratory; spreading; decreasing; remaining the same; about the wrong problem; or general (i.e. 'I hurt all over'). Some are pertinent in general, while others are pertinent to one specialty or not at all. Some are more important to the patient, while others are more important to the patient's health. Some are periodically related and some require investigation. All must be put into perspective. See also Present complaints.

Childish A term of reproach. It refers to any act that demonstrates foolishness or shows a lack of maturity. All of us have seen the rage of temper tantrums, unexpected disagreeableness, ill-temperedness and obstinacy. This is normal for a child but should be contained in adults.

Childish adult These individuals have childish traits (e.g. abnormally quick temper, thoughtless and ill-mannered).

Child-like This refers to a child's endearing traits such as innocence, trust, delicateness and the ability to love unconditionally. Associated with a child-like state is that of fun, fancy, imagination, seeing and speaking the truth, lack of deception and creativity. All of these are foundations for brilliance and genius when coupled with self-discipline. See also Self-discipline, Training.

Children's history The factors involved in a child's history are listed in Figure 2.

Chiropractic see Manipulation

Chronic *Chronos* is the Greek word for time and was the name of the ancient supreme god of the Greeks and father of Zeus. A chronic illness is a long-continuing disorder (e.g. chronic rheumatism) and usually starts with slow development that becomes deep seated or ingrained. Since chronic is something that continues for a long time, it may be *constant* (continually), *almost constant* (continually recurring) or *recurring*. There are three commonly used words for recurring: (1) *periodic*, or occurring at regular intervals but those intervals are of varying lengths throughout the total time; (2) *intermittent*, or occurring at intervals that constitute about half of the total time but are more or less regular; and (3) *occasional*, or occurring at infrequent and irregular intervals. Figures arbitrarily chosen to represent something that is chronic in medicine range from 3 to 6 months after an acute onset. See also Apportionment terms, Cumulative trauma, Primary gain.

Chronic orthopaedic pain syndrome see Dissociation

Circumstantial evidence Evidence based not on direct observation or knowledge, but rather implied from things already known. Circumstance is a word meaning 'that which stands around'. It is *indirect evidence* consisting of secondary facts by which a principle fact may be reasonably inferred. It is evidence that merely suggests something by implication. Fingerprints are physical evidence from which an inference can be drawn. By contrast, eyewitness testimony is *direct evidence* and this is the only other type of evidence. Without circumstantial evidence, no legal system could possibly work. Erroneous convictions are more likely to result from false testimony than from false inferences. Since in the Anglo-American legal tradition the accused is considered innocent until proven guilty, in the absence of a confession a conviction must be secured either on the basis of testimony, which can be unreliable, or circumstances. The murderer who is caught with a smoking gun or bloody knife bending over a dying victim must be convicted on the basis of circumstantial evidence. Even a confession is not enough for conviction; there has to be something to confess to (i.e. a 'circumstance'). As noted in newspapers, any major murder case is likely to inspire a rash of false confessions by the highly unstable and/or the publicity seeking. The evidence provided by circumstances remains, on the whole, the best, the most useful and the least likely to result in an unjust conviction. See also Direct evidence, Objective minus.

Civil action A lawsuit brought by an individual or group to, for example, recover money or property, to

Informant _____

A Child's History

Date _____ Name _____ Date of injury _____ Birth date _____

Complaints (read cover letter first)

History

Present complaints
    describe
    extent
    progress
    duration

Impairment from disability
    initial extent of disability
        school loss
        tasks unable to do

    presently
        unable to do
        trouble doing

    other pertinent disability
        limitations prior to date of injury
        prior injuries
        subsequent injuries
        compensation

Birth history
    weight _____ height _____ type of delivery _____
    perinatal complications

Developmental history
    held up head _____ sat alone _____
    crawled _____ walked _____
    exceptional qualities (mental and physical)
    talked in sentences

Past medical history
    illness
    allergies
    hospitalizations
    accidents
    operations

Social history
    education/grade
    future career

Family history
    defects, diseases, illnesses
    siblings

Review of systems
    HEENT
    cardiovascular/respiratory
    gastrointestinal
    genitourinary (including date menses)
    musculoskeletal
    psychiatric
    bleeding tendencies
    neurological
    general (health, skin problems)

Figure 2 Factors to be considered when taking a full history for a child

enforce or protect a civil right, or to prevent or redress a civil wrong, etc. A *civil procedure* is a process by which a civil case is tried and appealed, including the preparations for the trial, the rules of evidence and trial conduct, and the procedure for pursuing appeals. Criminal actions are different because the state prosecutes an individual for committing an offense against all the people.

Civil law This regulates relationships among people and does not involve the government directly. It pertains to lawsuits other than criminal practice and is concerned with the rights and duties of persons in contract and tort, etc. Civil law comes from *constitutions* (made by congress, federal and state authorities), *statutory law* (made by federal, state and local legislature) and *delegated law* (legislatures delegate some of its powers to governmental agencies and to other bodies). Confusion arises because this type of civil law is a term used differently than for the legal system derived from Roman law. Nations that utilise the experience and ideas of Roman law are found in most of Western Europe, in Latin America, Asia, North Africa, South Africa and the Soviet Union. See also Classification of law.

Civil procedure see Civil action

Civil trials see Trials

Claim A request or demand as to some right or supposed right related to, for example, a piece of land, an insurance payment or a tax refund, etc. See also Allegations of fact, Brief, Cause of action, Charge, Complaint, Counter claim, Declaration, Litigation.

Claim for reoccurance This implies that the original injury never healed properly. See also Recurrence.

Claimant Is one who makes a claim and then shows the existence of a right, an injury and damages. See also Claim, Litigant.

Claimed aggravation see Causation issues

Claimed pre-existing condition see Causation issues, Pre-existing

Claims administrator This is either (1) a self-administered insurer providing security for the payment of compensation; (2) group self-insurer or a third-party claims administrator; (3) a self-insured employer,

insurer, legally uninsured employer, group self-insurer; or (4) a joint powers authority. See also Adjustor, Contested claim.

Claque see Pardon

Classification From the Greek *kleiss*, meaning division. Originally it meant a way of organising things into groups, such as 'pigeonholing' information. Roman people were divided into six groups with each group being a class as in the school classroom. In this sense, classifying came to mean a way of organizing things — an arrangement into groups or categories on the basis of established criteria. Some criteria were required by authorities while others were for convenience only. In biology, plants and animals have been classified by the structure of their bodies. Medically, classifications are used to provide clarification of a disease's biological characteristics related to etiology, natural history and therapy. In general, classification is putting together things for the purpose of reasoning about them. The myriad of individual items are put into proper and logical division using some mental basis of connection. Classification proceeds from the principle that when many things resemble each other in a few basic qualities, we associate them in a class and use the class-concept in further reasoning. The mind will then use the resultant arrangement in its thought and memory processes. Classifications that represent a first step out of chaos, as is true of psychogenic mental disorders, start generally and broadly. As knowledge is gained, refinement occurs in the direction of the more particular and the more limited. See also Analysis.

Classification of law There is no agreement about the classification of law. Roughly, there are three broad categories: procedural law, substantive law and public law. *Procedural law*, also called *legal procedure, formal administration* and *due process justice*, is how the law is to be *enforced* outside and inside court. *Substantive law* are rules of law that define rights, duties and obligations (i.e. *what the law is*). Substantive law includes public law and private law (Table 1). *Public law* includes all rules related to matters in which the state or the community is directly involved. It relates to relationships between individuals and the government. Its major branches are constitutional law, administrative law, international law and criminal law (also called penal, punitive, vindictive and retributive justice). For example, the law of crimes pertains to offenses against the state. However, the offense may be a *tort* (part of private law) as well as a crime; this is the case for assault and battery. *Private law* relates to relationships

Table 1 Classification of law

(I) Substantive law (what the law is)

(A) Public law

    (1) Constitutional law

    (2) Administrative law

    (3) International law

    (4) Criminal law

(B) Private law, also called civil law

    (1) Domestic relations law

    (2) Property law

    (3) Contract law   } Law of obligations

    (4) Tort

(II) Procedural law, also called legal procedure

(how law is enforced)

(III) Equity jurisprudence (lawful fair play)

---

between one individual and another person or an *artificial person* (e.g. a corporation or state institution). It is sometimes called civil law, not to be confused with *civil law* systems derived from Roman law (see the entry for civil law). Its chief branches are the laws of property, of domestic relations, of contract and of tort. Contract and tort are sometimes grouped together as the *law of obligations*. See also Court of Chancery, Court of Equity, Law divisions, Law functions, Lawmakers, Laws general proprieties totem pole.

Classification of medical patients All medical students learn of one type of patient, the prototype I *textbook patient*. These individuals have 'benign' psychiatric problems, if any. They are characterized by having organic lesions. In practice, doctors learn about *self-deceivers* (prototype II patients), who believe that they have a medical lesion when they do not. They are not lying because they honestly believe they have a problem that does not exist. In the litigation arena, doctors learn about conscious deceivers (prototype III patients). They are trying to make others believe that they have some non-existent lesions but yet do not believe this themselves. Permutations of these three prototypes give seven main groups (Table 2). See also Six common clinical styles, Trophic changes.

Classifying crimes Crimes have been classified according to whether it is a: (1) *felony/misdemeanour*

Table 2 The classification of medical patients

Type I: textbook patients

(A) Honest and straightforward

(B) Stoic

Type II: self-deceivers

(A) Motor conversion

(B) Somatoform pain conversion

    (1) Somatoform pain disorders

        (a) Anxiety type

        (b) Neurotic depression type

        (c) Depression type

    (2) Hypochondriasis

    (3) Somatization disorders

        (a) Female type

        (b) Male type

    (4) Undifferentiated

(C) Body dysmorphic

Type III: conscious deceivers

(A) Classic malingerers

(B) Munchausen syndrome

(C) Deliberate deceitful exaggerators

Type IV: textbook/self-deceivers

(A) Psychophysiological (i.e. psychosomatic)

(B) Somatopsychic disorders

Type V: textbook/conscious deceivers

(A) Attention-seeking exaggerators

(B) Factitious disorders

(C) Paradoxical malingerers

Type VI: self-deceivers/conscious deceivers

(A) Pseudoanesthesia

(B) Pseudoparesis

(C) Combinations of pseudoanesthesia and pseudoparesis

Type VII: textbook/self-deceivers/conscious deceivers

(A) Organic lesions combined with textbook/self-deceiver

(B) Mentally ill (can involve types I, II, III, IV, V and/or VI)

(based on seriousness); (2) *crime against property or person*; and (3) *degrees* (first and second degree murder); and (4) *voluntary and involuntary*. See also Felony.

Classifying information　A hierarchy of terms can be used in order to classify information. These include feasible, possible, probable, reasonably certain and certain. *Feasible* is that which is capable of being done, otherwise it is impossible. *Possible* is that which is capable of happening, as when we say it is possible (not feasible) that it will rain today. *Probable* literally means that which has been tested and has the appearance of truth but there is still some room for doubt; hence, 'likely' to be true. What is likely appeals to the reason as being worthy of belief. Probable means that there are more points to favor believing than not believing and it guides us in matters where we lack certainty. This is particularly true in law where facts are sufficiently known to make the judge and jury moderately confident, as in 'probable guilt'. *Certain* signifies having existance, not merely in thought but in fact; we feel no doubt about it because it has happened or is happening.

It is possible to assign numerical ranges to these terms, based upon accumulated data from various fields. What they indicate is how we can classify information and how much we can rely on that information. Knowing both is fundamental to analysis and to communicating on a rational level. *Low possible* ranges from 1–20; *medium possible*, 21–34; *high possible*, 35–50. Any number over 50% and up to 69 is low probability; 70–89 is medium probability; and 90–96 is high probability. Whereas absolutely certain is 100%, certain with reservations – also called medically certain – ranges from 97–99. See also Medical-legal conceptual counterparts, Scientific method.

Clause　A particular and separate article, stipulation or proviso, and any formal or legal document.

Clean hands doctrine　see Court of Equity

Clear and convincing evidence　This is greater than the mere *preponderance* (or greater weight of evidence) and less than *beyond a reasonable doubt*. In the latter, the scales of justice are completely 'out of balance' towards guilt (for criminal cases); in the former, they are just 'out of balance'. A medical equivalent would be that clear and convincing evidence is between low medical probability (preponderance) and high medical probability (beyond reasonable doubt). See also Beyond reasonable doubt, Burden of proof, Classifying information,

Clerk　An assistant or a subordinate. A *court clerk* is an officer whose duties include keeping records, issuing processes and entering judgments. A *law clerk* is an assistant to a lawyer or a judge, whose primary job is to aid in researching and writing briefs or opinions, and in handling cases. See also American Disabilities Act.

Client　see Patient

Clinical laboratories　see Laboratory

Clinical manifestations　These are behaviors that are manifest. That which is *manifest* is etymological 'grasped by the hand' (i.e. palpable, obvious). Manifest comes, via old French, from the Latin *manifestus* (*manus* meaning hand plus *fetus* meaning gripped). Clinical manifestations are the displaying of that which has not necessarily been previously concealed but which has been evoked by occasion or circumstance to give characteristic signs or symptoms of an illness. They may reflect organic illness, the neurotic (with or without the psychophysiological component of self-deceivers), the psychotic tendencies of certain conscious deceivers, or the good/bad behaviors of any 'normal' patient. Clinical manifestations include not only the way in which a patient reacts to a doctor, the doctor's staff, society or the environment, but also the patient's extracorporeal attachments. Even those aspects of the patient that are capable of being observed by the intangible senses are clinical manifestations (e.g. the perception of what is going on in the patient's mind as it relates to mood, dispositions, attitudes, instincts, drives, predispositions, tendencies, habits and other aspects of mental health which specialists employ to account for the relatively enduring and consistent quality of behavior). See also Attachments, Extracorporent, Intangible, Manifestations, Manifestations of disability, Objective/ subjective scale, Psychogenic diseases.

Closing arguments　In a trial, this starts when neither party has any more evidence to present. The plaintiff's attorney has two chances to convince the jury (his or her opening and closing the argument). The defense argument occurs between. During the closing arguments both attorneys focus on the most pertinent facts and in the most persuasive manner.

Cognition　The intellectual functioning or ways of knowing and thinking, including the processes of perceiving, imagining, remembering, reasoning and judging. More of the left brain is devoted to cognition than is the right brain. See also Knowledge by description.

Collective bargaining The mechanism for settling labor disputes by negotiation between employer and representatives of employees.

Collusion The making of an agreement with another for the purposes of perpetuating a fraud, engaging in illegal activity, or in legal activity while having an illegal end in mind.

Color The hiding of a set of facts behind what purports to be a technically proper, legal theory.

Color of law Near semblance of legal right. An action done under color of law is one performed with the apparent authority of law, but is actually in contravention of law. A federal cause of action may be maintained against a state officer who deprives a person of his or her civil rights under 'color of law'.

Colorable That which presents an appearance different from reality or an appearance intended to conceal or to deceive.

Common ground see Medical fiction

Common law The strong monarchy that followed the Norman invasion of Britain in 1066 established the centralized royal court and jury systems. The jury system replaced trials by ordeals, battle and wager. Royal courts led to a definite legal tradition. All of the old Germanic customs and laws of each locality were consolidated into a uniform or 'common' system. This system was administered by the king's personal followers in his name. This body of rules was called *common law*. It grew from the decisions of judges in settling actual disputes. Thus, common law came to consist of both custom and tradition, as well as decisions by judges in specific cases and acts of parliament. A common law system based on the the English example is now also found in most English-speaking countries, including the United States. It is based primarily on two factors. First, *precedent*, where judge-made rules form the model for other judges to follow in similar cases. These judicial decisions become part of established law, but can be altered by legislature. Second, *custom*, where principles that have always been followed are used, although their origins may be obscure. These *custom laws* do not consist of absolute, fixed and inflexible rules, but rather broad and comprehensive principles based on justice, reason and common sense. Its principles have been determined by the social needs of the community and have changed with changes in such needs. See

also Court of Chancery, Court of Equity, Habeas corpus, Ration *decidendi*, Summary proceedings, Unwritten law.

Common sense Practical understanding and good judgment. See also Reasonable.

Common-law felonies see Felony

Comparative negligence The apportioning of negligence between the parties concerned (e.g. plaintiff and defendant). Thus, the plaintiff would get less money in proportion to the plaintiff's contributing fault. See also Apportionment, Contributory negligence, Negligence.

Compartmentalizing a concept see Abnormal

Compensation A comprehensive word signifying a return for a service provided. *Remuneration* is applied to matters of great amount or importance. *Recompense* has a wider meaning, with less suggestion of calculation and market value. For example, there are services for which affection and gratitude are the sole and sufficient recompense. Earnings, fees, pay, salary and wages are forms of compensation and may be included in compensation, remuneration or recompense. See also Employers liability acts, Malpractice.

Competence This, with jurisdiction, refers generally to the power of a court to act. No court has authority to hear all disputes. The subject matter and parties must be appropriate for a given court. See also Jurisdiction, Venue.

Competent It means sufficient, nothing more. It has a similar sense as moderate, reasonable, enough, fit, able, adequate, appropriate, satisfactory, suitable, capable and proficient. Medical-legally, competent is used mainly in the sense of legally qualified. Competent evidence is both relevant and proper to the issue being litigated. A competent court has proper jurisdiction over the person or property at issue. A criminal defendant is competent to stand trial if he or she is able to consult with a lawyer with a reasonable degree of rational understanding and has a rational as well as factual understanding of the proceedings against him or her. For example, a person is competent to make a will if he or she understands the extent of the property, the identity of the objects making up the property and the consequences of making a will. See also Competence, Courts, Evidence, Jurisdiction.

Competent court see Competent

Competent evidence see Competent

Complainant The party initiating the complaint in an action or proceeding. Whether it is the petitioner, plaintiff or applicant is determined by the nature of the proceeding and the court in which it is instituted. See also Applicant, Litigants, Petitioner, Plaintiff.

Complaint In a civil action, the first pleading of the plaintiff which sets out the facts on which the claim is based so that the defendant knows what is occurring. In criminal law it is the *preliminary charge* or accusation against another. See also Allegations of fact, Brief, Cause of action, Charge, Claims, Brief, Grievance, Pleading.

Complaint and petition see Declaration

Comprehensive medical-legal evaluation see Evaluation

Compromise Implies a mutual yielding of points on the part of those who stand for and against the question under deliberation. It denotes the adjustment of a controversy by mutual surrender of certain issues or by the modification of certain contingents. Lawsuits are frequently settled out of court by compromise, when the contending parties yield by mutual consent for the sake of private adjustment. See also Fair play.

Compromise and release A lump sum settlement which, if resolved against the applicant, would defeat the applicant's claim for all other pertinent benefits. See also Compromise, Case conclusion, Settlement.

Compromise settlement The pervading concept here is that of *agreement*. It can be either a word-of-mouth or a written arrangement, or a treaty; it may suggest intricate problems and bitter controversy, or genial and pleasant understanding (e.g. a gentleman's agreement). Thus mutual accord and assent, agreeable or otherwise, are to be respected as such in all cases where papers are signed, sealed and delivered. *Settlement* suggests conclusion or finality of that which is either agreed, adjusted or arbitrated.

Compulsory arbitration see Arbitration

Con artist see Conscious deceivers, Reasonable, Smoke screen

Concealed From the Latin *con*, meaning thoroughly, plus *celare*, meaning to hide. It is that which is covered, buried, camouflaged, enshrouded, guarded, incognito, inconspicuous, masked, obscured, screened, stashed, veiled or disguised. In medicine, these are the ways that certain organic conditions remain a mystery. Legally, *concealment* is the intentional suppression of truth or fact which is known to injure or prejudice another. For example, there may be intentional, or unintentional, non-disclosure by a party to an insurance agent of some vital information. See also Concealment in medicine, Deception, Latent, Occult, Smoke screen, Subclinical.

Concealment see Concealed

Concealment in medicine A family of words related to *hide* have great importance in medicine. Hide, an Indo-European word has given rise to apocalypse, cell, conceal, occult and probably color. Anything short of overt expressions is a form of hiding. Whether speaking anatomically (e.g. about the skin) or psychologically, the word 'hide' means covering. Synonyms include mask, bury, cloak, disguise, disassemble, screen, suppress and veil, etc. Something may be hidden by intention, by accident, or by the imperfection of the faculties of the person from whom it is hidden. A person may hide his or her face in anger, grief, abstraction or some other deceptive reason. Deceptive patients usually conceal their face when they fear recognition — an intentional act not to divulge. A thing is *covered* by putting something over or around it, whether by accident or design. Alternatively, it is *screened* when something is placed before it for purpose of protection from observation, inconvenience, attack or censure, etc. Anything which is effactually covered and hidden under any mask or accumulation is *buried*. In the figurative use, one conceals an evil or hostile intent. Self-deceivers tend to cover themselves. Conscious deceivers tend to conceal themselves. Both have buried destructive feelings. This implies that part of their true self is in hiding and usually is lost to awareness. In medicine, what is concealed is subclinical (e.g. an illness before it has manifested itself such as subclinical osteomyelitis). Concealed emotions are *repressed*. See Concealed, Deception, Euphemisms in medicine, Occult, Smoke screen, Subclinical.

Conceivable That for which the mind can entertain the possibility.

Conclusion This can relate to several things. For example, medically a case may come to an end because the patient was cured, died or became 'permanent and stationary'. A legal case may come to an end as a result of a *compromise and release*, a *findings and award*, a *stipulated award*, a *take nothing*, death or the dropping of a case. The conclusions in a medical report or a court trial could be a summary of the main points. Logically, conclusion is the last of the positions forming a syllogism, deduced from the premises. See also Case conclusion.

Concrete scientific minds see Reasonable

Concurrent Existing together. For example, in medicine *concurrent lesions* are two dissimilar lesions which exist together. In law, concurrent or *consecutive* are generally used to indicate the intention of the court. When used in ordinary legal parlance, the opposite of concurrent is consecutive and accumulative, particularly in criminal cases. For example, if the sentences are not concurrent, they are consecutive and accumulative. See also Apportionment terms.

Condition Something that necessarily precedes a result, but does not produce it. This is an important distinction from *proximate cause*, where the result follows the natural course of events. Legally, condition denotes something attached to and made a part of a grant or privilege. A condition is a conceivable future event, the occurrence of which will trigger the *performance* of a legal obligation. Conditions are important in contracts. See also Causes, Origin, Proximate cause.

Condonation exception see Horseplay

Confidence see Trust

Conflict of interest An inconsistency between a person's own interests and that person serving the interests of others pertinent to the situation.

Congenial job Is one where the injured lives a lifestyle consistent with the restrictions given by the doctor.

Congenital conditions Are those pathological lesions present at birth without etiological connotations. Compare with Acquired, Developmental, Heritable, Inherited. See also Genetic.

Congenital insensitivity to pain see Pain measurement test

Congenitally acquired lesions see Acquired medical conditions

Conjecture An inference, presumption or judgment that is acknowledged to result from incomplete or insufficient data or evidence. It is better founded than a guess, which is merely a hit-or-miss or random opinion based on little, if any, evidence. Conjecture is more substantial than a *surmise*, which contains the feeling of too much imagination and distrust. *Hypothesis* is a conjecture assumed to be true until proven otherwise and is used as a basis of discussion and reasoning and, perhaps, action. Just as a conjecture is more rational and systematic than a guess, so a hypothesis is broader and more realistic than a conjecture, but less accurate and authentic than a theory. See also Guess, Hypothesis, Scientific method.

Conscious deceivers These are prototype III patients who either have no lesion at all or have an insignificant one. In some cases an organic lesion can be consciously created (e.g. *factitious disorder*). Some of those with self-created, organic lesions consciously and destructively embellish their presentation. Compare with Self-deceivers. See also Classification of medical patients, Malingerers, Pathological lying, Postnatally acquired injuries, Prototype patients.

Consecutive see Concurrent

Consent in judgment see Judgment

Consequence of that action see Result

Conservatee An adult person, who, by reason of age, illness, mental weakness, intemperance or other cause, is unable to properly care for him or herself or his or her property. See also Incompetent, Minor.

Conservator In law, a person, official or institution (usually a bank) appointed by the courts to look after the interest of a minor or an incompetent. Conservator is used generally in the sense of *guardian*.

Constant see Chronic

Constitutions see Civil law

Constructive contempt see Contempt of court

Constructive notice see Constructive service, Notice

Constructive service see Notice, Service

Contempt of court   May be direct or indirect. Contempt is the attitude of despising or holding in disrespect. *Direct contempt* is that which is committed in the immediate presence of the court (e.g. an outburst in a crowded court room in the form of violence or an insult) or near enough to the court to obstruct its proceedings. *Indirect (constructive) contempt* usually refers to the failure or refusal to obey a lawful order, injunction or court decree. See also Discovery, Subpoena.

Contested claim   This is peculiar to the type of court in the state in which the proceeding is held. In the California workers' compensation scheme, a contested claim occurs when: (1) the claims administrator has rejected liability for a claimed benefit; (2) the claims administrator has failed to accept liability for a claim and the claim has become presumptively compensable under Section 5402 of the labor code; (3) the claims administrator has failed to respond to a demand for the payment of compensation after the expiration of any time period fixed by statue for the payment of indemnity benefits, including where the claims administrator has failed to either commence the payment of temporary disability indemnity or issue a notice of delay within 14 days after knowledge of an employee's injury and disability as provided in Section 4650 of the labor code; and (4) the claims administrator has accepted liability for a claim, and a disputed medical fact exists. See also Answer, Claims administrator, Disputed medical fact, Medical-legal.

Contingent liability   Is a liability that will come into being only upon the occurrence of some uncertain, future event.

Continuance   The adjournment or postponement of the proceedings in a case to a specified subsequent date.

Continuing trauma   Also called repetitive trauma, cumulative trauma or accumulative microtrauma. It is defined by California Labor Code, Section 3201.1, as repetitive mental and/or physical traumatic activities extending over a period of time, the combined effect of which causes disability or need for medical treatment. These activities include either minor successive injuries to the same part of the body, or normal activities which alone are insufficient to cause disability but whose total effect results in a condition causing disability. Examples include repetition against resistance, prolonged awkward positions and vibrations. Alternatively, cumulative trauma can be viewed as the occurrence of repetitive mentally and physically over-stressful or traumatic activities extending over a period of time that have caused slow cell death. That is, the patient gets progressively worse without realising the extent of the damage until the day of injury. Compare with Adaptation, Specific injury. See also Co-pilot injury, Cumulative exposure, Occupational disease, Occurrence, Stress.

Continuous   see Repeated, Vocational rehabilitation terms

Contribution   A right to demand another individual jointly responsible for an injury to compensate the victim.

Contributory cause   see Cause

Contributory evidence   see Facts

Contributory negligence   A legal doctrine that says that if the claimant in the civil action for negligence also was negligent, she or he cannot recover damages from the defendant for the defendant's negligence. Most jurisdictions have replaced this doctrine in favor of *comparative negligence*. See also Negligence.

Contusion   It derives from the Latin word *contundere*, meaning to crush. A contusion is an injury which results from a collision with something hard without breaking the skin (i.e. a *bruise*).

Conversion   Psychic conflict symbolically expressing themselves bodily. Psychogenic paralysis of a limb is an example of a *conversion sign*.

Conversion manifestation   These include conversion symptoms and signs. There are several types; for instance, a person may claim no sensation in non-anatomical distributions, or a weakness without an organic basis.

Conversion reactions   Some use this as a synonym for *somatization*, but this is confusing. A somatization makes reference not to the specific *'somatization disorders'* per se, but to the somatic effects originating from malignant psychic distress. Conversion reactions are not syndromes or discreet disorders with their own characteristic clinical pictures. They are individual manifestations occurring in response to stress in a wide variety of psychiatric or medical disorders. Inconsistencies in the physical examination in relation to known anatomical distributions or in relation to manifestations that vary from one examination to another are suggestive of conversion. However, such judgments are notoriously unreliable because of: (1) an incomplete history, physical examination or laboratory testing that do not allow for the diagnosis of subtle organic lesions; (2) limitations in our knowledge of pathoanatomy and pathophysiology; (3) wide variations in the presentation of organic disorders; and (4) limited methods for objective assessment, even if an organic lesion is correctly suspected. *Conversion symptoms* is an umbrella term. It contains a variety of clinical manifestations, many of which do not qualify as a 'symptom' or a 'sign'. Loss of sensory function or loss of vision are examples. Paresthesias and pain are metaphors and similes. Some patients show various types of affects (e.g. a frequent finding in somatization disorder is *la belle indifference*, with lack of concern about the effect of the pain on his or her lifestyle). Nevertheless, these differences in affect, complaints, sensory losses, etc., are generally included under the umbrella term 'conversion symptom'. Often, in contrast to the rest of medicine, those in the mental health specialties place 'signs' under the term 'symptom'. See also Dyaesthesia, Paresthesias, Psychogenic disease, Somatoform disorders, Umbrella term.

Conversion sign see Conversion

Conversion symptoms see Conversion reactions

Conviction see Conviction intima

Conviction intima Inner, deep-seated conviction. *Conviction* is frozen belief (i.e. a belief that has been confirmed and has thus become settled and established as a result of incontrovertible evidence). Conviction is often established by argument or evidence.

Co-pilot injury Is a cumulative microtrauma injury whereby a second payor is covering the same injury exposure. See also Passenger injuries, Pilot injuries.

Coronal plane The body is divided into front and back. See also Anatomical references, Transverse, Figure 1 (page 7).

Coroner Is a corruption of the word 'crowner', which is the old and proper spelling of this term. It formerly referred to an officer acting for the interest of the 'Crown in England'. A coroner now is a county officer whose duty is to inquire into the causes of violent or sudden deaths. See also Autopsy, Postmortem.

Corroborating evidence see Evidence

Costs see Court costs, Medical-legal expense, Memorandum of cost and disbursements, Projected orthopaedic expenses form, Punitive damages

Counsel Is a person who gives legal advice, prepares and manages cases and tries cases in court (i.e. a *lawyer*). See also Public defender.

Counter-claim Is a counter lawsuit within a lawsuit. The defendant makes a claim which seeks to reduce the plaintiff's claim or provide grounds for a judgment in favor of the defendant to whatever extent the counter-claim exceeds the plaintiff's claim. If the plaintiff's claim is defeated, judgment will be given on the counter-claim as if it were an entirely new lawsuit. See also Answer, Claim, Litigation.

Counter-traction see Traction

Counter-plaintiff/counter-defendant claim The plaintiff also becomes a counter-defendant and the defendant becomes a counter-plaintiff when a counter-claim is filed.

County medical society see Medical societies

Courage see Risk

Course see Pathological scope

Course of employment see Occurring in the course of employment

Court clerk see Clerk

Court costs Are the expenses of prosecuting or defending a lawsuit apart form the attorney's fees. A sum of money may be awarded to the successful (i.e. *prevailing*) party and may be recoverable from the losing party as reimbursement for court costs. See also Damages.

Court of Appeal This type of court gives judgments on lower courts such as a Court of First Instance. They are concerned with the record of the proceeding, the briefs of the parties and sometimes the oral argument of the attorney. As they are only concerned with questions of law, they determine if the lower court made a significant error. After the opinions of justices are announced, the case goes back to trial courts or the case ends completely. See also Court of First Instance.

Court of Chancery Written common law decisions were published in reports in the thirteenth century and centred around problems related to money and property. Kings were considered as the ultimate head of justice. All requests for help went to the king. When those requests were of the nature of fraud, broken promises, threatened wrongs and similar *private law* matters, a request for help (called a *petition*) had to be made. Petitions involving private law were handed over to the 'Royal Chancery' for special handling. This was required because the strict rules of common law failed in these *equity cases*. There were so many petitions that the chancellor developed the *Court of Chancery* where equity decisions were made. This has persisted today as *Courts of Equity*. See also Classification of law.

Court of Equity A court having jurisdiction in cases where a plain, adequate and complete remedy cannot be had at law. Originally, they were common law courts that had their own principles (e.g. *clean hand doctrine*) and their own unique remedies. For example, they could: (1) grant an *injunction* (a decree forbidding the defendant to do some act); (2) grant a *specific performance* ordering the defendant to perform his contract; (3) generate a *reformation* (rewrite a contract to conform to the actual intent of the parties); or (4) instigate a *partition* (to divide disputed property). In this sense, Courts of Equity were similar to the ancient Greeks who stressed that the *spirit of the law* was more important than the *letter of the law*. Courts of Equity were more interested in the merits of the case and the justice of the decision, while *common law courts* emphasized form and 'the letter of the law'. See also Equity, Spirit of the law.

Court of First Instance Where the case is originally tried. The outcome may be challenged either by appeal to a higher court or by a request for some form of review. See also Court of Appeal.

Court proceeding see Proceeding

Courts see Competent courts, Federal courts, Local courts, Municipal courts, State courts.

Covered see Concealment in medicine

Covetous see Greedy

Creative reporting This is undertaken by master doctors who invent or create concepts through observations. These observations and concepts are then used

in novel combinations not previously considered. See also Master doctors.

Credibility see Impeach

Creditor The person to whom money is owed by the debtor or to whom an obligation exists. See also Liability, Lien, Debtor.

Creeping modified work This is an 'on the job', gradual, work-hardening return to the usual and customary occupation of the injured worker. Always to the point just short of pain, injured workers push themselves to the limit. The principle is similar to gradually strengthening a muscle by progressive resistive muscle strengthening exercises.

Crime of passion Is a crime committed under the influence of extreme or sudden passion. This negates the element of premeditation, a necessary element of murder.

Crimes Along with *public offenses*, these are acts committed or omitted in violation of the law forbidding or commanding it. They are classified as: (1) *a felony or misdemeanour* (depending upon seriousness); (2) *crimes against property or persons* ; (3) according to the *degree* (e.g. first and second degree murders); and (4) whether it was *voluntary or involuntary*. Upon conviction the punishments can be either death, imprisonment, fines, removal from office or disqualification to hold and enjoy any office of honour, trust or profit. See also Crime of passion, Felony, *Mala in se*, Manslaughter, Misdemeanour, Murder.

Criminal This is either an act done with malicious intent, with a disposition to injure persons or property, or a person convicted of a violating a criminal law.

Criminal insanity Insanity is an obsolete term for psychosis (state of mental disorder), but is still used in strictly legal context such as an *insanity defense*. *Insane* individuals have a deranged mental condition that deprives them of their capacity to comprehend the nature and consequences of a particular act or to distinguish right from wrong. Compare with Health, Sanity. See also Incompetent, Insanity.

Criminal trials see Trial

Crocks Deceptive patients (prototypes II and III) choose certain emotions and certain behaviors to represent their *style of presentation* to the doctor. In certain patients, these styles may be more or less consistent; others are inconsistent for a particular style or switch styles. As a whole, this group has been referred to as 'crocks' by certain hospital staff members. This is a somewhat insulting term to describe patients who complain in excess of what the staff believes is appropriate to their actual ailments. Compassionate doctors always recall the tombstone that reads, 'This old crock was really sick'. See also Euphemisms in medicine.

Cross examination Is the questioning of a witness by the opposition concerning matters about which the witness has testified during *direct examination*. The purpose is to discredit or clarify testimony already given so as to neutralize damaging testimony or present facts in a light more favorable to the party against whom the direct testimony was offered. Compare with Direct examination, Redirect examination. See also Leading question.

Cultural reasons see Pain measurement test

Cumulative evidence see Evidence

Cumulative exposure As an occupational disease, is a form of cumulative trauma. It can have four important components in workers' compensation application: (1) the exposure itself, for example, to asbestos, which may need observation and management; (2) its resultant disease or injury which may or may not cause detectable disability; (3) when the resultant disability becomes evident, with or without the cause being known (called the *time of injury*); and (4) the disease and its disability, when they are medically and legally connected (technically the date of injury). The *date of injury* may be the same as time of injury, but it could be months or years later. See also Date of injury, Occupational disease, Occurrence.

Cumulative injury see Date of injury

Cumulative trauma Is the same as that of *continuing trauma* or *microtrauma*. Cumulative comes from Latin *cumulus*, meaning heap, and also lead to accumulate and cumulus clouds, which look like a 'heap' or pile. Cumulative should be compared with *continuous* (going on without interruption) and *continual* (recurrent at intervals over a period of time). To avoid confusion it is often best to use intermittent or recurring instead of continual, and uninterrupted instead of continuous. See also Apportionment terms, Continuing trauma, Date of injury, Occupational disease, Occurrence.

Curriculum vitae An outline of a person's career listing relevant achievements, education, positions held, etc. When sent as an application for a position, it is a very short account of a career and qualifications that are pertinent for the position. A *dossier* (a French word meaning literally a bundle of papers) is a set of papers giving information about one particular subject, especially one person's personal record. See also Dossier.

Custody see Bailiff

Custom see Common law

Custom laws see Common law

Customer see Patient

D

Damages This is money awarded by a court to an injured individual because of an unlawful act or the negligence of another person. See also Affirmative defense, Average, Award liability, Contributory negligence, Courts, Extenuating Circumstances, Judgements *in personam*, Pain and suffering, Punitive damages.

Date of injury The date that the incident or exposure occurred. For specific injuries most patients know when some manifestations of disability first became apparent. Sometimes, however, the patient's specific memory of the moment is unclear because it had, for example, occurred during physically strenuous activity. This is particularly the case if his or her adrenaline (epinephrine) level was high. These individuals may not notice pain or discomfort until the following day or even longer, depending upon the type of lesions. In a *cumulative injury* or *occupational illness* the date of injury is the time when the employee first suffered disability from the exposure and either knew, or in the exercise of reasonable diligence should have known, that the disability was caused by present or previous employment. A worker may have had symptoms resulting from the cumulative injury or the occupational disease for days, months or years before the date of injury is ascertained. The date of injury determines the law or regulations to be applied for the employee's claim. See also Cumulative exposure, Doctor's first report of injury.

Death The ancient concept for death was *expire*, when a person became so exhausted that he or she could not take another breath. The term *dwindle* was associated with the act or process of dying, in the same way as *birth* means 'the act or process of bearing.' Until recently, death was easy to define. However, the medical advancement of transplantations has meant that it has required refinement. Concerning the diagnosis of death of potential donors, the question is raised as to how far resuscitation should be continued. Every effort must be made to restore the heartbeat following sud-

den cardiac arrest, or breathing if the patient is suffocating, until it is clear the brain is dead. Most physicians consider that beyond this point efforts at resuscitation are useless. A further question concerns the stage when *brain death* has occurred (i.e. irreversible destruction of the brain). Most agree that there is no recovery after destruction of the *brain stem*, which controls the vital function of breathing and the reflexes of the eyes and ears, as well as transmitting all information between the brain and the rest of the body. Final determination is made by a trained clinician who is not concerned directly with the operation. Death is now defined as *the permanent cessation of all vital bodily functions*, including irreversible cessation of cerebral, respiratory and circulatory systems. See also Disease, End, Exhaustion.

Debridement This French term was introduced into the English language in the nineteenth century. It is used in surgery to designate the removal of foreign material and devitalized tissue from a wound. The term was used originally to designate the cutting of constricting bands of tissue. Its literal meaning is an 'unbridling'.

Debtor One who owes another, and this can be anything. Compare with Creditor. See also Liability, Lien.

Deceptive patients Those motivated to avoid something or achieve something through deviance. *Deviance* is a violation of rules and expectations. Deviants, the people who carry out deviance, become 'outsiders' of some sort when compared with those who conform to the norm and are accepted as members-in-good-standing. Viewed with suspicion, deviants are reacted to in a number of ways — they are either given more attention to rehabilitate them, stared at, shunned, ostracized, physically attacked or tried and imprisoned in some way. In a modified form, many doctors act in a similar manner to deceptive patients because such deviance has challenged their fundamental expectations. Doctors trying to improve in the art of medicine must balance the need for caring and empathy with non-judgmental professionalism. This requires the avoidance of value judgments on either the rules that deceptive patients have violated or on deceptive patients themselves. Decept-ive patients require just as thorough an evaluation as any other patient and they require even more understanding. See also Art of medicine, Facts, Functional overlay, Classification of patients.

Decimeters See Metric system

Decision From Latin *de*, meaning down, plus *caedere* to cut, it originally meant to 'cut the knot.' However, it became a strong word of action — the blow that cut down the opposition — a *decisive action*. In the ancient agricultural practice of winnowing, wheat was exposed to the wind so that the chaff blew away and the grains remained. From this developed 'separate the wheat from the chaff,' which implied that it is important to distinguish the wanted from the unwanted, the valuable from the relatively valueless. The concept of decision spread to include the mental action of cutting away all that is worthless to leave one possibility. This idea is even recorded in the *Bible* (Matthew 25:31) where the sheep were separated from the goats. From this sense came the mental action of distinguishing one thing from another and segregating them, when vacillation has come to an end and thought is redirected into action, a decision has been made. The process of eliminating uncertainty and vagueness by determining what not to do, while fashioning an intention of what to do, is *the decision-making process*. In medicine it is called making a diagnosis. In law, a decision is the *judgment* of a court on a dispute tried before it or submitted to it for review. The word *decree* is used for a decision made in a Court of Equity. See also Diagnosis, Findings, Judgment.

Decision-making process see Decision, Process

Decision making see Decision, Ethics

Decisive action see Decision

Declaration This is filed to let the defendant know what is happening. When completed, the declaration has in separate, numbered paragraphs the plaintiff's claim in full, as well as the remedy requested (e.g. money for damages). The defendant then submits an *answer* which, paragraph by paragraph, either admits or denies each matter stated in the declaration. If the answer denies any point in the declaration, the plaintiff must prove his or her point in the *reply*. A declaration is

also called a *complaint and petition*. In the reply, a defendant can file an *affirmative defense*. See also Answer, Claim, Complaint.

Declaratory judgment Although no action is taken, it is what the court indicates would happen if anticipated action does occur. This is also called *declaratory relief*. See also Judgment.

Declaratory relief see Declaratory judgment

Decree Is a decision of a Court of Equity, Court of Admiralty, Court of Divorce or Court of Probate. An *interlocutory decree* is a preliminary order that often disposes of only part of a lawsuit. A final decree is one that fully and finally disposes of the litigation. See also Decision.

Deductive reasoning Is the process of going from a whole to a part. It started in ancient times before the age of experimentation and was perfected by Plato using the *dialectical method* (the ability to pose and answer questions about the essence of things in order to replace hypothesis with secure knowledge). It uses the syllogism method with its major premise, minor premise and conclusion. Problems occur if a person does not pay close attention to the major premise (i.e. main statement, the assumption and the hypotheses). Compare with Analogy reasoning. See also A priori, Conclusion, Inductive reasoning.

Default Is to trick, cheat or swindle something (e.g. another's property) by fraud as opposed to intimidation or force. See also Bad faith.

Default judgment Is a judgment against defendants who have failed to respond to plaintiff's action or to appear at the trial or hearing. See also Conclusion, Judgment.

Defendant In criminal proceedings it is the accused. In civil proceedings it is the person being sued. See also Answer, Competent, Declaration, Litigants.

Defense A denial, answer or plea disputing the validity of the plaintiff's case. See also Affirmative defense, Allegations of fact, Answer, Defendant, Declaration.

Definable injury see Specific injury

Definition That which exactly delimits a concept. See also Abnormal.

Degenerative arthritis   see Cervical spondylosis, Osteoarthritis

Degenerative joint disease see Osteoarthritis

Delegated law see Civil law

Deletion see Mutation

Deliberations The process by which the reasons for and against a verdict are weighed by jurors.

Delusions see Pathological lying

Demarcate Separate by boundaries. See also End.

Demonstration see Certainty

Demonstrative evidence Also called real or objective evidence or tangible physical evidence, this is naturally the most direct evidence since objects in question are inspected by the judge or the jury themselves. It must be logically relevant and completely genuine before it can be admitted as proof. It can be directly connected with the case (e.g. the sponge removed from a patient in a malpractice case or the murder weapon in a criminal case). Alternatively, it may involve something used to illustrate testimony (e.g. model or skeleton to clarify testimony about an injury). Real evidence may not be accepted as legal proof unless it is authenticated by the testimony of witnesses. See also Beyond a shadow of a doubt.

Demurrer A motion to dismiss a civil case because of the alleged legal insufficiency of a complaint. See also Conclusion.

De novo Means anew, afresh. In medicine, *de novo* means the first onset of a lesion. In law, a *trial de novo* is a new trial of a case. See also Injury, New injuries.

Deponent Is a witness who gives pretrial testimony under oath that is set down in writing. It is usually at a lawyer's office. See also Affidavit, Deposition, Witness.

Deposed see Deposition

Deposition Is the pretrial questioning of a deponent by the opposing attorney in the presence of the witness's own counsel and a court reporter. This sworn testimony of a witness is the most common form of discovery and may be taken from any witness (whether or not he or she is a party to the action). In addition to an *oral deposition*, it can also take the form of a written *interrogatory*, where the questions are read to the witness by the officer who is taking the deposition. The person to whom the questions are being asked is said to be *deposed*. Deposed persons say whatever is in their memory, to the best of their ability, at the time the information is being recorded; it is not a take-home test or research project. The questions must be relevant to the litigated issues understood by the deposed. Corrections to the deposition can be provided during or after the deposition and, if the deposed remembers a vital detail later, an alteration can be made in the form of a correction or clarification. See also Deponent, Discovery.

Depression The fact that depression has plagued mankind since the beginning of recorded history is evident from ancient medical texts and through literary portrayal. The ancient Greeks attributed depression to *black bile* and the resultant clinical manifestation was called *melancholia*. Throughout the ages melancholia was thought, among other theories, to be the result of moral weaknesses or possession by evil spirits. This led to the placing of a stigma on mental illnesses. Today, depression is actually an umbrella term and its original meaning has been lost. It derives from the late Latin word *depressare*, to press down, an area sunk below its surroundings. In the fourteenth century it meant to exert force as in pushing down or casting down. It is now accepted that the usual meaning of depression is that ones spirit or mind is literally weighted or pressed down so that one is low in spirits, disheartened, saddened, etc. In the wider sense, depression can be neutral or even good. For example, humans used depression for energy conservation, not only in survival situations but out of respect (e.g. a reverent awe) and to gain peace. *Malignant depression*, however, occurs when somebody 'gives up' from *being pressed down*. This leads to feelings of hopelessness, worthlessness and powerlessness. What the patient is saying in so many words is, 'expect and demand nothing of me because life is not worth living' (i.e. *low life esteem*). See also Suffer.

Derivative injuries see Unrelated injuries

Design see Intent

Desire Once desires were originally thought to be influenced by the stars. In fact, the word desire comes from the Latin *desiderare* (from *de*, meaning away, from, plus *desiderare*, meaning star, constellation). Desire has in its core various combinations of feelings (with its magnitude), sensations (with its intensity) and mood. Thus, desires are filled with life, throbbing, longing, wanting, craving, insisting and ever pressing forward into action. Desire chooses the path and supplies the energy for action. Synonyms include ambition, aspiration, longing for, attainment, etc. It is the feeling sensation that excites desire, and that excitement is an act of tension which passes imperceptibly into will. In other words, *desire is a concentrated feeling sensation*. It is the build up of tension in desire that triggers will into action. Thus, desire merges and blends into the activities of the will which is observed by outsiders as will power. See also Malice, Malicious.

Desmitis Inflammation or irritation of ligaments.

Destructive aggression see Behavior methods

Destructive inner manifestations see Suffer

Detoxification For *addicts*, it is the treatment designed to free them from their drug habit. In *metabolic* detoxification there is a reduction of the toxic properties of a substance by chemical changes induced in the body. Its purpose is to produce a compound which is less poisonous or is more readily eliminated. See also Twelve-step program.

Developmental see Acquired, Congenital, Inherited, Postnatally acquired

Deviants see Deceptive patients

Diagnosis Is the art of distinguishing one disease from another and determining the nature of the disease. It is the doctor's preference after he or she has weighed the probabilities. A diagnosis is made when indecision has come to an end and can be made on the basis of clinical, laboratory and/or pathological evaluations. See also Diagnosis, Diagnostic impression, Differential diagnosis, Etiology, Extracorporeal attachments.

Diagnostic hypothesis see Scientific method

Diagnostic impressions This is a doctor's *tentative explanation/hypothetical diagnosis* when there is a significant degree of uncertainty. It is equivalent to a high degree of medical possibility or a low degree of medical probability. If, for whatever reason, further

diagnostic tools cannot be used for the advancement of diagnostic considerations, the most likely diagnostic impression is used in any medical-legal case so that the legal aspects can progress towards a conclusion. The law does not like *'questionable' medical decisions* that characterize a differential diagnosis and, for legal purposes, the doctor must choose the most probable cause. Medical probability starts at 50.1%, which is equivalent to the preponderance of evidence. See also Framing conclusion, Medical certainty, Medical-legal conceptual counterparts, Medical probability, Medical possibility.

Dialectical method see Deductive reasoning

Difference Obvious distinctions. See also Discern

Differential diagnosis From the patient's clinical manifestations, listing the most likely diagnostic labels for possible disease considerations is called differential diagnosis. Each disease is then analysed in light of all the evidence. Finally, the most likely disease is selected to give a diagnosis or diagnostic impression. Once indecision has ended, thought is transferred to the most appropriate therapeutic methods. If the diagnosis is incorrect and incomplete, then medical and/or surgical treatment is haphazard, usually ineffective and occasionally dangerous. See also Diagnostic impressions.

Differentiate Separate by quantities

Diffuse idiopathic skeletal hyperostosis see Cervical spondylosis

Diligence The degree of personal care, attention, time or effort given by a person to his personal or professional affairs. Three degrees of diligence and three corresponding degrees of negligence are recognized by the law. These include: (1) common or ordinary; (2) high or great; and (3) low or slight. See also Fiduciary, Legal, Loyal.

Direct contempt see Contempt of court

Direct contempt of court see Competence of court

Direct enforcers see Lawmakers

Direct evidence Testimony of an eyewitness who saw the criminal offense; for example, he or she saw the defendant throw a bottle through the window. This should be contrasted with circumstantial evidence when, for example, a fingerprint expert finds the defendant's fingerprints on the bottle that was thrown through the window. See also Circumstantial evidence.

Direct examination Is the initial examination of a witness, usually by the friendly attorney or the party who has called the witness to testify in a trial. It is also called examination in chief. Compare with Cross examination, Redirect examination. See also Leading question.

Direct players see Lawmakers

Directed verdict A request for a directed verdict is made by the defense attorney when the plaintiff's attorney has completed his or her presentation to the jury. The defense attorney asks the court to rule as a matter of law that the evidence presented does not provide sufficient proof for a reasonable jury to give an award to the plaintiff (or for the party having the burden of proof). When a judge supports this request, he or she may 'direct a verdict' and, thus, in effect, withhold from the jury the right to rule independently on the issues at all. Granting a directed verdict results in the final judgment and the termination of the trial. If overruled the trial proceeds. See also Overrule, Sustained.

Disability Literally means 'not able' and derives from Latin *dis*, meaning not, plus *habilis* meaning able, fit or adapted. Disability *is defined in terms of the relationship of the patient's varied medical effects to their environment.* Those varied medical effects that significantly disturb this relationship are called a patient's overall disability. Disability is an actual incapacity to perform the tasks usually encountered in employment and the wage loss that results. Included is mental impairment and physical impairment of the body (California Labor Code, Section 4750). Although impairment is the core of disability, disability is not a purely medical condition but, rather, administrative. Administrative vision perceives limitations in the ability to compete in the open labor market, whether this is from an impairment in earning capacity, impairment of the normal use of a member or competitive handicap. In California, disability occurs when an injured person's actual or presumed ability to engage in gainful activities (in any work) is reduced or absent because of impairment, with or without other factors. These other factors may include age, gender, education, race, economic development and social environment, as well as how the injured person's thoughts, ambitions and actions are affected by his or her current or future condition. The World Health

resulting from an impairment in the ability to perform an activity in the manner or within the range considered normal for a human being. According to the American Medical Association, a disability is an alteration of ones capacity to meet personal, social or occupational demands, or statutory or regulatory requirements, because of an impairment. Disability is a gap between what a person can do and what a person needs to, wants to, or has to do. See also Date of injury, Manifestations of disability, Morbidity, Open labor market, Pathology scope, Prophylactic, Psychiatric injury, Rehabilitation, Sensations.

Disability, American Medical Association see Disability

Disability pie see Apportionment

Disability, Social Security see Social security federal guidelines

Disability, World Health Organization see Disability

Disabled handicapped see Handicap

Discernment Seeing subtle distinctions. See Difference, Discrimination

Disclaimer Establishing formally and under oath of what is truly or falsely imputed to a person or supposed to belong to him or her.

Discovery The pretrial procedure by which one party to a lawsuit tries to gain information that is relevant to the case from the opposing party. Depositions, interrogatories, subpoenas, medical examination, etc., are designed to gain facts, deeds and documents that are exclusively within the opponents possession or knowledge. Each side is trying to gain the necessary information so they can build their case while lessening the opponents position. See also Admission, Conceal, Deposition, Evidence, Exhibits, Interrogatories, Litigants, Motion to produce, Subpoena.

Discretion see Reasonable

Discrimination Is to separate by qualities using our senses and reasoning intellect. Some use it to mean *discernment*, implying accuracy rather as a result of study and experience than of native quality. Discrimination also suggests distinctions and differential; the power to select and thus to reject rightly and profitably. When this becomes destructive and based on emotions there is unfair treatment of a group of people due to race, sex, nationality, religion, etc. Unfair treatment may be omissions or commissions. The majority's denial of privileges to certain minority groups is an example. Practically all state and federal laws do not permit discrimination against workers who are injured in the course and scope of their employment. Discrimination is the failure to treat all persons equally so as to gain a personal advantage or to put the other person at a disadvantage. See also American Disabilities Act, Differentiate, Demarcate.

Disease Is to be distinguished from injury, although the same principles apply when defining the term. Disease is 'negative ease' resulting from interruption, cessation or disorder of body or brain functions, systems, organs or parts. To understand disease is to first know what it is not. *Health*, with its homeostatic mechanisms, is the opposite of disease (or injury). Disease occurs when normal body or mind homeostasis breaks down because the contributing stimuli (usually from one or more causes) become more severe and/or the adaptive response of the individual is inadequate. It is a process that can be broken down into origin, beginning, middle, end and effect. *The origins of a disease are its causes.* This idea developed largely from the discovery of specific infectious agents as the causes of specific diseases, although the concept of one cause leading to one disease is now outdated. Various injuries or diseases may cause injury to cells and thus damage to cells may have many causes. *The beginnings of disease pertain to its pathogenesis*, which is the mechanism of disease development from the initial stimulus to clinical manifestations. Different cell types show differences in their vulnerability to specific stimuli and in their responsive mechanisms. *The middle portions of a disease relate to the morphological changes*; these can occur at any time in the disease process between the beginning and the end. Morphological changes are structural alterations induced in the cells and organs of the body or brain which are characteristic of that disease or are diagnostic. Resultant *lesions* often serve to distinguish one disease from another, as fingerprints identify criminals. Morphological changes that create lesions result in *clinical manifestations. The ending of the disease* can be predicted (a priori) or known by experience (a posteriori). A priori predictions are *prognoses* based upon the *natural history of the disease* in general and the *natural progression of the disease* for the specific patient. If the adaptive health harmony returns, the patient's dis-

ease or injury has ended. Otherwise, if imbalance persists and affected parts are not essential for survival, the condition becomes *chronic*. If imbalance is severe and disrupts vital functions, the patient can *die. Effects of a disease* give rise to impairment, disability and/or handicap; they can also cause death. See also A priori, Disorder, Epidemiology, Health, Injury, Pain, Pathology, Process, Prophylactic, Subclinical disease, Suffer.

DISH (diffuse idiopathic skeletal hyperostosis)   see Cervical spondylosis

Dishonest see Bad faith, Prevaricate, Smoke screen

Dislocation From the Latin *dis*, meaning apart, plus *locus*, meaning place, it is literally designating the state of being out of joint. This term came into English via the French in the fourteenth century. While the ancient Greek and Roman physicians knew and treated dislocations, they did not use this term. Instead, they called them *subluxation*. Later they were called *luxation*.

Disorder Under the broad category of disease, disorder is an alteration of the function or structure of an organ or the body as a whole. Causes of a disorder are: (1) losses; (2) reductions; (3) rearrangements; (4) excesses; (5) reversals; (6) mutations and (7) acquired substitutions. Other similar terms are *malady* (which nearly always refers to a deeply rooted disease, one that is chronic and usually serious) and *infirmity* (although this is often considered to imply a general breakdown of the body through age, it also refers to a bodily defect, perhaps resulting from disease in one who is otherwise physically sound). So, while deafness is an infirmity and epilepsy is a malady, a chromosomal abnormality is a disorder. Malignant thought disturbances are *functional disorders* because they are not associated with clearly defined physical cause or structural change; there is no detectable organic basis.

Disorientation Spatial orientation, which depends upon visual, tactile and kinesthetic perceptions, is often disturbed in parietal lobe dysfunction. Such patients may lose their way in familiar surroundings, develop an inability to interpret a road map, be unable to distinguish right from left or to park or garage a car or a boat. They may have difficulty in arranging a table cloth or dressing. *Disorientation is a special failure to orient the body with that of the surrounding space.*

Disposition The giving up of or the relinquishment of anything. In addition, it is the action of setting in good order the parts or elements of a whole. See also Education.

Disputed medical fact A medical issue under legal dispute. In a worker's compensation case examples would be: (1) the employee's medical condition; (2) the cause of the employee's medical condition; (3) treatment of the employee's medical condition; (4) the existence, nature, duration or extent of temporary or permanent disability caused by the employee's medical condition; and (5) the employee's medical eligibility for rehabilitation services. See also Contested medical claim.

Dissociation The separation of clusters of mental contents from conscious awareness (e.g. the separation of an idea from its emotional significance). An example is the schizophrenic patient who makes inappropriate responses. Even though the mental items are separated, they continue to produce responses in feeling tone as well as in motor and/or sensory pseudoabnormality. This is particularly true in emotional areas, where any of the numerous contents of an emotion can be dissociated to give an *emotional content dissociative syndrome*. If pain perception has been set free, then it can take on a life of its own; this is seen in *chronic orthopaedic pain syndrome*. See also Emotional distress, Empathy.

Distal see Anatomical references, Figure 1 (page 7)

Distinctive The peculiar characteristics or identifying markings of a thing. See also Difference, Discern.

Distinguish To separate the things by quantity and quality. See also Differentiate.

Distress see Anxiety, Emotional distress, Guilt

Diversions see Smoke screen

Divine providence see Providence, Reasonable

Dizzy see Vertigo

Doctor Refers to anyone who has been granted a doctor's degree by a state-approved institution. Non-medical doctors include doctors of the church, a learned or authoritative teacher, a person who has earned one of the highest academic degrees conferred by a university (e.g. PhD), a person awarded an honorary doctorate by a college or university and one skilled or specialized in healing arts (e.g. veterinarians, dentists, physicians and surgeons). Thus, all qualified physicians and surgeons are doctors of medicine, but not all doctors are engaged in the general practice of medicine. Physicians and surgeons are those trained to handle life- or limb-threatening situations and they distinguish themselves by placing MD (medical doctor) or DO (doctor of osteopathy) at the end of their names. In general, the title of doctor primarily and originally meant a teacher from the Latin *deceo*, meaning to teach. See also Physician.

Doctor–patient relationship The patient is a fellow human being in need of help and seeking comfort for a problem which may be of a physical and/or mental nature. The problem may be expressed appropriately or inappropriately. One of the doctor's duties is to guide patients through their illnesses to a cure. If a cure is not possible, the approach in decreasing order of importance is to: (1) improve the patient's health; (2) slow adverse progression; (3) stop adverse progression; and (4) make the patient as comfortable as possible despite adverse progression. The attainment of these goals is the *art of medicine*. It requires a combination of medical knowledge, intuition and judgment, as well as the ability to relate to the patient at the patient's level. Relating appropriately to the patient is caring about the patient's health and feelings and involves establishing a *rapport* that includes mutual trust and respect. How doctors approach patients determines, to a large degree, the amount and accuracy of the information provided by the patient. Any personal attacks on the patient or negative-value judgments about what the patient has done will cause the majority of patients to withdraw. The same principle applies when attorneys are taking the deposition from a doctor. Other factors in establishing a good doctor–patient relationship include the general appearance of the examiner, a kind and considerate approach, a professional attitude, integrity and humility. See also Art of medicine, Deceptive patients, Empathy, Illness, Narcotic, Sweat, Treatment, Trust.

Document A document is a record (i.e. words of great significance applying to any writing, mark or impression that serves as a *memorial* giving enduring attestation of an event or fact). Documents are generally considered as legal records, preserved in a public or official depository. The word *archives* is applied to the place where documents are regularly deposited and preserved. If a doctor uses documents in court, the authenticity of the documents must be established before its contents are admissible as evidence. See also Exhibit.

Dormant From the Latin *dormire*, meaning to sleep, it is when a lesion is in a state of suspended activity. This has a similar meaning to latent (from the Latin, *latere*, to be low), which refers to something that exists but is not apparent (i.e. it lies hidden and dormant as an occult infection). Medically, dormant means that a disease could go on for years without predictably resulting in disability, but it has a continuing susceptibility to aggravation by trauma or stress. In other words, although pre-existing or underlying dormant lesions are present, they would never progress beyond a subclinical level unless certain outside factors occur, such as a relatively minor work injury. See also Aggravation, Apportionment terms, Subclinical.

Dorsal see Anatomical references, Posterior, Figure 1 (page 7)

Dossier A French word containing the idea of bulging, now used to denote any batch of papers relevant to some situation, or a set of documents (or records) with a bearing upon a case that are bulging with details and supplements. Dossier is sometimes used as a synonym for curriculum vitae.

Draconian A descriptive term for strict and unreasonably harsh rules, laws and penalties. Graco, after whom draconian measures were named, was a law giver in ancient Athens.

Drug abuse see Drugs

Druggist see Drugs

Drugs The early origin of 'drug' is uncertain and a number of possibilities have been given: (1) it derived from the Spanish word *dragea* meaning sweet breads, because these were frequently sold by the early druggists; (2) it stemmed from the Dutch word *droog* or dry, because most of the early drugs consisted of dried herbs; (3) more logically, it may be derived from the Persian word *droa* or *odour* because they have a strong odour; and (4) drug may have come from Latin, via French, from the translations of the Arabic medical text during the twelfth century. Indeed, this period of time coincides with the appearance of the term in our medical vocabulary. The word *druggist* did not appear until about the sixteenth century. As far back as records occur, every society has used drugs that produced effects on mood, thought and feelings. Thus, drugs were used for medical and non-medical purposes. From this, developed the following definition: *drugs are chemical substances that affect the functioning of living things and the organisms (e.g. bacteria, fungi and protozoans) that infect them.* Conveying the notion of social disapproval, *drug abuse* refers to the use of any drug in a manner that deviates from the approved medical or social patterns within a given culture. See also Twelve-step program.

Duces tecum From a Latin expression meaning 'you bring with you,' it is the name of a variety of writs or legal orders. For example, a '*subpoena duces tecum*' requires someone ordered into court to bring with her or him those papers or things mentioned in the order.

Due care The degree of care which would be exercised by a person of ordinary prudence and reason (*the reasonable man*) under the same set of circumstances. *Negligence*, as part of *tort* law, is a deviation from due care as determined by the standard of the community or by some specific duty required by law. See Legal, Negligence, Reasonable.

Due process of law The principle that the government may not deprive an individual of life, liberty or property, unless certain rules and procedures required by law are followed. Individuals have rights to receive the guarantees and safeguards of the law and the judicial process. The phrase does not have a fixed meaning, but embodies society's fundamental notions of legal fairness, including adequate notice, assistance of counsel, the right to remain silent under certain circumstances, a speedy and public trial, an impartial jury, and the right to confront and to secure witnesses. This is guaranteed in the fifth and fourteenth amendments to the United States constitution. In short, it is the following of procedural law. See also Habeas corpus.

Durability see Viable

Duress Is the compelling of another person, by whatever means (e.g. threats or physical harm) to carry out what he or she need not otherwise do. It is a recognized defense to any act such as a crime, contractual breach or tort. These acts must be voluntary to create liability. See also Affirmative defense, Bad faith.

Dwarfs For centuries, all abnormally short individuals were called achondroplastic dwarfs. In 1879, two major groups were recognised: the proportionate short stature group (midgets) and the disproportionate short stature group (still called achondroplastic). Then, in 1929, the latter group was further divided into the short-limb (*chondrodystrophy*) and short-trunk (*osteochondrodystrophy*) types. It soon became apparent there were some dwarfs in the achondroplastic category who combined the short-limb features of the achondrodystrophy group and the spinal changes of the osteochondrodystrophy group. These 'transitional' dwarfs were placed in the group called 'pseudoachondroplastic spondyloepiphysial dysplasia'. Subsequently, all three groups were further split and gave rise to numerous specific conditions. An extremely important clinical point is that the osteochondrodystrophy group should be evaluated very carefully for a hypoplastic odontoid in the neck. Under-development of the odontoid can lead to sudden death following either 'whiplash' injuries or general anesthesia. (Reference: Bailey, J.A. II: *Disproportionate Short Stature. Diagnosis and Management.* 1973. WB Saunders).

Dynamic interaction see Effect, What is medical-legal

Dysaesthesia These are sensory phenomena which cannot be classified as simple paresthesias, hyperaesthesia or anesthesia. Patients complain of coldness, wetness and numbness, as well as burning, pricking and pain. There are tactile, thermal, postural, as well as painful dysaesthesias. They exhibit variations in degree, in extent and duration, which is common to all sensory manifestations. However, they are not clear cut and simple, but are often combinations of pain with thermal or tactile disturbances. Thus, the essential differences are that *dysaesthesias encompass a broader group of abnormal sensations and painful sensations and are initiated only after some cutaneous stimulation.* In everyday practice, dysaesthesias and paresthesias are used almost synonymously but paresthesias are non-pain sensations while dysaesthesias are combined pain and non-pain sensations. Compare with Anesthesia, Hyperesthesia, Paresthesia. See also Conversion reaction, Disability, Sensations, Sensation classification — Painful type, Subjective non-pain.

E

Early operative treatment see Acute

Eccrine see Sweat

Edema Hippocrates used the term *oideo* to designate a swelling or tumor. Subsequently, this meaning was limited to designate the puffy swelling of tissues due to accumulated fluids from any cause, including venous or lymphatic obstruction or increased vascular permeability. Special names are given according to the site where edema is located; for example, ascites (peritoneal cavity), *hydrothorax* (plural cavity) and *hydropericardium* (pericardial sack). A massive generalized edema is called an *anasarca*.

Educated estimate Is a professional opinion judgement. For example if the uninjured part of a limb (e.g. right hand) to which the contralateral injured limb (e.g. left hand) is being compared and yet is itself not normal, give an estimated normal value for the uninjured part. See also Estimate, Measurement, Pre-injury capacity.

Effect Effect is part of the *law of causality* which states that, 'All actions are caused by entities.' The etymological derivation of 'cause' means origination as it pertained to a trampled road bed and later a paved way. Cause, that which brings about a result, created the word effect, to bring about (a verb). Effect then took on its own identity and meant an accomplishment (a noun). In most non-medical fields there is nothing intervening between cause and effect; that is, for most discussions in philosophy, religion, many of the non-medical sciences and frequently in law (practically always with blame), effect is that which is directly produced by the action of an efficient cause. In medicine, however, focus is placed primarily on the intervening aspects between cause and effect. Nevertheless, an effect is an act, an exercise of power that can itself initiate a cause, resulting in its own ramifications that are transient or enduring. In the medical-legal arena, effect is the opposite of cause and is divided into *impairment and disability*. A physical component is

at the basis of impairment and disability in *normal patients*, while a mental or psychogenic component is present in deceptive patients. Both mental and physical impairment and disability result in *dynamic interaction*, where the patient affects society and society affects the patient. See also Cause, Effect, Result.

Effects of a disease see Effect

Efferent From the Latin *ef*, meaning out of, plus *fero*, meaning to bear or carry (it is the 'carrying away'). Efferent is used in medicine to descriptively designate those nerves which convey impulses away from the central nervous system and the lymphatics which carry lymph away from the lymph nodes. This is to be compared with afferent (from the Latin *ad*, meaning toward, plus *fero*, to carry). Afferent nerves, blood vessels and lymphatics carry their contents toward the centre of the body or an organ.

Emotional content dissociation see Emotional distress, Dissociation

Emotional distress Mood has a thought plus a feeling tone that can either be pleasant or unpleasant. A malignant magnitude of an unpleasant feeling tone results in distress, with the thought content determining the type of emotional distress. As a gross oversimplification, the pervading thought of anxiety is uncertainty; of anger/revenge; of depression/worthlessness; and of emotional pain/self-pity. In these four basic types of emotional distress, there is the absence of pleasurable thoughts. However, it is possible to disassociate yourself and actually like the unpleasantness (this is an example of *emotional content dissociation*). See also Dissociation, Guilt, Pain, Punishment, Suffering.

Emotional overlay see Functional overlay

Emotional pain see Suffer

Emotional vindication see Malpractice, Retaliation

Emotional wounds see Psychic scar, Trauma

Emotions Excited feelings related to the enhancement or defense of self-preservation and perceived as likes or dislikes. The contents of an emotion contain psychological (mood/affect) and physiological (autonomic nervous system) activities, both of which meet at the hypothalamus and limbic portion of the brain. The psychological component contains a feeling tone that is pleasant or unpleasant, plus a thought that has harmony or disharmony. It is the different arrangements of these four components, along with their intensity, that distinguishes an emotion. If the intensity of desire and will is great enough, an emotion will be expressed externally. It was in this sense that the ancient philosophers equated emotions with physical movement. Latin used the phrase *motus anima*, literally meaning movement of the spirit (where 'spirit' refers to will). Later, from the common Latin term exmovere (move out) came the sense of 'excite'. When the word 'emotion' moved from France to England, it meant moving or agitation — as in, 'the waters continuing in the caverns caused the emotion or earthquake.' By the late seventeenth century, emotion referred to a strong feeling. While keeping this concept, the term emotion has been applied in different ways. This included emote (to give out emotionally), *emotive* (a cause which leads to an emotional response) and emotional (relating to the emotions). See Autonomic nervous system, Emotional distress, Rage, Values.

Emotive see Emotions

Empathetic understanding see Empathy

Empathy From the Greek *empatheia*, meaning affection, passion, it is a psychological term referring to the projection of a persons own personality into the mind or personality of another in order to understand another better. T. Lipps (1851–1914), a German psychologist, defined the concept of empathy as a person who appreciates another's reaction by a projection of the self into the other. Empathy is most obvious when an actor or singer genuinely feels the part she is performing. An empathetic doctor enters the patient's world and views the patient's complaints from the patient's own frame of reference. This is a vicarious or indirect sharing in the suffering of others. As a result of being in the patient's world, the doctor feels personal distress (e.g. concern, sadness, helplessness, alarm,

etc.). Well-trained doctors separate their own personal reactions from the suffering of others and, instead, focus on the patient. Failure to separate the doctor's own distress from the empathetic concern (e.g. caring) will lead to the doctor losing her or his objectivity which is necessary for effective problem solving. Isolated empathetic concern can be reduced only by actually helping the person in need. There are several types of situations where empathy can be applied: (1) *relationship empathy*, the caring with a feeling connection; (2) *rational empathy*, getting in the thought flow of another person; (3) *philosophical empathy*, the removing of words from an idea, thought, or concept so that one can 'feel' these; and (4) *empathetic understanding*, the ability to 'hear' the patient at all levels of communication — in words, thoughts, feelings and unspoken cries for help. See also Art of medicine, Attachments, Dissociation, Doctor–patient relationship, Knowledge by acquaintance, Sympathy, Trust.

Empiric see A priori, Practical/practice

Empiricism see A priori, Practical/practice

Employee It is defined differently under different legal systems. In California's workers' compensation scheme, an employee means every person in the service of an employer under any appointment, contract of hire or apprenticeship. This maybe expressed or implied, oral or written, whether lawfully or unlawfully employed. This includes aliens, minors, elected and appointment-paid public officials, officers and members of boards of directors (with some exceptions), babysitters, incarcerated persons engaged in assigned work, working members of a partnership and persons being evaluated for a job even though he or she has not been hired on a full-time basis. The test is whether the person was rendering a service under another person's direction, assignment or control. See also American Disabilities Act.

Employer According to California's workers' compensations scheme, this includes the state and every state agency; each city, county, district, and all public and quasi-public corporations, and public agencies therein; every person including any public service corporation, which has any natural person in service; and the legal representative of any deceased employer, etc. See also American Disabilities Act.

Employer's Liability Acts Statutes specifying the extent to which employers shall be *liable* to give com-

pensation for medical problems sustained by their employees in the course of employment. This is complicated and specific state laws that are referable should be consulted. See also Compensation, Shall.

En banc   All the judges of a court sitting together. Appellate courts can consist of a dozen or more judges, but the panel often just consists of three. When a case is heard or re-heard by the full court, it is heard *en banc*. See also Bench, Justice.

End/ending   It can be viewed in many ways. For example, an aim or goal, a conclusion, the termination of an act, the completion of an act, when you are out of options, expiration, close-up, relinquish; the most remote part of an extremity; and a demarcation point or boundary beyond which something does not extend or occur, etc. End is an ancient word which derives form the Indo-European *antjo* and Greek *endon* meaning within (similar to the word *esoteric*). As used here, end is the *relative or absolute cessation of an action*. Since medicine is a biological process, a *medical end* is the actual outcome at some arbitrary point in time without determining what has already occurred. There could have been multiple causes, more than one beginning, and a great diversity of possible occurrences in the middle. This differs greatly from the legal system which tends to view end as a necessary, natural or logical termination point. An *absolute end* in medicine is death, but because of life-saving measures available today the moment of death is not always easy to determine. Death is not considered the absolute end in mysticism. In law, an absolute end is where there can be no appeal on a final judgment. In most cases, law would consider a *work product* as something that can be defined and therefore representing an *objective end*. In medical-legal work, end may be used as a noun or verb. See also Death, Result, Term.

End result   see Result

Endocrine reasons   see Pain measurement test

Endogenous   Originating inside the body. See also Homeostasis.

Enemy   see Revenge

Enforced   see Classification of law

Enjoyment   Is the experience of expanding *harmony*. It gives an alive and pleasurable feeling. See also Emotion, Magnitude, Pleasure.

Envious   see Greedy

Epidemiology   From *epi* (meaning upon), *demos* (meaning people) and *logy* (meaning science), it has been variously defined over the last 65 years. Basically, it is the study of the distribution, transmission and control of disease in populations. It is something more than the total of its established facts. It includes their orderly arrangement into chains of inference which extend more or less beyond the bounds of direct observation. *No disease has a single simple cause.* Rather, it is the result of a complex interaction of factors including those related to the biology of the host, exposure to possible infecting agents, circumstances in the environment and psychosocial dynamics. See also Disease, Etiology, Incidence, Koch's postulates.

Equal Employment Opportunities Commission (EEOC)   see American Disabilities Act

Equality   Refers to an amount or quantity. *Equity* adds the element of fairness to equality. Consider a wealthy and a poor group of people. In society, both have equal rights to shop in any store, eat in any restaurant and go to any movie. Equality of opportunity exists in all areas of life for both groups. However, as extremely poor people cannot take advantage of their equality, the arrangement is not equitable. Some argue that the only responsibility of a society is to provide its citizens with equality. Others believe that equality is meaningless in the life of the poor without equity. Patients who agree with the latter concept may become angry and seek redress.

Equity   A body of rules or customs based on general principles of *fair play* rather than on common law or statutory law. It is justice administered between opposing parties based on the concept of natural reason, ethics and fairness, independent of any formulated body of law. The principle is that equity will find a way to achieve a lawful result when the legal procedures are inadequate. In the United States, the distinction between law and equity has lost much of its meaning. The equity and law courts are now merged in most jurisdictions through *equity jurisprudence*. However, equity doctrines are still independently viable and capable of functioning. See also Bad faith, Case, Court of Chancery (for historical development), Decree, Equality (for the distinction between equality and equity), Fair play, Jurisprudence, Justice, Lawful, Legal, Spirit of the law.

Equity jurisprudence   see Equity

Ergonomics The study and design of work situations, taking into account the anatomical, physiological and psychological variables of the people who will work within the given environment. Typists, for example, may require a better chair or for the computer terminal to be positioned more appropriately. See also American Disabilities Act, Job tasks, Relative rest, Subtrials.

Erosive arthritis see Osteoarthritis

Esoteric An ancient concept deriving from Greek *estero* (inner meaning, 'pertaining to those within'). It originated with Pythagoras, who stood behind a curtain when he gave his lectures. Those allowed to go behind the curtain or veil were called his esoteric disciples. *Esoteric knowledge* came to be associated with knowledge hidden by a veil. The veil was just enough to dissuade most students from seeing and hearing what was behind it. Only exceptionally sharp students would step behind the veil. Once there, they learned the subtleties and nuances of how to handle 'impossible' problems.

Esoteric knowledge see Esoteric

Essential functions Is defined by the Equal Employment Opportunities Commission (EEOC) as 'the fundamental job duties of the employment position.' This includes job descriptions, job analyses, collective bargaining agreements and established work experiences of co-workers. Essential functions do not include incidental duties or functions. See also American Disabilities Act, Disability, Job tasks.

Estimation Involves the idea of calculation or appraisal which can either be subjective (e.g. esteem and regard) or objective. It is based on something you have an opportunity to see, feel or perceive in some way to make a calculation or judgment as to the value, size, quality or quantity. An estimation is only an approximation of the time, place or description, but it can sometimes be accurate. Compare with Guess, Medical probability, Speculation. See also Centigrade, Educated estimate, Fahrenheit, Measurements, Metric system, Pre-injury capacity, Quantity.

Ethics These are the fundamental issues of practical decision making. Its major concerns include the nature of ultimate value and the standards by which human actions can be judged proper/appropriate or improper/inappropriate. It is closely related to moral philosophy. *Morals* refers to standards or accepted conduct and generally applies to what is considered the right way of living in a society. Today, morals are more likely to have a religious application and a sexual connotation than ethics. To say that someone is a person of the highest ethics implies that he or she is honorable and upright in her or his private life and business dealings. However, a person of the highest morals would probably suggest that he or she is not guilty of sexual laxity. When referring to the moral sciences as a whole, ethics is a plural noun. However, it may also be used with a singular verb when it refers to fitness or propriety (e.g. the ethics of his decision is debatable). See also Beyond reasonable doubt, Evidence, Honesty, Integrity, Moral certainty, Pain, Probity, Professionalism, Reasonable trust.

Etiology From the late Latin *aiti*, meaning cause, origin, plus *logia*, meaning a philosophy of telling, a giving of proof or causes, it is the study or the causation of a particular disease or injury (i.e. their immediate, precipitating and predisposing causes). The information gathered through the science of etiology created and then outdated the concept of 'one cause, one disease.' Thus, although cause and etiology are used synonymously, they are different; cause is the initiation of lesions, while etiology studies the various causes that can give rise to the lesion. Etiology also establishes the significant sequential associations between two events without implications of logical or transcendental necessity or waiting until precise mechanisms are elaborated at a cellular or molecular level, which is the *pathogenesis*. Knowledge, particularly of primary causes, remains the backbone on which a diagnosis can be made, a disease understood or a treatment developed. See also Cause, Disease, Epidemiology, Koch's postulates, Pathogenesis, Pathology scope.

Euphemisms in law From the Greek *eu*, meaning well or sounding good, plus *pheme*, meaning speech, they are mild, agreeable or indirect words used in place of coarse, painful, offensive or unacceptable ones. Particularly in law, euphemisms are used to protect the lawyer, the client or the audience from embarrassment or other emotional discomfort. They can also be a synonym for a word or phrase of lower status or used to raise the level of a concept. For example, *counsel* is used instead of lawyers, *plausible denial* instead of official lying, *covert operations* instead of burglaries, *launder* instead of cleaning dirty money, and *protective custody* instead of imprisonment. See also Concealed.

Euphemisms in medicine In medicine, euphemisms like *camille* (being melodramatic about a illness), *gomer* or *gork* are motivated by a combination of irritation, consideration and mordant humour. It helps the caring profession maintain their morale in the face of daily exposure to sometimes sordid conditions, to pain and to death. Expressions like FUF (feces under fingernails) and FOF (found on the floor) represent both an in-group language and a convenient shorthand by which staff distance themselves from their own emotions. It also helps to conceal their feelings of annoyance or disgust. See also Concealment in medicine, Dissociation.

Evaluation Is the determination of the value or worth of something. However, its meaning can vary according to the type of disability assessment. In California's workers' compensation scheme, a *comprehensive medical-legal evaluation* of an employee is the preparation of a narrative medical report, prepared and 'attested to' in accordance with the labor codes, which proves or disproves a contested claim. See also Examination, Interpretation.

Event That which either has been accomplished, is the consequence of anything or is a noteworthy happening or occurrence (e.g. an earthquake or flood). Compare with Act (the product of will), Effect, Fact, Fear.

Evidence Is that which tends to show a thing to be true. In its widest sense, which includes self-evidence, it is the basis of all knowledge. Legal evidence includes testimony, documents and objects that are used to prove matters of fact at a trial. *Proof*, in the strict sense, is complete, irresistible evidence; for example, 'There was much evidence against the accused, but not amounting to proof of guilt.' In practice, however, a conviction can sometimes be made on *moral certainty*, or evidence that puts a matter beyond reasonable doubt while not so irresistible as demonstration. Particular types of evidence are: (1) *cumulative evidence*, or that which reinforces or proves something that has been established by other evidence; (2) *corroborating evidence*, which is supplementary evidence that tends to strengthen or confirm the initial evidence; (3) *direct evidence*, or proof of 'facts' by witnesses who saw acts done or heard words spoken; (4) *best* (primary) *evidence*, or that which is original (e.g. a hand-written letter) as opposed to *secondary evidence* (e.g. a photocopy); and (5) *clear and convincing evidence*, which is the standard of proof commonly used in civil lawsuits and in regulatory agency cases. It governs the amount of proof that must be offered in order for the plaintiff to *prevail* (win the case). See also Admissible evidence, Burden of proof, Clear and

convincing evidence, Competent, Factoids, Hearsay evidence, Impeach, Inadmissible, Incompetent, Preponderance of evidence, Prima facie, Proof, Reasonable doubt, Relevant evidence, Rule of evidence, Suppress.

Ex parte A Latin phrase meaning 'from or in the interest of one side only.' This is not permissible in an adversary proceeding. For example, an agreed medical examiner is not legally allowed to talk with either the defense or the applicant's side without notifying the other for permission. There are circumstances when it is permissible, such as in 'ex parte proceedings', when the legal procedure is that only one side is presented, or when an 'ex parte order' is granted by a court at the request of one party to a judicial proceeding without prior notification to the other party involved. A *search or bench warrant* is an *ex parte* proceeding, since the person subject to the search is not notified of the proceeding and is not present at the hearing. See also Bench warrant, Privileged communication, Provisional remedies, Temporary injunction.

Ex parte order see Bench warrant, *Ex parte*, Search warrant

Ex parte proceeding see *Ex parte*

Ex post facto This is Latin for 'after the fact'. It is not constitutionally legal to permit conviction and punishment if an unlawful act was performed before the law was changed and the act was made illegal. Compare with A priori. See also Retroactive prophylactic work restriction.

Exacerbation Is (temporary) pain occurring from the natural progression of disease. It does not make a condition more serious on a permanent basis and, hence, cannot be apportioned because it is not a new injury. However, *aggravations* make a condition more serious in terms of pain, lesions or clinical signs, and so can be apportioned because they are considered new injuries. The precise definition of exacerbations is that it is reflection of the natural history of relatively non-progressive active pathological processes independent of and uninfluenced by aggravation. See also Apportionment terms, Future medical treatment, Reoccurrence of an injury.

Examination From the Latin noun *exagmen*, meaning the tongue of a balance used for weighing, and from this came the Latin word *examinare*, meaning to try by weight. Hence, when doctors examine patients they literally make a careful observation and inspection of the patient as if they were 'weighing the patient's physical condition.' To legally order a physical examination it has to be reasonable and necessary with careful attention to the rights of the patient; this would have to include pertinent facts and reasons to justify the examination. An examination should not be performed if it is not needed to prove, or disprove, a claim. It should be conducted without considerable pain and danger to the patient, and the patient's privacy should always to be respected. However, the patient has a duty to be co-operative within this framework. See also Evaluation, Examination report, Physical examination.

Examination in chief see Direct examination

Examination report The generic format requires that the following information is included:

(1)   Claim number(s);

(2)   The patient's name, address, social security number, age and important identifying information;

(3)   The date(s) of the injury(ies) or date(s) of disability and occupational disease claim(s);

(4)   The allowed condition;

(5)   The purpose(s) of examination;

(6)   The capacity in which the doctor is evaluating the patient (e.g. agreed medical examiner, defense evaluator, applicant evaluator, independent medical examiner or treating doctor);

(7)   The history of the injury, including any treatment recommended or carried out;

(8)   The work history;

(9)   Other medical history;

(10)   Any medication prescribed for the injury and in general;

(11)   The results of the physical examination;

(12)   Any findings following diagnostic testing; and

(13)   Any comments on pertinent findings, diagnoses, conclusion or medical-legal issues.

See also Report comments.

Excessive see Vocational rehabilitation terms

Exercise Originally, this meant to let people, slaves or animals out of confinement, in order to put them to work or to give them a chance to play. From the Latin *ex*, meaning out, plus *arcere*, meaning to confine, it literally means to 'let out of confinement.' Today, exercise refers to the performance of physical exertion for the correction of physical deformity, the improvement of health or the attainment of a sense of well being.

Exhaustion This is the main issue in many claims of cumulative trauma and even death. From the Latin *ex*, meaning out of, plus *haustus*, meaning drained or emptied, it is literally when a person is drained or emptied of his or her vital or nervous power. See also Death.

Exhibit Any document or object introduced as evidence in court. See also Demonstrable, Discovery, Document, Evidence.

Existing condition see Pre-existing

Exogenous Produced or otherwise originating outside the organism. Compare with Endogenous.

Expert A person who has gained special knowledge, or skill, from experience which has resulted in him or her being regarded as an authority or a specialist. See also Facts, Framing conclusions, Legal opinion fact.

Expert witness A person who is well informed about science or some other specialized field beyond the competence of a layman. Due to the skills of the expert, their factual testimony and opinions relating to the field are received as evidence. See also Valid, Witness, What is medical-legal.

Exponential This is to be distinguished from arithmetical and geometrical progressions. An example of an *arithmetical progression* is a series of numbers which begins with 2 and then each subsequent number is the preceding number plus 2 (e.g. 2, 4, 6, 8, etc.). In a *geometrical progression* each number in the progression is the preceding number multiplied by a constant (e.g. 2, 4, 8, 16, 32, etc., if the constant is 2). An *exponential progression* is one in which the numbers increase according to the value of an exponent, which is a constant indicating the number of times the number is multiplied by itself (e.g. if the exponent is 2, the progression would begin 2, 4, 16, 256, 65536). Exponential growth is growth of a system in which the amount being added to the system is proportional to the amount already present.

Expire see Death

Exponential progression see Exponential

Exposure The word has had a bad connotation since its use for the old Greek and Roman practice of abandoning sickly or deformed children for the improvement of racial stock. This has resulted in primarily unfavourable application socially, politically and medically. In law, it means discreditable and embarrassing disclosure or revelation. Medically, exposure relates to the harmful subjection to something (e.g. an infectious agent, extremes of weather or radiation or hazardous conditions). See also Bad faith.

Expungement Official and formal erasure of a record or partial content of a record. See also Amendment.

Extenuating circumstances Unusual factors tending to contribute to the consummation of an illegal act over which the suspect had little or no control. These factors therefore reduce the responsibility of the suspect and serve to mitigate punishment or payment of damages. See also Affirmative defense, Damages.

External see Internal

Extracorporeal attachments These include clothing, jewellery, possessions and other items the patient brings to the evaluation. Some of them can be clues to the diagnosis and management.

Extracorticospinal tract see System — extrapyramidal

Extrapyramidal tract see System — extrapyramidal

Extreme cruelty Grave and serious misconduct by one spouse towards the other (e.g. physical violence, threats of violence, abuse that impairs mental health, etc.) which defeats the marital relationship.

Eyewitness A person who can testify as to what he or she has experienced by his or her presence at an event. See also Direct evidence, Witness.

F

Face saving see Primary gain

Facet joints see Mobilization

Factitious disorders see Con artist, Malingerers

Factoids see Evidence, Facts

Facts Can be absolute or relative. *Absolute facts* are those which are actual in existence. *Facts of reality* are called *truths*. *Relative facts* are those believed to be true, whether of a spiritual or worldly nature. 'Fact' referred originally to a work product, an objective thing, and derived from the Latin *factum*, meaning a thing done (as in facts of arrival). Subsequently, the word referred to the making of a thing, as in the Latin *facere*, to do, to make, to prepare (as in facts of becoming). For those objective things, the standard for comparison was concrete and ordinarily attainable, being a measure to which all else of its kind had to conform. Examples included the standard for weights and measures of corn or cotton, etc. Such objective facts were true for the individual as well as by the consensus of others. In the meantime, there was sporadic evidence in classical Latin of the use of 'fact' for 'something that happened, an event.' In post-classical times, this developed into 'what actually is.' For a given individual 'what actually is' could be true in actual existence, could have been a distortion or could have been fantasy. Yet it was true for the individual. Thus, a separation has occurred between what was true for the individual and what was true as determined by the consensus of others. Throughout the ages authorities in religion, science and government used their individual opinions as to what they believe to be true to argue about facts of reality. Obviously, this resulted in a great deal of disagreement about the 'facts'. Furthermore, in trying to reconstruct what happened in a legal setting, various types of objective, tangible, intangible and subjective evidence had to be relied upon. If this evidence was determined to be substantive and predominant, especially by the prudent lay witnesses and expert witnesses, such evidence, when compared with conflicting evidence, was considered as 'facts'. Each piece of contributory evidence was called a 'fact', even though it may not have been objective by consensus agreement (maybe they should be called *factoids*, evidence presented as if it were a fact). As a result *legal facts* came to include any combination of subdivisions in the 'objective/subjective scale'. By contrast, scientific facts tended to be a combination of objectivity and subjectivity. Perhaps this started when Newton (1642–1726) formulated a *scientific conjecture* for occurrences in nature. After repeatedly being tested and proven, the conjecture was accepted as a *scientific law*. This meant that scientific facts were reproducible theories, strongly supported by a large amount of evidence. Yet, even these scientific laws were relative facts, because scientific certainty never reaches absolute certainty; future evidence may lead to what was considered a scientific law being demoted in status back to a theory. This occurred with the introduction of Einstein's theory of relativity. An example of where the meaning of medical and legal fact diverges can be seen in the perception of a patient's functional abnormalities and anatomical abnormalities. In law, these are facts because patients are considered as their own witnesses. The law assumes that patients are as prudent as they used to be. No such medical assumptions are made. Medically, functional and anatomical abnormalities are not considered to be 'objective' across the board, although they can be at times. Functional losses and anatomical losses are *true medical-legal facts*, because they are provable by consensus agreement. See also Hypotheses, Legal fact, Legal opinion fact, Experts, Scientific method, Trial components, Valid assumptions.

Facts of reality see Facts

Fahrenheit see Centigrade, Metric system

Failure see Risk

Failure to respond This can have many different meanings. A legal example occurs when necessary information is not sent within a reasonable time period. This can impede the patient's right to due process by unnecessarily delaying her collection of evidence within the time restriction. See also Due process.

Fair Honest conduct. See also Honesty.

Fair hearing A special administrative procedure set up to ensure that a person will not be harmed or denied his or her rights without due process of law before a court can intervene.

Fair play Is an important medical-legal concept. Prudent people operate with the concept of fair play in business and legal affairs. Among most people, a prevailing cry today is 'that's not fair.' Yet, the majority do not know the real meaning of fairness. The origins of the word do not clarify the situation, as it was used in diverse situations. For example, in the early nineteenth century, the British used the term 'fair play' for fornication, while Americans used 'fair shake' in reference to having 'honest' dice. Today, fair play can be objective or subjective. Comparing apples with apples and dividing them equally is an example of *objective fair play*. *Subjective fair play* occurs when there is satisfaction between opposing parties because of equitable or impartial treatment pertaining to things of like or unlike kind. An *impartial arbitrator* 'objectively' discerns and compares the evidence and then renders a considered opinion as an equitable adjustment of disputes. A good *compromise* is where both parties received more than they feared in the worse scenario, but obtained less than they had hoped. In other words a 'fair' compromise occurs when both parties lose on some points but gain on others, yet both say 'that's fair enough.' See Bad faith, Fair hearing, Feeling tone, Habeas corpus, Happy, Honesty, Integrity, Justice.

Faith See Beyond reasonable doubt, Bad faith

Faker signs Numerous tests have been developed in order to detect *malingerers*. One of the best is the *Burns' bench test*. The patient is instructed to kneel as far forward as possible on a bench. The doctor grasps the back of the patient's ankles, while asking the patient to bend over and touch the floor with his or her fingertips. If he says he cannot do this because of low back pain, malingering is suspected. The reason is that flexion in this particular posture will not affect the low back specifically, as primary motion occurs at the hip joints

and not the lumbosacral spine. Another is the *Hoover test*, in which the supine patient is asked to raise the painful right lower leg while it is straight. Meanwhile, the palm of the doctor's hand is under the patient's left heel. If the patient is making a genuine effort to lift his or her right leg, he or she will push down with the left heel. If the patient is pretending to do a straight-leg raising and not trying, he or she will not press down with the left heel.

False negative In health care, an incorrect diagnosis that the patient does not have a disease or condition. In other words, the patient has a problem but it is not detected due to an incorrect report of a test or procedure. Outside of medicine, a trade test may also give a false-negative result because of its imperfect validity, resulting in the exclusion of otherwise qualified people who make a low score on the trade test. See also Sensitivity, Specificity.

False oath see Oath

False positive In health care, an incorrect diagnosis that the patient has a disease or condition. For this reason, if a laboratory reports that a patient has, for example, diabetes, then it is wise to repeat the test either at the same laboratory (they may have had a bad day when analyzing the first test) or at another laboratory. The repeat diabetes test frequently proves to be negative and further evaluation may confirm that the patient is not diabetic. Outside of medicine, a false positive may be the inclusion of an unqualified case because of imperfection in the selection criterion. Thus, an unqualified student may be admitted to medical school because of imperfect selective standards. See also Sensitivity, Specificity.

False testimony see Oath

Fantasies The fabrication of facts and/or values. These are a series of fanciful images or designs presented artistically. See also Pathological lying.

Fear Originally, it meant a disaster — a terrible event related to malevolent astral influence. This developed from the idea that a person's *lucky star* gave loving guidance. If a person did not find his or her lucky star, then there was the absence of love, placing them in the realm where fear could develop. By the eighth century, fear related to old Saxon word *var*, meaning ambush, as in one who lies in wait to bring on a sudden calamity. By the thirteenth century, it had switched from a noun to a verb and referred to a person going through the experience of the process resulting from a cause. From the thing undergone, the meaning has since shifted to signify the feeling of the cause — the dread of the event. Today, *fear is an unpleasant emotional and physiological response to a recognized source of danger.* See also Illness, Sickness.

Feasible see Classifying information

Federal cause of action see Color of law

Federal courts Are United States courts, including District Courts (federal trial courts), Courts of Appeal (appellate review courts) and the Supreme Court (the court of last resort in the federal system). Others include Court of Claims (against the United States Government), Court of Customs and Patent Appeals (reviews Custom Court decisions) and Customs Court (reviews decisions of the customs' collectors).

Feel A word used by the ancient Greeks to mean vibrate, shake, stir or excite at its root.

Feeling tone see Emotional distress, Fair play, Magnitude

Fellow–servant rule Precludes an injured employee from recovering damages from her employer where the injury resulted from the negligence of another employee.

Felony A crime of graver nature than a misdemeanor and crimes declared to be serious by statute or to be 'true crimes' by the common law. Statutes often define felony as an offense punishable by imprisonment for more than 1 year, by death or by imprisonment generally. The original *common-law felonies* were felonious homicide, mayhem, arson, rape, robbery, burglary, larceny, prison breach (escape) and rescue of a felon. See also Crime, Misdemeanor, Pain.

Fiduciary Involves a person acting for the benefit of another in a relationship involving confidence and trust in the handling of another's money or property. Examples are executors, guardians, trustees and the trust departments of banks. See also Guardian, Honesty, Integrity, Probity, Trust.

Final decree see Decree

Finding A court decision that answers questions raised by the pleading or charges. It discloses the grounds on which the judgment rests. *Findings of fact* are made by a jury or judge. See also Decision, Judgments.

Finding of fact see Finding

Findings and award see Case conclusion

Fingers see Figures 6 and 7 (page 59), Impairment

First-aid treatment Is the initial emergency treatment of injured or ill persons prior to the arrival of trained medical personnel. It remains first aid if it is a one-time event that adequately cares for minor scratches, burns, splinters or other minor work injury not requiring the attention of a physician.

First cause see Origin

First-degree murder see Murder

Flare ups see Future medical treatment

Floating impairment see Impairment

Follow-up medical-legal evaluation Is an evaluation which includes an examination of an employee and the preparation of a narrative report within 1 year.

Foot The different bones in the foot are shown in Figure 3. Figure 4 (overleaf) clarifies the terminology for the different types of movement.

Forensic medicine Medical knowledge and technology applied to questions of law. See also Medicine/medical, What is medical-legal.

Foreseeable risk Risk whose consequences should be known to a person of ordinary prudence. This is a concept used in various areas of the law to limit *liability* of a party for the consequences of his or her acts that are in the realm of foreseeability. In tort law, a party's actions may be deemed *negligent* if the injurious consequences of those actions were 'foreseeable.' Foreseeability is the main issue in *proximate cause.* See also Affirmative defense, Proximate cause, Prudent person, Reasonable, Reasonable person, Tort.

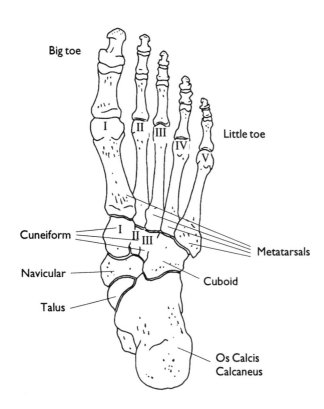

Figure 3 The bones in the foot

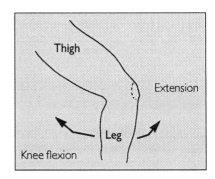

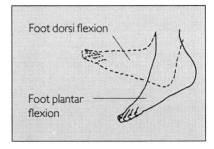

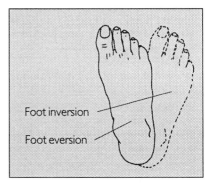

Figure 4 The terminology associated with movement of the foot

Foresight see Reasonable

Forethought see Reasonable

Forgive see Pardon

Fragile bone diseases Metabolic condition (genetic, congenital or acquired) that causes moderate or severe osteomalacia, osteopenia, brittle bones or thin bones.

Framing medical-legal conclusion Are methods used for complex questionable decisions. In the *reasonable medical probability method*, the legal system is looking for what is most likely (i.e. when one situation is more likely to be the situation than another with a 51% or more chance that such a relationship exists). This allows for a broad margin of uncertainty. Of course, the closer opinions can come to reasonable medical certainty, the more weight those opinions carry. Another approach is the *'if-then method'*, where if a certain situation is the case, one opinion is appropriate but, if another occurs, then an alternative opinion would apply. Both methods are used when there are inconsistencies and contradictions in the case evaluation. See also Diagnostic impression, Legal opinion fact, Preponderance of evidence, Report comments.

Fraud Intentional deception that deprives someone of a right, causes harm or induces another to part with something of value. See also Bad faith, Conceal, Deception.

Frequently see Vocational rehabilitation terms

Friend of the court see Amicus curiae

Front see Anatomical references, Figure I (page 7)

Function, seven factors see Aging, Subjective non-pain disability

Functional abnormalities All body parts are present but work in an unusual manner because of pathophysiological (e.g. disordered neuromuscular systems) and/or psychological (e.g. bizarre gait) factors. The patient's voluntary input can play a part or, if psychologically based, can actually be the cause. Compare with Anatomical loss, Functional loss. See also Anatomical abnormalities, Facts, Impairments, Objective minus.

Functional disorders see Disorder, Psychogenic disease

Functional limitation This is an individual's inability to perform certain actions due to *impairment*. The comments in a report would be solely due to the allowed conditions in the claim(s). For example, the situation of a patient whose low back injury restricts her to flexion of 55°, extension of 15°, and to rotation and lateral bending of 15°, with slight/moderate pain if the back moves beyond these limits or when sitting or standing for over 45 minutes. In these circumstances, the report can include comments about the type of work the patient can perform and the reason for that opinion. For example, 'This patient would have difficulties in occupations requiring more than occasional bending and lifting of objects from below the level of the knee, extreme rotation action of the spine and performing overhead activities. I would not expect the patient to have difficulties in the use of the upper limbs nor with walking, sitting, or standing as long as the latter two are not required more than periodically throughout the day.' See also Impairment, Subjective non-pain disability.

Functional loss All body parts are present and look the same as they did before the injury, but the part does not work well anatomically. An example would be an objective. Compare with Anatomical abnormality, Functional abnormalities. See also Facts, True medical-legal facts.

Functional overlay Also called psychogenic overlay, emotional overlay and physiological overlay, it is generally considered to be symptoms expressed by the patient that the doctor believes are not based upon any detectable alterations in the structure of the brain, nervous system or body. Others have used it as a diagnostic term for the *exaggeration* of a low level or arrested lesion, as well as when relatively minor body injuries are excessively amplified. Functional overlay is a psychiatric diagnosis in the legal arena and is equal to being dishonest. It is roughly in the category of a *somatoform disorder*. See also Deceptive patients, Overlay, Self-deceivers, Subjective non-pain disability.

Functional prolongation Excessive enduring quality and quantity of manifestations. See also Functional overlay.

Fungi see Drugs

Furnucle see Sweat

Fury see Rage

Future medical treatment This is treatment to: (1) cure or relieve the effects of the permanent 'pilot' injury (e.g. to increase function, reduce pain); (2) maintain the workers' therapeutic and/or natural healing gain; (3) slow adverse progression, and (4) to relieve the effects of exacerbations or recurrences that are reasonably expected from the work-related lesions for which a finding and an award has been given. In other words, future medical care is recommended when it is *reasonably medically probable* (more likely than not) that the patient will either need treatment for anticipated flare ups (i.e. *bad days*), with or without *adverse progression* (i.e. deterioration), or to prevent or minimize these from occurring. See also Appliance, Home remedies, Medical necessity, Medical possibility, Physical mobility aids, Projected orthopaedic expenses form,

G

Gag order A court-imposed order to restrict information leakage about a case.

Gainful employment An occupation suited to the ability and potentiality of the worker.

Gap in the statute No existing rule relevant to the points in dispute. See also Informational gaps, Interpreting legislation, Jurist.

Gated law see Civil law

Genetic The branch of biology which deals with the phenomenon of heredity and variation is called *genetics*. It is derived from the Latin word *genus*, meaning race or kind. It includes heritable and inherited conditions. Compare with Acquired, Congenital, Development, Postnatally acquired.

Genetic congenital conditions Are heritable disorders which convey the sense that in a given individual the gene and/or the disease, although transmittable to the offspring, may not have been inherited but arose by mutation. See also Mutation.

Genetic congenital/development lesions The tarda heritable developmental lesions are genetic problems with origins present before birth (e.g. from mutation) but not manifested until sometime after birth. See also Mutation.

Genotype The genetic constitution of an individual. The genotype does not necessarily predict the *phenotype* (the individual's observed characteristics). That is, genotype, like *character*, determines what a person really is, while phenotype, like *reputation*, is what a person appears to be. See also Phenotype.

Genu valgum see Valgus body position, Figure 5

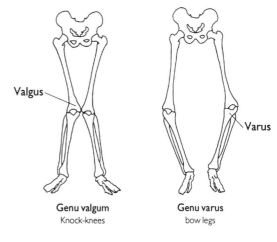

Valgus

Varus

Genu valgum
Knock-knees

Genu varus
bow legs

Figure 5 The difference between genu valgum and genu varus

Genu varum see Varus, Figure 5

Geometrical progression see Exponential

Gold bricker see Malingerer

Gork see Euphemisms in medicine

Gomer see Euphemisms in medicine

Good cause A legally sufficient and substantial reason for doing something. For example, a case might be reopened when the existence can be shown of fraud, lack of notice to the parties or significant evidence is discovered.

Good faith Is honesty in dealings when fulfiling an obligation as well as observing reasonable standards of fair play. Compare with Bad faith. See also Equity, Fair play, Justice.

Grade see Pathological scope

Gram see Metric system

Grand jury A jury of between 12 and 23 people who are empowered to look into possible criminal activity, report on it, and indict individuals when it finds evidence that they have committed crimes. See also Jury.

Grandfather clause A provision permitting persons engaged in an activity to continue, despite the presence of a new law affecting that activity.

Gratuitous promise A person who gives his or her word to do something, or to refrain from an activity, without requiring any consideration in return.

Gratuitous service (volunteer) The person rendering gratuitous service as a volunteer to another person (i.e. not an employee under California's workers' compensation scheme). See also Mandate.

Great probative value Something of importance in establishing officially the authenticity or validity of a case. For example, a medical report containing: (1) complete and accurate history; (2) review of records; (3) consistent statements regarding causal relationship; (4) careful analysis; and (4) medical rational for the opinion. See also Report comments, Well-reasoned report.

Greedy From an Anglo-Saxon word (*graeding*) that emphasizes the idea of selfish satisfaction or lack of self-restraint. Greedy people want everything for themselves. They are keenly and excessively aggrandizing for food and material things. This makes 'greed' an *umbrella term*. Some similar words under the umbrella are: *miserly* (given to hoarding, chiefly for its own sake, but also out of fear and in defense, to the extent of self-denial and often times hardship), *avaricious* (bent upon gain of any sort, money as well as other material things), *rapacious* (violently seizing and carrying off what a person wants), *covetous* (the uncontrollable desire for what belongs to another), and *envious* (which goes beyond covetous in denoting not only an inordinate

desire to have something that another possesses, but implies a feeling of spite and malice towards the other). These and similar concepts are important in understanding the minds of deceptive patients. See also Smoke screen.

Greet the court see Address the court

Grief see Anger

Grievance An allegation that something imposes an illegal burden, denies some equitable or legal right, or causes injustice. See also Bad faith, Complaint.

Grievant The one filing a grievance.

Grip see Measurement, Objective minus

Guardian A person entrusted to look after the interests of a minor or an incompetent person. The specific fiduciary relationship is defined by law and court orders. See also Fiduciary, Trust.

Guess Is a time, place or description of something about which a person has no information on which to base his or her answer. Guesses, in contrast to estimates and medical probabilities, are not acceptable in the medical-legal arena. See also Conjecture, Estimate, Hypothesis, Inference, Scientific method, Speculation.

Guilt The sense of anguish felt after a person has fallen short of his or her own standards. Consisting of the pervading emotions of anxiety and concealed anger, guilt is perhaps the most common form of distress in our culture. Guilt may be *benign* (i.e. mild or slight) or *malignant* (i.e. moderate or severe). Malignant guilt concerns itself with the conflict of values beyond 'normal' qualitative or quantitative proportions (too intense and/or too long). This is true whether a person's standards are realistic, unrealistic, adopted from other people, or created by the individual. See also Anguish, Distress.

H

Habeas corpus From the Latin for 'you have the body,' it is an ancient common law writ. It is issued by a court or judge directing the person who holds another in custody to produce the body of the person before the court for some specific purpose. During the Middle Ages it was employed to bring cases from inferior tribunals into the King's courts. During the reign of Henry VII (1485-1509) it was a device for the protection of personal liberty against official authority. For example, it prevented the detention of persons without trial. The judge would order to have a prisoner brought into court to determine the legality of the imprisonment. Subsequently, these aspects have persisted and expanded to include those held under private authority, those in mental institutions and situations involving child custody, etc. Habeas corpus is, in essence, a constitutional guarantee against imprisonment without a cause being shown (i.e. make the arrest official or release the person). See also Fair hearing, Fair play, Good faith.

Hallux varus see Varus

Hand The different bones in the hand are shown in Figure 6 . Figure 7 clarifies the terminology for the different types of movement. A normal hand has four fingers and a thumb – not five fingers.

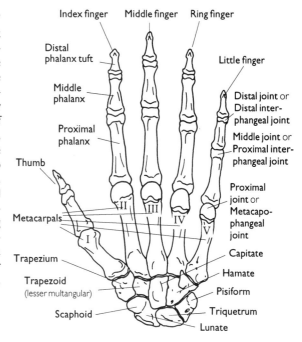

Figure 6 The bones in the hand

Figure 7 The terminology associated with movement of the hand

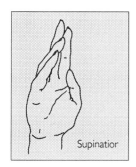
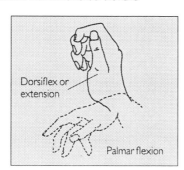
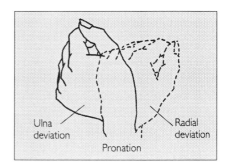

Handicap Also called physically challenged, it is any genetic, congenital or acquired physical or mental defect or characteristic preventing or limiting a person from participating in 'normal life'. It refers to what the patient cannot do compared with non-handicapped people. Six conditions which include the vast majority of handicaps are: (1) blindness and partial blindness; (2) deafness and partial deafness; (3) cardiac disorders; (4) tuberculosis; (5) mental retardation and socioemotional disturbances; and (6) severe orthopaedic problems (chiefly neuromuscular). *Impaired handicapped* persons can accommodate for the 'activities of daily living' obstacles, while *disabled handicapped* cannot. With either, the ability to accomplish a specific task with or without accommodation means they are neither handicapped or disabled with regard to that task. See also Disability, Disabled, Impaired, Impairment.

Handicapped employee One with a physical or mental impairment that interferes with obtaining employment or re-employment should the worker become unemployed. See American Disabilities Act, Handicapped, Open labor market.

Happening see Occurrence

Happy see Fair play, Health, Justice, Negative pleasures, Pleasures

Harmless error An error committed during a trial that was either corrected or not serious enough to effect the outcome of a trial. Thus, it was not sufficiently harmful (prejudicial) to be reversed on appeal.

Harmony From the Greek harmonia, meaning joining in agreement. See also Enjoyment, Yin and yang.

Hazardous substance see Substance

Health Is from the Anglo-Saxon word *hal*, meaning heal, whole or sound in body and mind. Health first meant well being, as in those who were able to cope with any stress life has to offer while enjoying a sense of well being as long as it lasts. It is a biological term relating to a state of being, a state of becoming and a state of adaptation. As a state of being, health involves harmony within a person (e.g. mind, cells, fluids, organs and tissues) plus harmony between the person and the person's environment. As a state of becoming, Emile Coue (1857–1926) encapsulated the meaning in, 'Every day, in every way, I am getting better and

better.' To maintain a state of adaptation, a person's homeostatic mechanisms must be fully operational in maintaining a state of being and a state of becoming. Health is happiness and although happy people have the same problems as unhappy people, the former handle their emotions and thoughts differently. People who are mentally healthy have learned how to handle the confusion and chaos of life but not be a part of it. They also know how to enjoy the good times. *Mental toughness* is the maintenance of mental health and mental discipline during adversity, while keeping a realistic framework on good times. See also Safety, Sanity, Illness.

Hearing A proceeding where evidence is taken to determine an issue of fact and to reach a decision on the basis of the evidence in or outside the court.

Hearsay evidence Statements made by one person in court about what another said when the speaker is not available for cross-examination. This indirect statement is hearsay and, with few exceptions, will not be admissible as evidence in any form (including oral or written statements, non-verbal conduct intended as a substitute for words). Since the demeanor of the person who is supposed to have provided the evidence cannot be assessed by the judge or jury, there is generally no adequate basis for determining whether it is true. See also Evidence.

Hematoma A localised collection of blood, usually clotted, in an organ, space or tissue as a result of the violation of a blood vessel wall. By contrast, a seroma is a tumor-like mass containing serous (serum) fluid. *Serum* is a Latin word meaning *whey* and applies to the watery part of clotted blood because of its obvious resemblance to the watery part of curdled milk.

Heritable Although used as essentially synonymous with 'genetic' and 'inherited,' the term 'heritable' implies that not only are genes transferred from parent to child, but that new genes may be present in a zygote as a result of new mutations. In other words, 'inherited' implies hereditary transmission from parent to child, while heritable includes new mutations with the inherited material. Compare with Acquired, Congenital, Development, Inherited, Postnatally acquired. See also Zygote.

Heritable disorders of connective tissue Generalized defects involving primarily one element of connective tissue (i.e. collagen, elastin or mucopolysaccharides). They are transmissible in a simple *Mendelian* manner.

Hide see Concealed, Concealment in medicine, Smoke screen

Hippocratic oath see Medicine, Professional

Histrionics Deliberate displays of emotional drama. *Verbal histrionics* are vivid similes, such as 'being jabbed like an ice pick.'

Hit see Hurt

Homeostasis From the Greek *homeo*, meaning changing, plus *statis*, meaning standing, it refers to the way the internal environment is maintained in a stable condition. An example is that the production of new cells is regulated to match cell-death rates. See also Disease, Endogenous, Health, Injury.

Home remedies That area of treatment ranging between no need for further medical care and the need for formal medical care by a doctor. They include hot showers, getting into a Jacuzzi, family members giving massages, over-the-counter medication, etc. See also Future medical treatment, Treatment.

Homicide The killing of a human being by the act, by omission or by negligence under circumstances which may be justifiable, excusable or felonious. See also Classification of crimes.

Honesty Acting with regard for the rights of others, honest people adhere to their integrity and what they believe to be true, even if it is not, hence 'honest men can differ'. Being *candid* relates to an honest statement, while being *fair* applies to honest conduct. *Probity* is honesty tried and proved, especially in those things that are beyond the reach of legal requirement. Compare with Bad faith, Impeach. See also Bonafide, Fair play, Good faith, Integrity, Probity, Professionalism.

Honorable people see Bad faith

Hoover test see Faker signs

Horizontal plane The body is divided into top and bottom. This should be compared with the *coronal plane* (which divides the body into front and back) and the *sagittal plane* (which divides the body into right and left halves). See also Anatomical references, Figure I (page 7).

Horseplay Implies rough, boisterous play at work, which can involve *skylarking* (the performing of tricks or frolicking). Injuries sustained while an employee is engaged in horseplay or skylarking are not usually compensable. However, if an employee voluntarily participates in horseplay or skylarking and the employer does not object, a resultant *proximate injury* may be compensable under the *condonation exception*. Condonation means the voluntary overlooking of an offense as if the offender has not committed an offense. This implies forgiveness and pardon for the offense. See also Proximate cause.

Hostile witness A witness whose testimony is not favorable to the party who called her or him as a witness. However, she or he may be asked leading questions and may be cross-examined by the party who calls her or him to the stand. See also Leading question.

House of Representatives The lower house of the US Congress. It is the most representative body in the Federal Government. See also Checks and balances

Humane see Sympathy

Humanistic qualities see Art of medicine, Attachment

Humble see Presume

Hurt The English borrowed 'hurt' from old French word *hunter*, meaning to knock, to hit. What was knocked or hit would hurt in a physical or mental sense. As a verb, the meaning of hurt disappeared in seventeenth century England. What remained was only the metaphorically extended noun of wound or harm. In the medical-legal arena, hurt is not restricted to physical injuries, but includes also mental pain as well as discomfort or annoyance. See also Psychic, Trauma.

Hidradenitis suppurativa see Sweat

Hydropericardium see Edema

Hydrothorax see Edema

Hypersensitivity In the medical-legal field, this is a massive word with far-reaching ramifications in diagnosis and management. In the figurative sense, it implies excess or above-normal. The Greek prefix hyper means over and above and beyond, in excess of normal. People may be hypersensitive as a result of psychogenic factors, endocrine disturbances, as part of their temperament, to drafts, to poison ivy or as a result of an abnormal autoimmune system, etc. As generally used, hypersensitivity reactions are pathological processes induced by immune responses, immediate or delayed. Sharp clinicians can use the subject of hypersensitivity to point out why rules of thumb are dangerous in medicine. See also Pain measurement test, Rules of thumb, Valleix phenomenon.

Hypertrophic arthritis see Osteoarthritis

Hypothesis From the Greek *hupo*, meaning under, plus *tithenai*, meaning put, to place, it is a foundation or a putting under. Literally, this is placing a tentative explanation, or *educated guess*, under a theory. A hypothesis is a statement of what is deemed possibly true and serves as a starting point for further investigation. If observation and experimentation explain all of the facts the hypothesis is regarded as *verified*. Until then, it is regarded as a *working hypothesis* (i.e. an educated guess or medium possibility of truth which is used at that time for practical purposes). When more known facts fit, a hypothesis becomes a theory that is probably true. See also Conjecture, Facts, Guess, Inductive reasoning, Scientific conjecture, Scientific methods, Supposition.

Hypothetical question A question based upon assumed or supposed facts for which a witness is asked for an opinion in court. This question is not supported by the essential facts of the case at hand that would prove its truth. Compare with Leading question.

I

Ideal surgical candidate Is one who exists only as a concept. Included would be: (1) an honest and straight-forward patient; (2) a patient that intensely dislikes being sick; (3) a patient who has no hidden agendas of secondary gain; (4) a patient with clear-cut pathological lesions that are causing clinically recognizable manifestations; (5) lesions which are relatively easy to reach surgically; (6) lesions that do not lend themselves to non-operative treatment; (7) a patient who is in good health naturally or by medical control; (8) a patient who has confidence in the operating surgeon; (9) a patient whose peripheral problems (e.g. family matters, finances, etc.) are under control; (10) a patient that is anxious to get back to work of whatever type; and (11) a patient that has appropriately chosen the surgeon suitable for the patient's lesion.

'If-then' method see Framing conclusions

Illness and sickness As early man viewed illness as divine punishment for being evil or wicked and healing as purification, medicine and religion were inextricably linked for centuries. A person became ill because he or she lost favor with a god. Physical and spiritual purging was necessary to regain that god's grace, and this would lead to improved health. This notion is apparent in the origin of our word *pharmacy*, which derives from the greek *pharmakon*, meaning 'purification through purging.' Today, ill and sick mean of unsound physical or mental health, unhealthy, but ill is the more formal term. In Great Britain, sick implies nauseated. Doctors must take cultural and language differences into consideration when evaluating different patients. See also Disability, Doctor-patient relationship, Fear, Suffer.

Immediate cause see Cause, Cause and effect, Proximate cause

Immediate operative treatment see Acute

Impaired handicap see Handicap

Impairment Is a vague legal concept and this is further confused when using criteria for the condition outlined by the Social Security, vocational rehabilitation, non-workers' compensation insurance companies, veteran's pensions, non-workers' compensation but industrial pensions (e.g. teamsters) and in workers' compensation. The American Medical Association defines impairment as an alteration in a person's health status as assessed by medical means; the World Health Organization says that it is any loss or abnormality of psychological, physiological or anatomical structure or function; and the California workers' compensation scheme states that impairment is purely a medical condition characterized by any anatomical and/or functional abnormality or loss — a reduction or loss of using this whether subjective, objective, physical or mental. Subjective and objective impairment are important topics in their own right. An 'impaired' individual is not necessarily 'handicapped' or 'disabled'. Loss of a finger in a laborer has fewer ramifications than if it occurred in a musician. Further, if loss of a finger prevented a surgeon from operating, the surgeon might make a *lateral job transfer* (e.g. into radiology or teaching). Impairment, even when localized, cannot have its consequences fully understood without knowing the patient's activities at, and away from, work. Some impairment is 'stable and permanent,' while other impairment is 'floating' or 'sliding' despite being stable and permanent. There is 'reversible' impairment. California's Labor Code defines *impairment as not an unknown condition, but one that causes loss of function of the body in whole or in part. In general, impairment is the amount of a patient's anatomical and/or mental loss of function caused by the allowed injuries in the claim.* However, the law uses 'disability' for legal disability and medical impairment, without making a distinction between the two. A doctor should remember that in law all medical statement/opinions address impairment, not disability. In using the American Medical Association rating system, impairments are to be given based on the whole person, not the body part. See also American Disabilities Act, Disability, Disabled,

Functional abnormalities, Handicapped, Loss of use awards.

Impartial arbitrator see Fair play

Impassive To give no sign of emotion whatsoever, even though a feeling, reaction, may be strong within. See also Stoic.

Impeach Call and question about damaging evidence. This can be *impeachment of a witness*, when an attack on their credibility (believability) is made by offering evidence for that purpose. It can also be a challenge to the authenticity or accuracy of a document, decree, judgment, etc. See also Evidence.

Impeachment of a witness see Impeach

Impunity see Penalty

Inadmissible Under the rules of evidence, that which cannot be admitted or received as evidence. See also Evidence.

In camera In Latin this means 'in a room' and it refers to a hearing in the judge's chambers or private office outside the presence of the jury and the public. See also Chambers.

Incidence An epidemiological term. It is the rate of occurrence of new cases during a defined interval. It is a more specific indicator of the *risk* of acquiring a disease than is *prevalence* (the ratio of known cases to the population at risk at a particular point or over an interval). Prevalence also reflects factors that influence disease duration and is calculated by multiplying incidence by the average duration of disease. Therefore, incidence is preferable to prevalence for inferring mechanisms of cause or host predisposition to onset. See also Epidemiology, Prevalence, Risk.

Incite Also referred to as abetting, in criminal law it is to urge or instigate another to commit a crime.

Inciting cause see Cause

Incompetence A lack of ability, fitness or of some legal qualification necessary for the performance of an act or the discharge of a responsibility. *Incompetent evidence* is that which the court will not permit the counsel to present during the trial because of some defect that relates

to the witness or to the evidence. Compare with Competence. See also Criminal insanity, Evidence, Insanity.

Incompetent evidence see Incompetence

Incompetents see Conservatee, Minor

Indecision Inability to make a decision. See also Diagnosis, Diagnostic impression, Differential diagnosis, Waffling.

Independent contractor A person engaged to utilize her or his own judgment and skill to perform an agreed task without control by the employer, except as to the result or the product of the work.

Indictment see Complaint, Prosecution

Indirect contempt of court see Contempt of court

Indirect contempt see Contempt of court

Indirect evidence see Circumstantial evidence

Indirect players see Lawmakers

Inductive reasoning Goes from a part to a whole. Inductive reasoning heralded the scientific method during the Renaissance. It is complimentary to deductive reasoning. Proof by induction involves using a conclusion as the premise for a new deduction. Thus, what is ordinarily known as scientific induction is a constant interchange of induction and deduction. Induction is based on the logical axiom: *what is true of the many is true of the whole.* Based upon our perception of nature's universal and uniform laws, induction goes through the steps of observation, hypothesis, testing and verification (i.e. accounting for all the facts which properly are related to it). The major premise of reasoning by deduction is nothing more nor less than the hypothesis, theory, law or principle discovered in the process of reasoning by induction. Deductive reasoning accepts this major premise as a fact and then proceeds to draw conclusions from it based on the axiom: *what is true of the whole is true of its parts.* See also A priori, Analogy reasoning, Deductive reasoning, Facts, Scientific Method, Valid.

Inference Is deducing what is being implied by 'reading between the lines'. It is a probable conclusion towards which known facts, statements or admissions point, but which they do not absolutely establish. To *infer* is to reason from the known to the unknown and to then form judgments based on the deductions. For example, 'from the study of Indian relics, we infer that some tribes had highly developed arts;' or 'your haste infers your eagerness.' There are multiple places for error between what your messenger collected for information and your conclusion. These include errors in the information obtained by the messenger, the messenger's interpretation, the messenger's intention in selecting the information and relating it to you, the actual relating of the information, your interpretation of what you think you heard and your expressing of the information based upon your interpretation. Drawing inferences is frequently used in right brain or 'subjective' thinking. If incorrect and then acted upon, it can be quite damaging to others (e.g. rumors, punishment as from circumstantial evidence, etc.). It can also be damaging to you. For example, a man with dark glasses, a cane, and a dog may be blind as you guess or may be in disguise. Inferences may be good for emergency or short-term decision making, but are generally not good for life-shaping decisions. See also Guess.

Inferior/lower/caudad Are used to designate parts of the body away from the head end. See also Anatomical references, Figure 1 (page 7).

Infirmity see Disorder

Informational gaps Leaving out essential information (e.g. the reasons for opinions) because, for example, the operative or pathology reports are not available for review. See also Comments, Gap in statute, Report.

Informational mess Chaotic information. See also Process.

Informed consent Consent given only after full disclosure of what is being consented to in order to avoid violation of a person's right. See also Probity, Professionalism, What is medical-legal.

Infractions It concerns the violation of private rights and pertains to laws, rights, agreements, acts or treaties, etc. This is a much broader and more general violation than *infringement*, which refers to a particular article in an act or certain terms in a negotiation.

Infringement That which violates the rights of others through deed. See also Public offense.

Inheritance of acquired characteristics In the early nineteenth century, Lamarke proposed that acquired characteristics could be passed on to succeeding generations. This has, until recently, been out of favor. Cairns has reported that bacteria threatened with starvation can, in effect, size up their troubles and mutate in ways that enable them to survive. Thus, life-saving mutations are produced in response to the stressful situation. He believes that this is unlikely to occur in higher animals. Darwin's theory of natural selection, which stands in opposition to Lamarckism, states mutations arise spontaneously in organisms. Furthermore, by chance, some of these mutations may allow an organism to survive better than others of its kind.

Inherited Those characteristics that are transmitted from parent to offspring through the genes. This process is also called *transmission*. Compare with Acquired development, Congenital, Heritable, Postnatally acquired.

Injunction see Court of Equity

Injury May be specific, cumulative or an occupational disease (California Labor Code, sections 3208, 3212-3213). Medically, injury is defined as any adverse influence which deranges the cell's ability to maintain a steady, normal or adaptive homeostasis. *Homeostasis* refers to the way the internal environment of the body is maintained in a stable condition. Injury may be *de novo* (i.e. new, fresh) or it can be *superimposed on a pre-existing lesion*. Most *specific traumatic injuries* (e.g. an accident) arise *de novo* and this is called a *precipitated injury*. *Superimposed injuries* on pre-existing lesions are either *aggravations* or *accelerations*. An aggravation 'lights up' or 'makes worse' a pre-existing lesion. An acceleration increases the expected speed of progression in a pre-existing lesion that was either asymptomatic or symptomatic, but known to be progressive in nature (e.g. asbestosis). See also Apportionment terms, Cumulative trauma, Disease, Occupational disease, Pathology scope, Serious injury, Specific injury.

In network To catch or entangle in a net.

In rem The subject matter of litigation. See also *Res*

Insane see Anger

Insanity In law, it is a condition of the mind that causes a person to be incapable of attending to his or her own affairs or not responsible for his conduct. *Incompetency* is the more usual term in a civil procedure. *Insanity* is used largely in the use of criminal matters. See also Criminal insanity, Incompetence, *Non-compos mentis*.

Inscription see Prescribed, Prescription

Inspection see Physical examination

Instructions to the jury Before the first witness is sworn, counsel for the respective parties must deliver to the trial judge and serve upon opposing counsel all proposed instructions to the jury covering the law as disclosed by the pleading. As evidence is developed, there are additional instructions to the jury about questions of law that have not been disclosed by the pleading. Before beginning the argument, the court on request of counsel must: (1) decide whether to give, refuse or modify the proposed instructions; (2) decide which shall be given in addition to those proposed; and (3) advise counsel of all instructions to be given. If, however, during argument issues are raised which have not been covered by instructions given, the court may give additional instructions on the subject matter. See also Reasonable person.

Insufficiency Being inadequate to perform allotted duties.

Intangible Sight and touch are used to determine what is objective. Touch without sight is used to determine what is tangible. Those things that have presence but are determined only by hearing, smell and taste are intangible. *Presence*, the quality or quantity emitted by an object or thing, is that which is detectable or capable of being detectable by the senses. The absence of presence, if it cannot be measured, is *subjective*. Thus, subjective includes what is thought. What is felt can either be subjective or subjective/intangible (as when a person has empathy for another's feelings). The sensing of pheromones is a prime example of something intangible. In law, *intangible property* is associated with a document, such as stock certificate, bonds, accounts receivable or pattern rights. The document itself is not the property interest or the rights owned, but merely evidence of them. Even if the document is destroyed the property may still exist. Compare with Objective, Subjective, Tangible.

Intangible property see Intangible

Integrity Doing what a person knows to be right, even if he or she has to give up an advantage or put him or herself at a disadvantage. See also Fair play, Honesty, Probity, Professionalism.

Intensity From the Latin *intensus*, meaning stretched tight, it refers to the increasing of relative strength, degree or force. This makes it a quantitative or qualitative attribute. See also Emotion, Magnitude.

Intent Refers especially to the state of mind — having the mind strenuously bent upon something; the mind straining or stretching forth towards an object is a mind directed with keen attention and tension. Intent is forming a plan or purpose – i.e. what one plans to do or accomplish. Intent fastens on the end itself. This is to be compared with *purpose* (referring to the result of the action) and *design* (referring to the adaptation of means to an end). For example, a person decides to kill a man or women (intent) and forms a plan to entrap the victim (design) to bring about the victim's death (purpose). As the law cannot read the heart, it can only infer the intent from the evidences of design. See also Inference, Malice, Malicious, Malicious prosecution, Malingerers, Manslaughter, Motive, Premeditation.

Interim permanent disability awards Are given when workers will inevitably have adverse progression of their pathological condition. Factors of impairment are offered when the patient's condition has medically stabilized within a reasonable period of time. If the worker's condition deteriorates significantly, the court amends the award because of further disability. Examples which may lead to this are avascular necrosis (osteonecrosis) of the hips and progressive heart or lung disease. See also Adverse progression, Permanent and stationary.

Interlocutory Temporary or provisional, not final.

Interlocutory decree see Decree

Intermittent see Chronic, Vocational rehabilitation terms

Internal body structures Those that are inside the body or its parts (e.g. the heart, lung, liver, etc.). They are said to be internal organs. *External* defines structures related to the outside of the body or its parts (e.g. hair, nails, etc.). See also Endogenous, Exogenous.

Interpretation 'Feeling evaluations' i.e. determining meanings of emotions, preferences, tastes and other subjective things to distinguish them from logical evaluations. See also Evaluation.

Interpreting legislation Statute books, the records of legislation, contain tens of thousands of rules. Even when the relevant rules have been identified, their precise significance usually has to be established. One reason is that few statutes are indisputably clear. *Interpreting legislation (deciding the meaning) is one of the functions of the judge.* He looks to prior legislation on the same topic to discover what legislators had in mind in modifying the law. He studies their choice of words with great care. When there is a *gap in the statute*, he devises a rule that is in accord with the principles of the law. See also Gap in the statute.

Interrogation The process by which suspects are rigorously questioned by the police.

Interrogatories This is a type of discovery procedure in which a person is commanded to answer written questions provided by the opposing party in a lawsuit. See also Deposition, Discovery.

Intuitional intelligence A connecting of two or more unrelated ideas/thoughts without the use of reason and without knowing why such connections are possible.

See Associational intelligence, Knowledge by acquaintance, Spacial intelligence.

Invalid see Valid

Involuntary manslaughter see Manslaughter

Involuntary nervous system see Autonomic nervous system

Ipso facto A Latin phrase meaning 'by the fact itself' or 'by the mere effort of an act or fact.'

Irrelevant Whereas *relevant* is used as a legal term for 'connected with,' irrelevant means not pertinent to anything of consequence in the proof of facts under dispute. Irrelevance is a valid reason for objection to a question in a trial. See also Objection.

Issue A disputed point of question between opposing parties. When the plaintiff affirms and the defense denies (or vice versa), they are said to be 'at issue.' When the defendant has filed an answer denying all or part of the allegations of the complaint, the issue has been *joined* and the case is ready to be set for trial. See also Medical-legal.

J

Jekyll and Hyde In a classic book, Dr Jekyll, a London doctor of repute, discovered a drug that would change him almost instantly into an evil dwarf (Mr Hyde). He was able to reconvert, but this diminishes after repeated dosages, so that he becomes more Mr Hyde than Dr Jekyll. Eventually, Hyde committed murder and, after the trial in which Jekyll's lawyer revealed the secret, Hyde committed suicide. 'Jekyll and Hyde' is often loosely used to refer to a case of 'split personality,' more accurately termed *schizophrenic* or *'schizoid personality'*.

Job analysis A detailed official outline of a job, including the essential functions.

Job description A semi-official summary of a job

Job requirement see Essential functions, Job analysis, Repeated

Job tasks Essential functions that are vital to the job, particularly those done every day. See also Americans with Disabilities Acts, Disability, Essential functions

Job trials Also called 'job try outs', it is the utilization of actual jobs in a real employment situation for the purpose of work evaluation. These may be quite realistic and effective in determining job opportunities for the handicapped. The author predicts that job trials will become more popular as the Americans with Disabilities Act rises to prominence. Compare with Work hardening in return to work status. See also Americans with Disabilities Acts, Lateral job transfer.

Job try outs see Job trials, Lateral job transfers

Joined issue see Issue

Joint and several tort feasors see Liability

Joint binding see Mobilization

Joint dysfunction see Manipulation, Mobilization

Joint play see Mobilization

Journeyman doctors Are those with significant experience to the point that they are able to bring complex medical-legal issues into manageable proportions for all parties concerned. They have the knowledge and use it in the correct way, in the right system and at the appropriate time. See also What is medical-legal.

Judgment The selection of the seemingly best option is a judgment. The Romans had two words for law: *lex* (legal, law-abiding) and *jus* (judge). *Jus* referred to somebody who either spoke the law for its application or who practiced the law as a judge. Legal judgments are final determinations or decisions of the court as to: (1) the rights and duties of the parties in a lawsuit; or (2) the sentence or final order of a court in a civil or criminal proceeding. There are several types of legal judgment. A *default judgment* is the judgment rendered because of the defendant's failure to answer or appeal. A *summary judgment* is a decision on the basis of pleadings, affidavits and exhibits presented for the record without any need for a trial, and is used when there are no disputes as to the facts of the case, but one party is entitled to a judgment as a matter of the law. A *consent judgment* occurs when the provisions and terms of the judgment are agreed upon by the parties and submitted to the court for its sanction and appeal. A judgement *non obstante veredicto* (NOV) is literally a judgment not withstanding the verdict, when the judge decides a case contrary to the verdict of the jury. This can be made in a civil or criminal case. In general, a *judgment is the final deposition of a lawsuit*. See also A priori, A priori findings, Decision necessities, Declaratory judgment, Default judgment, Oath opinion reversal, Summary judgment.

Judgment and law see Normal, Preface

Judgment *in personam* This is a personal judgment and is the type most commonly rendered by courts. It imposes a personal obligation on the losing party (e.g. to pay a sum of money) or it may be a 'take nothing'. See also Case conclusion, Conclusion, *In rem*, *Quasi in rem*.

Judgment *non obstante veredicto* (NOV) see Judgment

Judicial reviews These were used in federal court systems for federal or state matters (e.g. when state laws conflict with the United States Constitution) or in state courts. Parties who have lost in the trial court can appeal to appellate courts which have control over the trial court. This is particularly likely if the trial judge refuses to follow a precedent that seems clearly applicable. *Appeals* are used in all state and federal court systems except the Supreme Court to correct errors of law made by inferior courts. *Appellate judges* sit in groups of three to nine or more, depending upon the court, so biases are likely to be cancelled out. The necessity of appeal courts to publish a written opinion is a check and balance, as is a judge's need to be re-elected. In this respect the media has also had a powerful influence. See also Appeal, Check and balance.

Jurisdiction The authority of the court or other government agency to decide a controversy and to award appropriate remedies. See also Competence, Venue.

Jurisprudence Prudence is a very powerful word and incorporates, but is more comprehensive than, *providence*. *Prude* (Latin) originally meant wise with foresight, forethought and discretion. All of this implied a quality that enabled a person to choose a sensible course, particularly when managing practical affairs. *Prudence* implies a habitual deliberateness, caution and circumspection in action. It is said that the law declared itself to be wise and then crystallized the wisdom of the law in the term jurisprudence, the science of law. It studies the structure of legal systems (e.g. equity) and of the principles underlying that system. It is a collective term denoting the course of judicial decision (i.e. case law) as opposed to legislation. Sometimes it is used as a synonym for law. See also Case law, What is medical-legal.

Jurist A person having a thorough knowledge of law. One of their jobs is to research the definition of legal terms. Typically, they research the records, from the earliest to the most recent cases, in order to find those pertinent words that were defined in other courts. It is customary for legal decision makers to build on each others works. When this cannot be done, then justices elaborate on the meanings of a word. See also Gap in the statute.

Juror A person either selected or sworn for jury duty. See also Deliberation, Witnesses.

Jury A representative group of people who determine issues of facts at a trial. See also Beyond reasonable doubt, Findings, Grand jury, Summons.

Jury instructions see Instructions to jury, Prudent person, Reasonable, Reasonable doubt, Reasonable person

Jury summons see Summons

Justice The constant and perpetual disposition to render all people their due through judicial administration of law. Justice is founded in equity, honesty and right. It is the attempt of honorable people to have fair play. Ideally, the law is the means to justice and justice is the goal of law. Justice is, however, dependent upon society's concept of right and wrong. Its purpose is to secure life, liberty and the pursuit of happiness for all. See also Adversary, Equity, Good faith, Law, Lawful, Obstruction of justice.

Justices Those judges reviewing cases in the Court of Appeal or the Supreme Court. See also *En banc*.

K

Kilogram One kilogram equals 2.2046 pounds (lb) or 1000 grams. To convert pounds into kilograms multiply by 0.4535924.

Knock knee see Figure 5 (page 57), Valgus body position

Knowledge by acquaintance This is intuitive cognition that is global, immediate and reaching into the heart of a thing by empathy. Intuition opens the conceptual and perceptual doors. See also Empathy, Intuitional intelligence.

Knowledge by description This is abstractive cognition, which involves scientific analysis, specialization and conceptualization; it tends to see things as solid and discontinuous. Such a process is useful for getting things done, but it fails to reach the essential reality of things precisely because it leaves out duration with its perpetual flux (which can be grasped only by intuition). See also Cognition.

Koch's postulates Robert Koch (1843–1910) devised the medical rule that four conditions must be satisfied to establish the causative organism of a specific disease: (1) the organism must be present in every case of the disease; (2) the organism must be isolated and grown in pure culture; (3) pure culture must produce the disease when it is inoculated into a susceptible animal; and (4) the organism must be removed from the infected animal and grown again in pure culture. This was also called the *law of specificity of bacteria*. See also Cause, Epidemiology, Etiology.

L

Laboratory Originally spelt 'elaboratory' in seventeenth century English, it derived from the French word *elaborataire*, meaning workshop. Nowadays it denotes a place for experimental work in any branch of science, as well as for the preparation of drugs and chemicals. *Clinical laboratories* examine materials derived from the human body for the purpose of providing information on diagnosis, prevention or treatment.

Latent Not visible or apparent; it is something that is hidden or dormant. In law, a *latent defect* is one that is present but undetectable by a reasonably careful inspection. For the medical sense of the term see Concealed, Deception, Dormant, Occult and Smoke screen.

Latent defect see Latent

Lateral Also called radial, it describes body parts furthest from the saggital plane, which divides the body vertically into the right and the left half. For example, as the thumb is anatomically away from the sagittal plane, it would be considered lateral (or radial). See Anatomical references, Figure 1 (page 7).

Lateral job transfers see Americans with Disabilities Act, Impairment

Launder see Euphemisms

Law A rule of conduct imposed by authority. See also Justice, Retroactive law.

Law clerk see Clerk

Law functions The functions of the law include: (1) keeping the peace; (2) influencing and enforcing standards of conduct; (3) maintaining the status quo, (4) facilitating orderly change; (5) maximizing individual self-assertion; (6) facilitating the planning and realiza-tion of reasonable expectations; (7) promoting social justice; and (8) providing compromised solutions for disputes. See also Classification of law.

Law's general proprieties totem pole Constitutions prevail over statutes, but statutes prevail over common-law principles established in court decisions (i.e. a court will not use a case decision for law if a statute is directly applicable). Constitutions, federal or state, are the basic source of law for the jurisdiction and not only specify the structure and delegation of power to the government, but also allocate power between levels of government (e.g. between federal and state in the United States Constitution, and between state and local ruling bodies in state constitutions). If the state laws and actions are in conflict with United States Constitution, the Constitution will be enforced. If ambiguities exist in the Constitution, the Supreme Court will make a decision on how to precede, although this is subject to legislative change or overruling by the court. See Classification of law, Lawmaker division, State courts.

Law of causality see Cause, Effect, Etiology

Law of obligation see Classification of law

Law of specificity of bacteria see Koch's postulates

Lawful An ambiguous word which, in its strictest sense, means legality. This may not be *justice*, which is the rendering to everyone what is due or merited, whether in act, word or thought. However, lawfulness also signifies accordance with the supreme law of *right*, which denotes conformity of personal conduct to the moral law and thus, necessarily, includes justice. For example, the rightful owner is lawfully entitled to his or her possessions. See also Equity, Justice, Legal.

Lawmaker division This includes the federal, state and local governments. The federal judicial system is simple and unique to the United States of America. The *district courts* (i.e. the courts of general jurisdiction) are the foundation. They are accountable to a *Court of Appeal* which, in turn, is accountable to the *Supreme Court*. In addition, the *tax courts* are accountable to a Court of Appeal, the *Custom Courts* are accountable to *Court of Customs* while patent appeals are accountable to the Supreme Court. Then there are the *Court of Claims* (which hears suits against the United States Government and is accountable to the Supreme Court) and the *Court of Military Appeals* (which hears cases from the military tribunals). See also Classification of law.

Lawmakers Legislatures, such as the United States Congress, State Assembly and a City Board of Alderman (or City Council), are the lawmaking branches of federal, state and local government. Although the executive branch of the federal, state and local governments (i.e. the President, the Governor and the Mayor) have no power to pass laws, they can propose new laws, approve or disapprove laws that have been passed, and can enforce the statutes in existence. Furthermore, they can establish regulatory and administrative agencies that have a certain discretionary power to make and enforce regulations in particular areas. These can be: (1) *direct enforcers,* which include the police, the military and various security agencies; (2) *direct players,* who are the prime people involved in a trial (e.g. judges, reviewing courts, justices and juries); and (3) *indirect players,* who are numerous and variable people also associated with trials (e.g. doctors, witnesses, clerks, paralegals, court reporters, investigative agencies and translators, etc.). See also Classification of law.

Lawyer see Counsel

Lead see Leading question

Leading question The word 'lead' is far more complicated than most people realize. It originated from the idea that a person had a guiding star and later from sailors using the stars to navigate. More recently it has applied to the hunting field, when a person was shown the way over a fence. In law, a leading question is one that suggests the reply. For example, under direct examination during the trial, it is when the witness is asked, 'Isn't it true that you saw Sharon standing outside the store waiting for a friend when the robbery occurred?' The opposing counsel will object to this type of question as it is suggests how the witness should explain or recall the event, instead of simply inquiring

how the event actually took place. However, it is a valuable tool in the direct examination of a hostile witness or a cross examination, since the object of such examination is to test the credibility of the statement made during direct examination. See also Cross examination, Direct examination, Hostile witness, Objection.

Left brain thinkers See practical/practice

Legal From the Latin *legalis* (which is associated with *lex,* meaning law/loyal, one of the two Roman words for law), it means according to human law. This should be compared with the word, *lawful,* which is often used in a similar manner, but also means 'conforming to moral principles' in line with religious or ethical doctrines. It is, therefore, more common to say 'lawful marriage' than 'legal marriage'. Furthermore, *legal law* is chosen by authorities and so tends to become imposed, while lawful moral principles are followed voluntarily in accordance with a religious or other standard. *Loyal* was originally synonymous with legal and both referred to the faithful carrying out of obligations. See also Equity, Judgment, Justice, Lawful.

Legal causation see Cause, Cause and effect, Proximate cause

Legal concealment see Concealed

Legal conclusion see Conclusion, Decree

Legal dispute see Disputed medical facts

Legal facts These are events or things, the actual occurrence or existence of which is to be determined by procedural law (e.g. evidence). In law, fact refers to any information upon which people involved in the legal case base an opinion, whatever this may be. Decisions on questions of fact are made by the jury in deciding the outcome of a case. This should be compared with *questions of law,* which are determined by the court. As the non-legal sense of fact is a thing known to be true (from the Latin *factum,* meaning a thing done), be wary of the difference between the legal and non-legal meaning of facts, especially in depositions. See also Facts, Legal opinion fact, Medical information, Medical probability, Proof, Trial components.

Legal fiction see Medical fiction, Retroactive prophylactic restriction

Legal judgments see Judgment

Legal law see Legal

Legal normal see Normal

Legal opinion fact Is a: (1) professional judgment (i.e. reasoned opinion); (2) arrived at after weighing evidence; (3) with citations of legal reasons, precedents and principles to justify it to the satisfaction of the jury and judge. See also Assumptions, Facts, Framing medical-legal conclusions.

Legal procedure see Classification of law

Length see Metric system

Lesions These structural alterations in the tissues, which are recognisable by gross and microscopic examination, occur with most diseases and all injuries. Such alterations, and the functional disturbances which accompany them, result in the *clinical manifestations of disease* (the *signs* and *symptoms*). Signs and symptoms from the morphological changes influence the course and the prognosis of the disease. Frequently, the terms lesions and *pathology* are used synonymously. However, as pathology is a field of scientific study and is not an abnormality, it would more appropriate to say 'there is no evidence of abnormalities or lesions in the liver' than 'there is no evidence of pathology in the liver'. See also Disease, Pathogenesis, Pathology, Pathology scope, Subclinical disease.

Letter of the law This refers to the stated terms of legal guidelines. A Court of Equity would be more interested in the merits of the case and the justice of the decision, while common law courts place emphasis on 'the letter of the law' or the form of law as stated by law makers.

Liability An obligation to do, or refrain from doing, something (e.g. a debtor has the obligation for paying a creditor). A liability makes a person responsible for his or her conduct, whether this concerns a contractual, criminal or civil (tort) matter. It may also make somebody responsible for the conduct of another, as in a suit against *joint and several tort feasors* (persons who have committed torts), where a successful plaintiff could recover his or her damages from all of tort feasors, or from any one of them if the other parties responsible cannot pay. See also Creditor, Debtor, Tort.

Libel A tort consisting of a false, malicious publication, the purpose of which is to defame a living person or to

mar the memory of a dead one. Any printed material, written text, signs or pictures that tend to expose a person to public scorn, hatred, contempt or ridicule may be considered libellous. See also Slander, Tort.

Libman test see Pain measurement test

Lie detector see Polygraph

Lien A right to claim certain property in satisfaction of a debt. A lien does not convey ownership of the property, but does give the lien holder the right to have his or her debt satisfied out of the proceeds of the property if the debt is not otherwise payed. In the United States worker's compensation scheme, liens are submitted when a doctor provides self-procured medical treatment. See also Self-procured care.

Lighting up The activation of a non-progressive (i.e. staying the same), dormant (i.e. inactive) medical condition or lesion. This is a form of aggravation. With respect to apportionment, it means that factors have caused the underlying dormant condition to awaken or ignite to the point that the injured person becomes aware of signs and/or symptoms. It is assumed that in absence of these factors, the underlying dormant lesion would not have become symptomatic. Compare with exacerbation. See also Apportionment terms, Injury reoccurrence.

Limbo see Ambiguous

Liminal value see Value

Liter see Metric system

Litigants The plaintiffs or defendants involved in a lawsuit. See also Applicant, Complainant, Defendant, Party, Petitioner, Plaintiff, Standing.

Litigation A judicial contest aimed at determining and enforcing legal rights. See also Suit.

Local courts These include the traffic courts, the police courts, the small claims courts and the justice of the peace. Cases heard in these courts frequently cannot be appealed. See also Courts.

Logic conclusions see Conclusion

Long see Prolonged

Loss of use awards This refers to compensation by statute under the workers' compensation scheme in the United States for loss of a member or its usefulness. Any amputation or injury that renders a member (e.g. leg) medically and permanently useless would be considered for a loss of use award. Such compensation is solely for the loss of, or loss of use of, for example, an arm, and is considered first and separate from any percentage of permanent partial disability (e.g. residual impairment due to restrictions at the elbow). However, the worker's compensation schemes vary between states. See also Impairment.

Love see Fair play, Fear, Sympathy

Low back anomalies see Nerve, Roots

Low life esteem see Depression

Lower motor neuron disease see Motor neuron disease

Loyal see Legal

Lucky star see Desire, Fear, Leading question, Predominant

Luxation see Dislocation

Lying see Pathological lying, Prevaricate

M

Mad see Anger, Rage

Magistrate A public civil officer invested with some part of the legislative, executive or judicial power. In a strictest sense, the term includes only inferior judicial officers such as *justices of the peace*.

Magnitude From the Latin *maghus*, meaning large, and the ancient Germanic word *milil*, meaning much, it refers to the sense of expanding loftiness. Thus magnitude is both a *quality* and *quantity* word. It is an intensity which can be measured precisely, but is more expansive than intensity. The expansiveness has indefinite borders. The concept of intensity is extremely important in feeling tone and relates to sensations that can be pleasant (e.g. enjoyment) or unpleasant (e.g. suffering). Magnitude is part of the contents of enjoyment and suffering. See also Measurements.

Mala in se This means 'evil in itself' and refers to behavior that is universally regarded as criminal, such as murder. See also Crimes.

Malady see Disorder

Malfeasance The doing of a wrongful or unlawful act, especially official misconduct. See also Lawful, Misfeasance, Non-feasance.

Malice The intention or desire to injure another without justification. See also Intent, Punishment.

Malicious Characterized by malice. *Malicious injury* is intentional and without a good reason. *Malicious mischief* is damaging or destroying another's property out of revenge. See also Intent.

Malicious abuse of process see Malicious prosecution

Malicious injury see Malicious

Malicious mischief see Malicious

Malicious prosecution Is a sham lawsuit against a victim for the purpose of harassment. *Malicious abuse of process* is the wilful misapplication of the legal process to accomplish an unlawful purpose. See also Intent.

Malignant That which is moderately, severely or extremely destructive. See also Classification of medical patients, Guilt.

Malignant depression see Depression

Malignant guilt see Guilt

Malingerers/other conscious deceivers Centuries ago, French beggars who created artificial sores for financial gain were called *malingroux*. *Malingroux* derived from *malingre*, and meant sickly, sore, scabby, ugly and loathsome. In the early nineteenth century, malingerer or skulkers were fashionable names for soldiers and sailors who produced ulcers on their legs by artificial means in order to escape duty. An alternative term developed during the American gold rush, from 'cheaters' who sold gold-plated bricks or, if the gold brick was real, a sham brick was substituted after business had been concluded. These cheaters were called *gold brickers*. Subsequently, a number of colloquial terms have been developed to describe conscious deceivers and these include shirkers, clock-watchers, goof-offs, boondogglers, triflers and dodgers, etc. As medical diagnostic labels, psychiatrists preferred to use 'malingerer' and 'factitious disorder' for conscious deceivers. Members of both groups were considered to have an intention to deceive but, in contrast to those with a factitious disorder, malingerers had an external incentive (i.e. conscious secondary gain). Terms related closely to both include deliberate deceitful exaggerators,

Munchausen syndrome, attention-seeking exaggerators and paradoxical malingerers. See also Classification of medical patients, Faker signs, Intent, Secondary gain.

Malpractice A professional's improper or immoral conduct in the performance of his or her fiduciary duties, whether this is performed intentionally, as the result of carelessness or out of ignorance. Malpractice is commonly applied to lawyers, doctors and public officers to denote negligence or poor performance of duties where professional skills are obligatory on account of the fiduciary relationship with patients or clients. Medical malpractice actions have three basic functions: quality control, compensations for harm and emotional vindication. *Quality control* is probably best achieved, since the standard of care is set by physicians themselves and enforced by patients and juries. *Compensation for harm*, however, is skewed toward major injuries. Attorneys in the United States, for example, represent malpractice cases on a *contingency fee basis* (i.e. they are payed a proportion of compensation, usually 20-40% of the total amount awarded to the plaintiff). Patients who suffer less severe injuries may have little redress for compensation. *Emotional vindication* is a measure of the consumer's ability to make a complaint as well as to get a satisfactory response. See also Negligence, Professional, Retaliation, Revenge, Risk, Tort.

Mandate This is: (1) a judicial command; or (2) a contract by which one individual acts for another gratuitously. See also Gratuitous service.

Manifest see Clinical manifestations

Manifestation This is the 'presence' of something. Presence means appearance, bearing or that which is observable or capable of being observed whether intangible, tangible or objective. Presence pertains chiefly to the external, while *personality* refers of the expression of the internal. A *clinical manifestation* is the display of that which has not necessarily been concealed, but which has been evoked by circumstances to give characteristic signs or symptoms of an illness. They may reflect organic illness, the neurotic (with or without the psychophysiological component of self-deceivers), the psychotic tendencies of certain conscious deceivers or the good/bad behaviors of any patient. See also Abnormal, Clinical manifestations, Disease, Intangible, Lesions, Magnitude, Measurements, Medical probability, Objective, Tangible, Suffer.

Manifestations of disability Include: (1) the patient's complaint of pain as indicated by the patient, in the medical records or documented by the employer; (2) the patient having received medical treatment to the part of the body that is presently the subject of litigation; (3) the patient has missed time from work due to pain or discomfort to the part of the body that is the subject of litigation; (4) the patient has presented to a doctor because of a pertinent problem, even though there has been no treatment or work loss; (5) a doctor has given a pre-existing (i.e. before the 'pilot ' date of injury) prophylactic work restriction; (6) an actual work restriction has been in existence prior to the *pilot injury*; (7) the patient adhered to a self-imposed restriction prior to the pilot injury; and (8) there has been objective evidence of a pre-existing disability (e.g. amputation). See also Manifestation.

Manipulation From the Latin *manipulare*, meaning to handle, it is any manual operation in, for example, chemistry, pharmaceutics or 'bone setting'. *Bone setters* existed at the time of the earliest records. They were regarded as the orthopaedic surgeons of their day. However, as the art of medicine and surgery became transformed into a science, the respectability of bone setters waned. Nevertheless, bone manipulators did have some measure of success and this resulted in the development of two schools of manipulative treatment, osteopathic and chiropractic. At their best, these manipulators could treat *joint dysfunction*, the loss of one or more movements of an involuntary nature occurring at any synovial joint. As these joints are involuntary, they can only be restored by the use of normal movements that give normal function. A host of methods were developed for this purpose, ranging from the gentle examination movement on part of the joint to a frank assault on the entire joint. Therefore, *proper manipulation can be defined as a technique used to restore normal function to an impaired joint by the use of normal movements*. Its purpose is to reduce pain arising from joint dysfunction. It is possible to relieve pain in a joint or from a joint without materially affecting its voluntary range of motion. The symptoms of pain from joint dysfunction may be local to the joint or may be present as a pain referred from a joint to any other place which shares the nerve supply as the joint. Despite what seems to be a wide variety of movements, the maneuvers are actually limited to traction, compression, flexion, extension, rotation and lateral bending. Any of these carried out with violent or great force can be disastrous. This is particularly true when manipulation is used as a 'shotgun' type of care. See also Mobilization, Mobilization under anesthesia, Treatment.

Manslaughter Unlawful killing of another person without malice or intent to kill. *Voluntary manslaughter* is the intentional killing committed under circumstances (e.g. rage, terror or desperation) that, although they do not justify the homicide, reduce its evil intent. *Involuntary manslaughter* is a death caused by criminal carelessness or as an accident in the commission of some wrongful act. An example would be driving an vehicle at excessive speed which results in a fatal collision. The speeding may be unlawful, but does not amount to a felony. See also Classification of crimes, Mitigating circumstances.

Maritime law The law relating to shipping and boating on navigable waters. These laws are separate from every other jurisdiction. See also Admiralty law.

Masked depression The somatization of a malignant depressive emotion. This can also mean doing the opposite of what a person feels, such as during daredevil activities. See also Primary gain.

Masochism see Sick pleasure, Suffer

Master doctors Are those who have excellent skills in the areas diagnosis, treatment and reporting. They are able to take creative 'medical leaps' and contribute to the highest standards of the medical community. See also Apprentice doctors, Creative reporting, Journeyman doctors.

Masterful inactivity see Art of medicine, Masterful neglect

Masterful neglect Medical activity is discontinued, but a watchful eye is maintained during follow-up office visits to ensure that the situation continues to be satisfactory. See also Masterful inactivity, Therapies of medicine.

Material witness A person who can give unique testimony that might have a bearing on the case. See also Witness.

Maturity see Self-discipline

Maximum medical improvement A treatment plateau, static or well stabilized, at which no fundamental, functional or physiological change can be expected within reasonable medical probability, in spite of continuing medical or rehabilitated procedures. However, a patient may need supportive treatment to maintain this level of function or reduce

adverse progression. If a patient has *not* reached maximum medical improvement, then an explanation is required. For example, the present treatment program may need to be continued. In legal proceedings, if this is the case, an opinion should be rendered as to how much further treatment (i.e. intensity and frequency) and time will be needed. Alternatively, if the problem is an incomplete and/or wrong diagnosis, inadequate diagnostic analysis and/or inadequate or inappropriate treatment to date, these issues need to be clearly identified. An opinion would then be required to establish the steps needed for that patient to reach maximum medical improvement. The patient may accept the present incomplete diagnosis, treatment and response to that treatment, or no longer wants to continue with medical activity, in which case the patient has reached maximum medical improvement. See also Permanent and stationary.

May This is a discretionary term, but *shall* means must.

Mayhem The offense of violently injuring or maiming a person's body so as to render that person less able to defend himself.

Mean That which is between the two margins of deficiency and excess. See also Average, Middle

Measurements The determination of the magnitude, intensity, extent, degree or some quantitative determination of something that has *presence*. When evaluating a disorder or injury, it is often useful to state normal values, or at least make an educated 'estimate', to provide a comparison. For example, when evaluating grip effort for a legal case, if a doctor believes that the patient is not providing maximum effort, he or she should say why and give an estimated normal grip strength reading (or percentage loss) for the injury in question. Otherwise, they should explain what they believe to be causing the grip loss (e.g. reduced range of motion, pain, etc.). See also Educated estimate, Estimation, Intangible, Magnitude, Manifestation, Metric system, Physical examination, Quality.

Mechanism of injury This is the cause or process by which some adverse result (e.g. trauma) is achieved. It is what initiated the injury or disease. See Apportionment terms, Arising out of employment, Cause, Etiology, Pathology scope.

Mechanotherapy The use of a mechanical apparatus in the treatment of disease. See Physical modalities.

Medial see Anatomical references, Figure I (page 7), Ulnar

Medial sum See average

Mediation A form of alternative dispute resolution in which the opposing parties bring their dispute to a third party who will help them agree on a settlement. See also Arbiter, Arbitration.

Medical benefits Legitimately injured employees are entitled to receive the 'big four': (1) *therapy* (physical or mental), (2) *temporary disability benefits*; (3) *permanent disability benefits*; and (4) *rehabilitation*. Death benefits are payments provided to surviving dependants. When considering medical benefits, therapy can include all medical, dental, surgical and hospital treatments reasonably necessary to cure or relieve the effects of the pilot injury or problems deriving from pilot injury. See also What is medical-legal.

Medical causation see Cause

Medical certainty This is the point at which a high probability concerning a medical matter moves into the realm of certainty. It is arbitrarily determined as 97–99%. It is equivalent to *beyond a shadow of doubt*. See Certainty, Medical possibilities, Medical probability, Scientific certain, Scientific law, Scientific method.

Medical conclusion see Conclusion, Deductive reasoning, Inductive reasoning, Report comments, Scientific method

Medical end see End/ending

Medical fiction That which lacks medical validity. This frequently occurs in the legal arena when, for example: (1) certain terms and ideas are attributed to medicine, such as 'permanent and stationary', which are biologically impossible; (2) using 'all-or-nothing' thinking, which does not apply to medicine (e.g. describing a patient's presentation as subjective and/or objective); or (3) using *rules of thumb* in forming medical opinions. In the latter case, non-medical people often judge doctors on how well they conform to some fictitious rules of thumb. To avoid misunderstandings due to medical fiction, when writing persuasive opinions it is necessary to first establish *common ground* (the foundations); this may include a historical perspective of disease condition and/or the etymology of keywords. A word of warning, attorneys frequently apply medical fiction as cross examination

strategy in order to place the doctor in unfamiliar territory; this can be especially dangerous during depositions and courts. See also Allowed medical conditions, Report comments, Well-reasoned reports.

Medical history This involves pertinent problems indicated in the patient's chief complaints and in the referral source's cover letter. It covers the work history, medical history, present complaints and past medical history.

Medical illustrative testimony see Demonstrative evidence

Medical illogic see Cause, Medical fiction

Medical information The listing and acceptance of medical facts. Case law has mandated certain prerequisites in all combined-effects reviews necessary for those reviews to be considered as 'some medical evidence.' Thus, doctors must state in the report that they have reviewed all of the medical records on file, list the names and titles of persons who generated the medical information, and state which pieces of information have been accepted as factual. From a legal perspective, something that is factual is not necessarily the same as accepting its accuracy. This is an example of how *legal facts differ from medical facts*. If inaccuracies exist in the medical information contained within records, then this problem should be addressed either in the specific section of your report which concerns the appropriate allowed condition(s), in the discussion section of the report, or in both. It is simply a matter of mentioning the limitations found in the various doctors' reports. This is particularly true when such omissions can have an affect on accuracy. See also Facts, Legal facts, Report comments.

Medical issues see Rating report, Report, Treating report

Medical-legal Legal evidence of a medical nature. For a patient's case to be considered medical-legal, there must be: (1) a valid claim; (2) the doctor's report must meet requirements needed to resolve the *contested claim* (i.e. prove or disprove some disputed issue); and (3) the report must be delivered on time. See also Contested claim, Forensic medicine, What is medical-legal.

Medical-legal conceptual counterparts Although it is controversial to quantify abstractions it is useful to put a numerical value on certain basic medical and legal

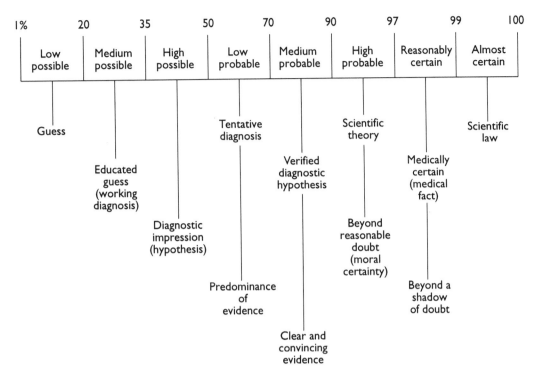

Figure 8 Medical-legal conceptual counterparts

concepts to show how they roughly relate to each other. None of the concepts are considered 100% certain, although scientific laws are just short at 99%. Legal facts can range from a low probability of reality and truth all the way to almost certain. Except for future predictions (e.g. the possibility of a need for surgery), the legal system has little use for concepts with possibility at its core. See Figure 8. See also Classifying information and individual entries, Facts, Hypothesis.

Medical-legal detective see Research

Medical-legal expense   Any cost or expenses incurred by, or on behalf of, any party or parties, the administrative director, the appeals board for radiographs, laboratory or other diagnostic tests, medical reports, medical records, medical testimony and interpreter's fees, if they are needed, but they must all be required to prove or disprove a contested claim. See also Costs.

Medical-legal reports see Rating report, Report comments, Treating report

Medical-legal research see Research

Medical luxury see Necessities

Medical necessity   see Future medical treatment, Medical benefits, Necessities, Objective impairment

Medical possibility   This is a guess concerning a medical matter, where chances of it actually occurring range from 1 to 50%. Although it is of no legal value in court, it can be of useful in the settlement of negotiations (e.g. a patient is believed to have a 35% chance of requiring surgery within the next 5 years).

Medical probability   Is the appearance of truth or reality without known certainty. There is a reasonable likelihood or grounds to presume conformity to a reason or experience either from superior evidence or from arguments adduced in its favor. If there is more evidence for the situation occurring than against, even if it is a 51:49 ratio, then an opinion should be given as medical probability, which will allow for doubt. See also Arising out of employment, Beyond reasonable doubt, Diagnostic impression, Framing conclusions, Future medical treatment, Preponderance of evidence.

Medical records In ancient times, records were kept in the minds of storytellers, reporters or messengers. To qualify, they literally had to learn pertinent information 'by heart'. Indeed, the word 'record' (from the Latin *recordarire*, again, plus *cor*, the heart) meant to be mindful of a thing or to remember it by internalizing it into the heart. Today, medical records are written documents containing sufficient information to identify the patient clearly, to justify the diagnosis and treatment, and to document the results accurately. See also Document, Knowledge, Messenger, Record, Report.

Table 3 The types of medical record listed in order of their usefulness (with the most useful at the top of the table).

Operative reports and pathology reports

The doctor's first report of injury

Reports that include the mechanism of the injury

Diagnostic tests, particularly the special tests (e.g. magnetic resonance imaging and computerized tomography scans) and those used by the medical community at large

Prior rating sheets

A job analysis

Records pertaining to all medical problems the patient may have had since birth

The 'summary of evidence'

All other records

Information about the rating system used by the referral source

---

Medically driven Medical information that is used to control key decision aspects in the medical-legal system.

Medical societies On admission to a medical society, a member assumes an obligation not only to conform to the rules and regulations of the society, but also to observe its standards of professional ethics. A *county medical society* in the United States usually has the authority to enforce discipline among its members so that they obey the society's rules and regulations. This includes the power to expel or otherwise discipline members not acting in the best interest of the society.

Medication see Medicine/medical

Medicine/medical These terms, which relate to the art and science of healing and concern all that is serious and grave, come from the Latin words *medicina* and *medicus*, which refer to heal. These roots also gave rise to the words *medication* and *physician*, both of which are based on the verb *mederi*, to heal. Initially, medicine meant savage magic. It was the *Hippocratic oath* that established the standard of ethics for most Western physicians. Its essence was the promise to relieve suffering and to prolong and protect life. As new discoveries were made, medicine branched into well over 31 subdivisions, with forensic medicine (medical knowledge and technology applied to questions of law) being one example. See Art of medicine.

MEDLARS A registered acronym for the 'Medical Literature Analysis Retrieval System'. It is used in various ways by libraries. Some of the stored information is printed in various medical bibliographies (e.g. *Index Medicus*) which are distributed worldwide. Direct access to the MEDLARS database is available on a subscription basis through MEDLINE, The National Library On-line Terminal Reference Retrieval System. This finds and retrieves articles published in medical journals or journals related to medical topics. MEDLARS is based on the citations in *Index Medicus*. This is made available through the United States National Library of Medicine in Bethesda, Maryland. See also Research.

Melancholia see Depression

Memorandum of cost and disbursements These are expenses incurred by parties in prosecuting or defending a suit. They are legally chargeable to the adverse party and are referred to as *costs*. The court may order the losing party to pay the successful party allowable costs. See also Costs.

Memorial see Document

Mental toughness see Health

Mentally healthy people see Health

Mesial (or medial) Describes the parts of the body that are nearest to the sagittal plane. See also Anatomical references, Figure 1 (page 7).

Mesomorph A type of human body form which has characteristics between those of the *ectomorph* and the *endomorph*. In contrast to the latter forms, the physique of mesomorphs is usually muscular and well proportioned. An endomorph has a relative preponderance of soft tissues and viscera, resulting in a rounded body shape. A ectomorph is tall, thin with long limbs and extremities, a narrow chest and small breasts.

Messenger see Inference

Metaphor The comparison of one thing to another without the use of 'like' or 'as' (e.g. 'a man is but a weak reed' or 'The road was a ribbon of moonlight'). This should be contrasted with a *simile,* which compares two things usually considered different, introducing most with a 'like' or 'as' (e.g. 'the realization hit me like a bucket of cold water' or 'sleeping like a dog'). Both metaphors and similes are *analogies* (i.e. they are similar, alike, resemble, compare, correspond, are parallel, correlate). Our brains appear to easily understand and use metaphors. From childhood we make life comprehensible by using comparisons when a straightforward explanation fails. Metaphors as figurative speech are a way to enrich or enlighten by stretching terminology beyond its conventional context. See also Security.

Metaphysical systems see Character, *A priori*

Metric system Originating in France at the time of the French revolution, it consists of only three words and a half dozen prefixes. The *meter* (m) is the unit of *length,* the *litre* (l) is the unit of *capacity*; and the *gram* (g) is the unit of *weight.* The subdivisions of each of these units have the Latin prefixes *milli-* (abbreviated to m, 1/1000), *centi-* (c, 1/100) and *deci-* (d, 1/10). The multiples for each of the units in the metric system come from the Greek prefixes *deka-* or *deca-* (D, 10), *hekto-* or *hecto-* (h, 100) and *kilo-* (k, 1000). When converting the old British imperial system into metric units it is worth remembering that: 1 m = 39.37 inches; 1 inch = 2.54 cm; 1 cm = approximately 0.4 inches; 1 l or 1000 cm^3 (also called cubic centimetres or cc) weighs 1 kg; and 1 cc water weighs 1 g.

Middle Deriving from the word *mean* (which was originally from the Latin *medius,* medium value), middle is that which is between the beginning and the end. Middle starts at the end of the beginning and ends at the beginning of the end. In general, the contents of the middle may relate to, for example, a number, quantity, degree, kind, value or quality. Biologically, the middle is always part of a process. Medically, it is primarily concerned with diagnosis and treatment or management.

In law it refers to the trial process. See also Disease, Process.

Millimeters see Metric system

Minimal pain see Pain grading

Minors or incompetents An infant or a person who is under the age of legal competence (e.g. under the age of 18 years) and is, therefore, considered a minor. An application for benefits for minors and incompetence in the California Worker's Compensation would be accompanied by a *petition for appointment* of a guardian *ad litem* and trustee. Forms are obtained at the Worker's Compensation Appeals Board. See also Conservatee.

MINT see Cause

Miracle A contradiction of the laws of nature as we understand them.

Miscarriage of justice Damage to the rights of one party in a legal action that results from errors made by the court during the trial and that is sufficiently substantial to require a retrial. See also Justice.

Misdemeanor Class of criminal offenses less serious than felonies with less severe penalties. See also Classifying crimes

Miserly see Greedy

Misfeasance The doing of a lawful act in an unlawful or improper way. See also Lawful, Malfeasance, Non-feasance.

Mistake Old Norse meaning 'taking wrongly', it is an act or omission caused by a misunderstanding of law or fact. See also Harmless error.

Mitigating circumstances A set of conditions that, while not exonerating the accused, might reduce the sentence or damages arising from the offense. See also Affirmative defense, Manslaughter.

Mobilization This is a 'hands on' procedure often used effectively for *joint binding.* A European physical therapist introduced the author to the procedure, particularly with respect of binding of the occipitocervical joint (as a cause of *orthopaedic headaches*) and binding in facet joints. For this technique to be useful, it is important to properly diagnose the condition and understand joint pathoanatomy. For example, facet joints are provided with a complete capsule and lined with a definite synovial membrane. On the medial superior aspect some of the ligamentum flavie blends into the capsule, which may prevent the capsule from being nipped between the two articular surfaces during movement and from protrusion into the spinal foramina. The synovial membrane of the facet joints is made up of synovial villi which vary in size, shape and appearance while containing a rich supply of blood vessels and nerves. These soft tissues which line the facet can undergo adaptive shortening and bind. Thus, when normal movement is attempted these structures are prematurely placed at full stretch, reducing the distance before the movement is stopped by ligamentous tension. Any overstretch of soft tissues from this point could lead to sufficient mechanical deformation of the free nerve endings in these tissues and cause pain. *Mobilization involves joint play* (movement not under voluntary control but necessary for painless free performance of active range of motion) *testing and stretch through slow methods.*

Mobilization under anesthesia (MUA) Putting the joint through its full range of movement during complete muscular relaxation. This is useful for rupturing adhesions. However, if too much force is used the capsule of the joint may also rupture. Although this method has many advocates, it can do a great deal of harm. See also Manipulation, Mobilization.

Moral certainty   see Beyond reasonable doubt, Certainty, Ethics, Evidence

Modal zero see Abnormal

Modalities   A therapeutic method, especially one employed in physical therapy. See also Physical modalities.

Moderate pain see Pain grading

Modified work Work which has fewer demands than a former occupation. A typical legal question is that, 'Given the allowed conditions recognized in the claim(s), even if the patient has not reached maximum medical improvement, is the patient capable of returning to modified work? If so, what medical restrictions would apply to such work?' An example for physically strenuous work would require comments regarding the appropriate limitations of physical activities (e.g. avoiding lifting and bending of over 10 pounds (4.5 kg)

five times in one hour, avoid twisting or stooping completely, etc.). If the allowed conditions are of a psychological nature, then the work restrictions would be defined in terms of necessary limitations to circumstances that would aggravate the psychological condition (e.g. avoid extreme psychological stress that comes from working with a certain individual). See also Americans with Disabilities Act.

Modus operandi   Latin for 'manner of operation', it refers to the means of accomplishing an act; especially the characteristic method employed by a defendant in repeated criminal acts.

Mononeuropathy   see Sensation classification — painful type

Mood see Emotional distress, Emotions, Pleasure

Moot To propose for discussion. A *moot court* is a mock court held by students for practice in legal procedure. A *moot point* is not subject to a judicial determination because it involves an abstract question or a pretended controversy that has not yet actually arisen or has already passed. Thus, it will not effect or be affected by the court's decision. A *moot case* involves an abstract question not arising from existing facts or rights.

Moot case see Moot

Moot court see Moot

Moot issues An issue becomes moot if later events show any decision by the court to be meaningless in regard to a specific case.

Moral certainty   see Beyond reasonable doubt, Certainty, Ethics, Evidence

Moral philosophy see Ethics

Moral sciences see Ethics

Morals see Ethics, Facts

Morbidity Disability (e.g. absence from work, economic loss, increased pain, delayed rehabilitation) as a result of a degree of sickness or the presence of complications following treatment (e.g. a surgical procedure). See also Disability, Impairment.

More likely than not see Arise out of employment, Medical probability

Morphological change see Disease

Motion An application for a rule or order made to the court or judge which is usually in favor of the applicant. Motions may be made orally or, more formally, in writing.

Motion to produce An order made by a court at the request of counsel compelling the defendant to provide specific evidence to the court. A type of discovery procedure. See Discovery.

Motive The cause or reason for either doing or not doing an act. Motive is not synonymous with criminal intent; intent is essential for crime, but a motive is not. See also Intent.

Motor neuron disease A group of conditions in which muscles may atrophy and motion may be hampered by spasticity, and both these may exist to various degrees and in a variety of combinations. The *upper motor neuron* (UMN) is the descending motor pathway (the *pyramidal track*) from the cerebral cortex to the motor nuclei of the brain stem and spinal cord. A lesion of the corticopontine fibers of the pyramidal track causing *upper motor neuron paralysis* may be located anywhere between the cortex and the middle of the pons. Interruption of this motor pathway leads to spasticity of the muscles and reduced motor power, so that, for example, while the eye can still be closed and the fore-

head wrinkled, the teeth cannot be bared on the affected side and there is weakness of the lips and buccinator muscles. This may result from many conditions (e.g. vascular accidents, neoplasms, cerebral contusion, degenerative cerebral disease, etc.). It is usually associated with hemiparesis, or with weakness of the upper limb owing to the condensation of fibers which occur in the pyramidal track and the internal capsule and below; but in cortical and subcortical lesions it may occur independently. The *lower motor neuron* (LMN) consists of the anterior horn cell in the spinal cord or the motor cranial nerve nucleus in the brain stem and their associated nerves. Destruction of either of these units leads to flaccidity, paralysis and atrophy of the muscle. The reaction of degeneration appears after paralysis has been present for 2–3 weeks, when contractures may occur.

Multiple mononeuropathy see Sensation classification — painful type

Municipal court A city court that administers the law within the city. See also Courts.

Murder Homicide with malice of forethought. *First degree murder* is unlawful killing that is deliberate and premeditated. *Second degree murder* is unlawful killing of another with malice of forethought but without deliberation and premeditation. See also Classifying crimes, Crimes, Lawful, Manslaughter, Premeditation.

Muscle grading Information about this can be obtained through books on muscle testing or techniques of

Table 4 The original system devised to grade muscle action during examination. It was proposed in March 1946.

Amount of muscle action (%)	Rating given	Action considered	Full description
100	5	Normal (n)	Complete range of motion against gravity with full resistance
75	4	Good (g)	Complete range of motion against gravity with some resistance
50	3	Fair (f)	Complete range of motion against gravity
25	2	Poor (p)	Complete range of motion with gravity eliminated
10	1	Trace (t)	Evidence of slight contractility. No joint motion
0	0	Zero	No evidence of contractility
Spasm		S or ss	Spasm or severe pain
Contracture		C or cc	Contracture or severe contracture

Table 5 A newer system for assessing muscle strength.

Grade	Description of grade
1	Complete range of motion against gravity and full resistance
2	Complete range of motion against gravity and some resistance, or reduced fine movements and motor control
3	Complete range of motion against gravity only, without any added resistance
4	Complete range of motion with gravity eliminated
5	Slight contractions with no joint motion
6	No detectible contractions

manual examination. There are numerous systems and each system has its own peculiarity. The National Foundation for Infantile Paralysis proposed a revised grading of muscle action during an examination in March 1946 and this is shown in Table 4. A somewhat newer system which grades muscle strength is shown in Table 5.

Musculoskeletal affections   These include: (1) traumas, both extrinsic and intrinsic; (2) inflammation; (3) metabolic disease; (4) neoplasms; (5) congenital anomalies/alterations; (6) neurological disorders; and (7) vascular disorders. They result in anatomical disorders of the body parts as well as physiological disorders in the functioning of body parts.

Musculoskeletal system structures   These include: (1) bone and its periosteum; (2) hyaline cartilage; (3) joint capsule; (4) ligaments, (5) muscles; (6) tendons; (7) tendon sheaths; (8) intra-articular menisci; (9) bursae; (10) fascia; (11) blood vessels; (12) nerves; (13) fat; and (14) skin.

Must see Should

Mutation   Semantically, mutate is probably the most direct English descendant of the Indo-European base *moi*, meaning change or exchange. In genetics a mutation is a permanent transmissible change in the genetic material, usually in a single gene. The change may be in a form of loss (*deletion*), gain (*translocation*) or exchange (*transduction*) of genetic material. See also Genetic congenital condition, Inheritance of acquired characteristics.

N

Narcotic It originally derived from the Greek *narke*, which meant 'numbness', but since the fourteenth century has referred to a substance which when swallowed, inhaled or injected into the system induces drowsiness, sleep, stupefaction or insensibility according to its strength and the amount taken. This includes opium or its derivatives such as morphine and heroin (a derivative of morphine). See also Art of medicine, Doctor/patient relationship, Drug rehabilitation, Twelve-step program.

Natural history of a disease This is the usual course of the disease, from its beginning to its end, without treatment or other interferences (e.g. superimposed conditions). See also Apportionment terms, Disease, Pathology scope.

Natural progression of disease (or injury) The course of the physical and/or psychological manifestation of the disease (i.e. the patient is getting better, worse or remaining the same). This assessment must be made in the light of patient's character, the patient's activities and the natural history of the disease. See also Apportionment terms, Cause, Disability, Disease, Lesions, Natural history of disease, Pathology, Pathology Scope, Prognosis.

Necessaries Those things which are indispensable, proper or useful for the sustenance and reasonable enjoyment of life. It is a relative term. If an appliance is judged to be a *medical necessity*, this is a subjective opinion of objective impairment. This appliance could be anything that cures or relieves the effects of the injury (e.g. it could be a van for transportation), to help the injured person become more competitive on the open labor market, etc. Medical necessity must be distinguished from *medical luxury*, which add to a patient's pleasure or comfort, but are not absolutely necessary (e.g. a jacuzzi).

Negative abnormal see Abnormal, Guilt

Negative abnormal people see Abnormal

Negative pleasures Whereas *sick pleasures* are more about destructive selfishness, negative pleasures are in the realm of constructive selfishness. One such pleasure is the desire for *retaliation*. To retaliate is to give like for like. Hammurabi (1792–1750 BC, King of Babylonia) gave us a standard for retaliation when he declared the punishment should be 'an eye for an eye.' However, this may also be necessary for self-defense and self-protection, which do not involve self-centered gratification. A legal example of a negative pleasure would be those legal actions taken against discriminatory harassment. A successful outcome would not only be self-satisfying, but also help similar victims. See also Sick pleasures.

Negligence Failure to exercise a degree of care that a person of ordinary prudence (*a reasonable man*) would exercise under the same circumstances. Thus, the injury would be a proximate and foreseeable result. In a suit to recover damages resulting from an unintentional 'tort', the plaintiff must prove negligence. See also Assumption of risk, Comparative negligence, Malpractice, Patient abandonment, Proximate cause, Reasonable person, Red herring, *Res ipsa loguitur*, Tort.

Negligent see Foreseeable risk

Nerve injuries see Seddon classification of nerve injuries, Sensation classification — painful type, Sunderland classification of nerve injuries

Nervi nervorum Nerves supplying nerves. See also Table 10 (page 124).

Neuralgias see Sensation classification — painful type

Neurapraxia   see Seddon classification of nerve injuries, Sensation classification — painful type, Sunderland classification of nerve injuries

Neuropathies   see Sensation classification — painful type, Stocking/glove anesthesia

Neurosis   see Psychogenic disease

Neurotics   see Psychogenic disease

Neurotmesis   see Seddon classification of nerve injuries, Sensation classification — painful type, Sunderland classification of nerve injuries

Neutralized   see Euphemisms, Euphemisms in medicine

Never   see Vocational rehabilitation terms

New injuries   Are traumatically induced lesions that occur de novo or are superimposed on other lesions. New injuries must be clearly distinguished from superimposed injuries in determining if new and further disability has arisen from de novo and/or superimposed injuries. See also Apportionment, De novo, Disease, Injury, Precipitated disease or injury.

Noble   see Character, Respect

Noble beliefs   see Character

No-fault   Is without regard to who was at fault. For example, persons injured in an car accident may receive compensation for their resulting injuries without determining who actually caused the accident.

Non-aggressive   see Behavior methods

Non-compos mentis   Not of sound mind or discretion. See also Insanity.

Non-feasance   The failure of a person to perform some act that he or she either should, or is required, to perform. It should be compared with misfeasance (the improper doing of an act that would otherwise be lawful) and malfeasance (carrying out an act that is wholly wrongful and unlawful). See also Lawful.

Non-genetic congenital/developmental lesions   Are affectations of an acquired nature present before or at birth but not manifest until some time after birth.

Non-genetic congenital lesions   Are pathological processes acquired in utero which are present at birth (e.g. thalidomide embryopathy).

Non-pain sensations   see Dysaethesias, Paresthesias, Sensation, Sensation classification — painful type.

Non-pertinent   see Red flag lesions, Red herring pathological lesions

Non-progressive   see Lighting up

Non-suit   Termination of a lawsuit without any judgment on the issues involved. This could be a judgment against the plaintiff when he or she cannot prove his or her case or does not proceed to a trial (a take nothing).

Non-work activities   All activities outside work. In legal terms, it tends to refer to mentally or physically strenuous hobbies or avocations. See also Activities of daily living.

Normal   Is the cornerstone of the medical-legal system. It is against the normal that the abnormal is compared (e.g. consider histology). According to the dictionary, normal is synonymous with health, reasonable, representative, typical, mediocre, etc., and thus appears to be an 'umbrella term' with a variety of meanings.
Medically, 'normal' can be used in two very different situations. First, it can be a biological term which relates to living organisms that continually change and grow. The 'normal' or 'physiological' state is achieved by adaptive responses to the ebb and flow of various stimuli. Adaptation permits the cells and tissues to adjust and to live in harmony with their micro-environment in order to preserve homeostasis (a stable state or normal). Second, in medicine normal also refers to individual characteristics in a range of values clustered closely around the average. This definition can be applied to the study of pathology, where it is important to know the normal value range for fasting blood sugar, so that an abnormal reading (which may be above or below) can be identified. With blood sugar levels, the normal is a range (60–100 mg per 100 ml blood) and not an absolute value. Even so, the range is only a guide, as someone with a fasting blood glucose of 99 mg per 100 ml blood is not necessarily free of diabetes, and a patient with 101 mg per 100 ml blood is not necessarily a diabetic.

Legally, normal is performing the proper functions according to established principles or rules. It is from this perspective that the word 'normal' originally arose (from the Latin *normalis*, meaning made according to the carpenter's square). When something was made according to the carpenter's square, it was made according to a pattern which conformed to a rule. Such a 'normal' design became the standard. In other words, the 'norm' was the standard and what was normal followed the ruler or the standard measure of person, place or thing. For example, it is the author's impression that the legal normal refers to the *prudent person* as applied to action or conducts; it is what most people would do under a given circumstance. This concept would extend into *professionalism* of any type. Compare with Abnormal, Normal variants. See also Health, Pre-injury capacity, Professional, Proof, Reasonable.

Normal hand see Thumb, Figure 6 (page 59)

Normal patients These are prototype I textbook patients (i.e. those studied in medical school and have organic lesions). When people are ill, they are not their 'normal' selves. 'Normal' patients have emotional problems as a result of their illness (or other problem), but these remain at a mild or slight level and are of appropriate duration. See also Classification of medical patients.

Normal values see Values

Normal variants Are mild or slight anatomical, physiological or biochemical deviation from what is considered normal which is not sufficiently different to be considered abnormal. Therefore, normal variants lie between what is normal and abnormal. Clinical pathological manifestations are generally not present when the normal variant is closer to the normal than the abnormal.

However, considerable confusion can exist as the normal variant approaches the abnormal. For example, the normal variant of a limbus vertebrae has often been confused with a fracture. Almost all medical normal variants have increased susceptibility to relatively minor trauma or disease. Compare with Abnormal, Normal.

Norms Rules and expectations that are proposed to provide regularity or patterns to social life. *Deviants* violate the rules and expectations. See also Deviants, Normal.

Notary public A public officer authorized to administer oaths, to attest to and certify certain types of documents, to take dispositions and to perform certain acts in commercial matters. The seal of a notary public authenticates a document. In some jurisdictions an attorney admitted to practice within the jurisdiction can act as a notary public.

Notice Communication sufficient to charge a reasonable person with the knowledge of some fact. *Actual notice* is knowledge that may be either positively proved to have been communicated to a person directly or personally, or that he or she is presumed to have received personally. *Constructive notice* is knowledge given to a person by law, regardless of the person's actual knowledge, because he or she could have obtained such knowledge and should have done so in that particular situation. See also Knowledge.

Nuisance Anything that disturbs the free use of a person's own property or that renders its ordinary use uncomfortable.

Nunc pro tunc The Latin phrase means 'now for then', and is used in reference to an act which is allowed to be performed after the time when it should have been performed.

Oath 'I do solemnly swear that the testimony I am about to give will be the truth, the whole truth, and nothing but the truth. So help me God.' For at least the last 3000 years there have been sacred or solemn voluntary promises made to some divine being in order to get something desired or to avoid something unwanted. These pledges have usually involved the penalty of divine retribution for intentional falsity. The swearing of an oath before divine symbols already existed during the Sumerian civilisation of the ancient 'Middle East' and in ancient Egypt. Here, a warrior often swore by his life or 'ankh' (oath), which literally means 'an utterance of life'. Ancient Germanic tribes, Greeks, Romans and Scythians swore by their swords or other weapons. They were actually evoking a symbol of the power of a war god as a guarantee of their trustworthiness. By the time of Jesus, oaths were sworn on the person's own soul, honor or faith. A false oath was considered a danger to that person's soul. During the medieval trials of 'ordeal and battle', God was appealed to as the highest judge. In these cases of the accused versus the people, it was believed that God would be on the side of the right and would pass on the judgment of guilt or innocence. Of course, this was there for everyone to see, for if the accused had God on his side he would successfully perform the test (i.e. the dangerous ordeal). Before the trials, the accused was ordered to swear before a number of witnesses as an offer to exonerate himself by oath. Hence, the word *witness* originally meant 'drawn in' to perform a legal act. Even though witnesses never gave testimony, they initiated a system that eventually lead to the more rational use of evidence. It has subsequently become a legal requirement that oaths consist of some conscious act of undertaking an obligation and are performed in the presence of an official. Witnesses must state an intention to give all pertinent information and to tell only the truth when relating it. Testimony will not be received unless the witness is subject to some sanction of falsity, either by giving affirmation or by taking an oath if they believe in God. Although oaths are usually taken upon the gospel or by swearing with the hand, no particular form is nec-

essary to make an oath binding. False testimony constitutes the crime of perjury, because it breaks a 'going together in agreement' — one of the original meanings of oath. See also Professionalism, Reasonable, Witness.

Objection An attorney asserts during a trial that a particular witness, line of questioning, piece of evidence or other matter is improper and should not be continued. Then the court rules on its impropriety or illegality. See also Irrelevant, Leading question.

Objective Is a very complicated word with many unexplained or poorly defined ramifications. As a result, most use a confusingly simplistic definition. Nevertheless, it is generally accepted in law that something is objective if it can be seen and/or measured. Even in medicine, objective findings are considered those which are independent of voluntary fashioning or creation, and can be seen, felt, heard and/or consistently measured by various doctors. Examples would be fever, crepitus, swelling, heart murmur, jaundice, ankylosis and amputation. To fully understand 'objective' is to include concepts and definitions of tangible, intangible, *objective minus* ('what is there but is not' and 'what is not there but is') and *subjective plus* (because it 'fits' or 'works,' the truth seems valid in advance of proof), rather than *subjective* (based on psychological processes) and *subjective minus* (it is untrue or not there). When in doubt, it is helpful to consider that something is objective if it has its perceptive origin outside the mind. Compare with Subjective, Symptoms. See also Anatomical abnormality, Anatomical loss, Intangible, Objective/subjective scale, Signs.

Objective appraisal see Estimation, Quantity

Objective end see End

Objective evidence see Demonstrative evidence

Objective facts see Facts

Objective fair play see Fair play

Objective impairment Consists of anatomical and/or functional losses and sometimes anatomical and/or functional abnormalities. An extension of this concept may include certain appliances as medical necessities.

Objective minus Are functional and anatomical abnormalities that would have been under a patient's control (e.g. loss of joint motion or hand grip) or represents a 'red herring' (e.g. atrophy). Non-medical people are often misled by objective minus factors of impairment because, although a deviation from normal is seen, it does not necessarily mean that the deviation is the cause of that patient's problems or the effect of the injury. In addition, they also include concealed or subtle factors that can only be detected by experts, special studies or through circumstantial evidence. Thus, objective minus consists of 'what is there but is not' and 'what is not there but is'. See also Anatomical abnormality, Circumstantial evidence, Red herring pathological lesions, Functional abnormality, Objective/subjective scale.

Objective/subjective scale This includes *objective* (i.e. it can be seen, touched or measured and has its perceptive origin outside the mind), *objective minus* ('what is there but is not' and 'what is not there but is'), *subjective plus* (because it 'fits' or 'works,' truth seems valid to experts in advance of proof), *subjective* (based on psychological processes) and *subjective minus* (it is untrue or not there).

Objective vertigo see Vertigo

Obligate To bind in a legal and/or moral sense.

OBMER Stands for origin, beginning, middle, end and result. See also Disease, Process, Underlying disease.

Obstruction of justice Is standing in the way of legal progress. This includes attempting to influence, intimidate or impede any juror, witness or officer in any court in the discharge of her/his duty. This could extend to police officers and other administrative officials. See also Lawful.

Occasional see Chronic, Vocational rehabilitation terms

Occult see Concealed

Occult medical lesions Are concealed lesions considered as undefined underlying medical conditions. They undergo the usual origin, beginning, middle and, possibly, end, but the external effects of these processes are not clinically detectable, either inconsistently or throughout. Usually such undefined occult lesions lie dormant or are continuing to unfold in an active state. See also Pathological scope, Process, Underlying disease (or pathology).

Occult minds see Reasonable

Occupational disease Is one in which the cumulative effect of the continual absorption of small quantities of deleterious substances from the environment of a person's place of employment ultimately results in manifest pathological lesions. Although any one exposure to the deleterious substance is inconsequential in itself, it is the accumulation of repeated absorption of the factor which brings about the disease (see California Labor Code sections 5500.5, 6302–6306 and 5412). An occupational illness is produced by exposure to various chemicals, infections and stress/strain, etc., when continued and repeated exposure to the causative agent exists beyond a single work day or a work shift. Industrial diseases are often slow to develop and the link with a specific material or process is hard to establish. Examples include asbestosis and radioactive materials. See also Occurrence.

Occupational illness see Date of injury

Occurrence Something that is 'run against'. It means anything that happens and is synonymous with *happening* and *event*, although event may have much larger significance (i.e. world events, but everyday occurrences). In the medical-legal arena, occurrence relates to small insults such as, for example, each tiny deposit of scar-like tissue which causes injury to a lung. Each insult-causing injury is an 'occurrence' for the purpose of determining which payor insurance coverage applies. See also Apportionment terms, Occupational disease, Reoccurrence.

Occurring in the course of employment see Course of employment

Offense Any violation of law for which a penalty is prescribed, including both felonies and misdemeanors.

Ombudsman   A Swedish word which denotes an 'investigator of public complaints'; literally 'administration man'. Ombudsmen are government officials appointed to receive, investigate and report upon grievances of private citizens against the government.

On pain of death   See Pain, Penalty

Open labor markets   In ancient Greece, open markets were called *agorot*. The word market itself derived from an early Roman trade word related to money. In English law, an open and public market was that place set apart by custom for the sale of particular goods. Today, it is where a group of productive enterprises make or supply goods. In an open market supply and demand are expressed in terms of price. Price can be paid for either goods or hire. Prospective workers go to the open labor market for hire. Disability refers to a reduction in the ability of a person to compete in the open labor market for jobs that are viable to the injured. See also Disability, Permanent disability.

Opening statements   At a trial, attorneys for the plaintiff and for the defense outline what they believe to be the nature of the case and what each hopes to prove as the trial proceeds. These contain only essential facts and are used to orientate the judge and jury in similar manner as the preface of a book.

Operative procedures   Operative is from the Latin *operari*, meaning to work, it literally means any work that is done by hand. Subsequently, the term came to mean an action or work done with the hands or with instruments upon the body (e.g. a surgical operation). The surgical sense was first recorded in the sixteenth century. An operation includes any procedure which uses instruments to semi-open or open a body to repair damage or to restore health by adding or removing something. See also Treatment.

Opinion   From the Latin *opinio*, meaning think, and possibly to choose. It is an expression, often in the form of a conclusion or judgment, of a person's beliefs, ideas, thoughts, feelings and emotions which seem true or probable to that person. Opinions are heavily influenced by background, aspirations, values, standards and integrity, and can be based on reality, partial reality or fantasy. Opinions range between faith and knowledge. There are several types: a *view* (an opinion affected by the way a person looks at things), a *sentiment* (an opinion that results from deliberation but is colored by emotions) and a *persuasion* (a more confident opinion,

involving the heart as well as the intellect). In law, an opinion is the reason given for a court's judgment, finding or conclusion as opposed to the decision, which is the judgment itself. Medically, the best and most professional opinions are formed when doctors suspend their personal feelings in order to gain neutral position and understand and analyze both sides of a significant issue (i.e. they suspend one issue while reasonably assessing another, to rationally analyze the advantages and disadvantage of both issues, to disregard any information that is misleading or incorrect, and to then arrive at an honest judgment). See also Judgments, Professionalism, Reason.

Opinion facts   See Legal opinion fact

Opinion rule   A judgment of belief on the part of a member or the majority of persons; what is generally thought about something.

Opium   see Narcotic

Oral testimony   That information which is given by experts, witnesses and the plaintiff. See also Witnesses.

Order   This originally denoted a row, line, series or other regular arrangement, but has subsequently given rise to many other metaphorical meanings (e.g. rank, class). Its use in the sense of a 'command, directive' was first recorded in England in the mid-sixteenth century, and presumably derives the notion of 'keeping in order'. In court, an order is an oral or written command directing or forbidding an action.

Order to show cause   see Show cause order

Origin   It has many meanings, but usually refers to an initial cause giving rise to a beginning, the start of an action. The opposite of cause is *effect* which etymologically means 'to bring about'. When referring to origin as a cause it is important to distinguish between its spiritual (e.g. *first cause*) and *worldly* subdivisions. In a worldly sense, as used in the medical-legal arena, origin is the giving of birth to forms of activity. See also Process.

Origins of disease   see Disease

Orthopaedic headaches   see Mobilization

Orthopaedics   Orthopaedics is the medical specialty that includes the investigation, preservation, restoration and development of the form and function of the extremities, spine and associated structures by medical, surgical and physical methods.

Osteoarthritis From the Greek *osteon*, meaning bone, *arthron*, meaning joint, and *itis*, meaning inflammation. For centuries, the term had been used for most, if not all, of the over 109 different arthritic conditions. Nowadays, however, what remains is an inflammatory type of arthritis (*erosive arthritis*) and a non-inflammatory type (*degenerative joint disease, degenerative arthritis* or *hypertrophic arthritis*). Erosive or inflammatory arthritis is most commonly seen in hands, particularly in women. Degenerative joint diseases can be seen all over the body but is usually most painful in the large weight-bearing joints such as hips, knees and ankles. Both types are characterized by degeneration of the articular cartilage, hypertrophy of bone at the margins and changes in the synovial membrane. Pain from degenerative joint disease tends to be associated with activity. See also Cervical spondylosis.

Osteopaths see Manipulation

Overgeneralization Assuming similar outcomes to different experiences.

Overlay, functional/psychogenic/emotional Overlay means an increment; a later addition superimposed upon an already existing condition, state, mass or lesion. Functional overlay is the emotionally determined increment to an existing symptom, impairment or disability which has been of an organic or of a physically traumatic origin. It reflects a reaction to the organic injury that is greater than would be expected from a person of normal stability (i.e. in terms of how much a person is bothered and worried by pain). Functional overlay is a psychiatric diagnosis and, in some instances, can be compensable. Thus, care should be taken on the use the term 'functional overlay' in court, in depositions or in reports. See Functional prolongation.

Overrule To overturn or make void. For example, to deny a motion, objection or other point raised to the court. Higher courts can overrule erroneous decisions of lower courts.

Overruled An objection is the act of calling the court's attention to something that the counsel to one of the parties in the lawsuit considers improper or illegal. If the judge says 'sustained', he is agreeing with the objecting attorney. If he says 'over-ruled', he or she is not in agreement and the witness must answer the opposing counsel's question. See also Directed verdict, Sustained.

Overt From the Latin *apert*, meaning to open, it is to open in order to view; to manifest; that which is observable.

Overt behavioral expressions Are those that are 'openly done', manifest and unconcealed. For example, an open overt expression of fear is flight; of rage is fight.

P

Pain From the Latin *poena*, meaning punishment or penalty, this word derives from an old belief that our troubles are the result of our sins. Punishment is the ancestral meaning of pain, with suffering as a secondary development. In early usage, suffering in purgatory or hell was inflicted as a punishment in a religious sense. During life, a person's sin would cause sorrow and from the meaning of sorrow it shifted to trouble. Disease was an example of trouble and a 'patient' literally means 'the victim who suffered'. Disease meant the patient was paying the penalty for his or her sins. Similarly, during those times when religion and law were closely related, people who committed crimes were considered sinners and, therefore, needed to suffer. Hence, a penalty or fine which was considered to be unpleasant or distressing was imposed. From this definition arose such legal expressions as 'on pain of death' (meaning under penalty of death) and 'pains of felony' (meaning the crime with which a person is liable to be charged). Pain then evolved away from moral law and became the trouble taken in attempting or accomplishing something such as childbirth. Nowadays, *pain is a general term for mental or physical deviation from a state of well-being.* This includes disturbing sensations resulting from injurious external interference (e.g. wound, bruise or harsh word), the lack of what a person needs, craves or cherishes (e.g. hunger pains or bereavement) or abnormal action of bodily or mental functions (e.g. pains of disease, envy or discontent). Suffering is one of the severe forms of pain, the others are: *Torment and torture* (intense and terrible suffering), *agony* (that with which the body struggles) and *anguish* (that by which it is crushed). See also Penalty, Punishment, Suffering.

Pain and suffering This is a legal concept related to damages. In trials, the plaintiff's attorneys promotes the concept of 'pain and suffering' that resulted from a wrong done or suffered. Even the loss of ability or capacity to work for reasons of physical pain or emotional/mental suffering has the potential for compensation. Advocates tend to exaggerate, using terms such as awful, dreadful, enormous, outrageous. As both pain and suffering encompass in their content intensity and magnitude, there can be different degrees of pain and suffering. For convenience these degrees are subdivided into mild, slight, moderate and extreme. The large number of synonyms for pain and suffering can be appropriately be placed into one of those four subdivisions (e.g. *tolerate* donates a mild type of suffering while the word *anguish* denotes an extreme degree). One of the duties of the medical-legal doctor is to appropriately assess the patient's level of pain and suffering and then apply the appropriate word. If, for example, we agree that the word 'tolerate' means forced acceptance and this is what the patient has done, then it would be inappropriate to use the term 'anguish'. In the United States, the adversarial trial system has lead some plaintiff's attorneys to persuade the doctor to upgrade terms of degree, while some defense attorneys may want an unrealistically downgrade it. In order for the doctor to formulate a solid concept of the degree of the patient's pain and suffering, the doctor needs to know who the patient is as a person, the scope of the patient's pathological lesions and the patient's activities.

Pain diagrams These are outline diagrams of both the front and back of the body which are used by patients to show the location of their pain and, using designated symbols, the degree of pain they feel.

Pain frequency rating California workers' compensations uses the pain frequency rating shown in Table 6.

Table 6 The pain frequency rating used in California worker's compensation.

Type of pain	Duration of pain
Occasional	Up to 25% of an 8-hour work day
Intermittent	50% of an 8-hour work day
Frequent	75% of a work day
Constant	90–100% of a work day.

Pain grading In California workers' compensation this includes: (1) *minimal pain* (an annoyance but no work handicap); (2) *slight pain* (tolerated despite some handicap in the performance of the activity precipitating the pain); (3) *moderate pain* (tolerated despite marked handicap); and (4) *severe pain* (includes the activity precipitating the pain).

Pain measurement test Objectively measuring pain is very difficult. The main problem is to distinguish between stoics, 'normal' patients and deceptive patients. As of yet, there are no tools to make such a distinction. Even with 'normal ' patients, some have *hypersensitivity for constitutional, cultural or endocrine reasons*. Thus, the psychogalvanic reflex test and the Libman test are extremely crude measures.
The aim of the *Libman test* is to determine the physical sensitivity to pain as it varies in different individuals. The doctor presses forcefully with his or her thumb tip upon the tip of the patient's styloid process (just behind the lobe of the ear). Average patients react and normally resent this pressure. If there is *congenital insensitivity to pain*, the patient is stolid and does not react. For those that react, they can be graded on a scale from one to four, where 1 is mild, 2 is slight, 3 is moderate and 4 is severe. A 2.5 numerical medical bridge is equivalent to 'slight to moderate.'
A *psychogalvanic reflex* utilizes an electrical stimulus to the skin and then records the skin resistance as well as the patient's response to a shock stimulus. Some researchers have noted that, when this technique was used, there was an objective medical difference between those known to be suffering from physical pain and those assumed to have psychogenic pain. However, the measurement of pain still requires more research and one possible place area of investigation is the autonomic nervous system.

Pain of death see Pain

Pain of felony see Pain

Pain sensations see Sensation, Sensation classification — painful type

Palpation see Physical examination

Paralegal A person who is not a member of the bar but is employed, usually by the law office, to perform a variety of tasks associated with a law practice, any one of which may be performed properly and conveniently by one not trained or authorized to practice law.

Paramedic A health care worker who provides services that are associated with, and compliment, those of medical practitioners.

Paramedical Those who are ancillary to the medical profession, such as occupational therapists, physical therapists, laboratory technicians and emergency medical technicians, etc.

Pardon The means to forgive. It is a *claque* or loan translation that was created by taking the components of a foreign word (the Latin term *perdonare*), translating it literally and then putting it back together to form a new word. 'Perdonare' was a compound verb formed from *per*, meaning thoroughly, and *donare*, meaning give, and it had an underlying sense of 'give wholeheartedly.' A pardon relaxes the punishment and removes guilt so that, legally, the offender is as innocent as if the offense had never been committed.

Paresthesia An abnormal tickling, prickling or burning non-painful sensation. See also Conversion reactions, Dysaesthesia, Sensation, Sensation classification — painful type, Subjective non-pain disability.

Paroxysm A term that applies to an alternately recurring and receding pain which occurs in waves. The paroxysm is the rising of the wave. Composed of the Greek prefix *para*, meaning beside, plus *oxyno*, meaning to shapen or to prick, paroxysm originally denoted a fit of rage or a seizure. It moved into English language during the sixteenth century and has subsequently denoted a severe sudden onset of a disease.

Partial rehabilitation see Self-rehabilitated

Partial temporary disability see Temporary disability

Partition To divide disputed property. See also Court of Equity.

Party A person, business or governmental agency actively involved in the prosecution or defense of a legal proceeding. See also Litigant.

Passenger injury(s) It is any injury, apart from the *pilot injury* (i.e. the main pathological condition), that is of significance to the same part of the body. They can occur before, simultaneously or after the pilot injury. Some passenger injuries may be the subject of litigation elsewhere (e.g. car accidents), have previously been compensated in worker's compensation or civil courts, or may be non-compensable (e.g. the result of falling off a ladder at home). Appropriate names can be applied to passenger injuries when their individuality is needed. See also Pilot injury.

Passive see Behavior methods

Passive aggression see Behavior methods

Past medical history At times important and sometimes vital information can be discovered from asking about illnesses, medications, allergies, operations, hospitalizations, accidents, military disabilities and a system review. A system review includes information about the problems to the head, to the cardiorespiratory, vascular, gastrointestinal and genitourinary systems, those that are psychiatric, neurological or musculoskeletal in nature, any bleeding tendencies and anything else that might influence a treatment plan. See also History form.

Pathogenesis Refers to the mechanisms by which the causative agent(s) brings about the ailment. It is the sequence of events and the response of the cells and the tissues, or the whole person, to the cause(s) from the initial stimulus to the ultimate expression of the clinical manifestations, including the factors which influence its development. In practical terms, this is how the disease came about and the resultant ramifications leading to a *lesion* (i.e. an abnormal change in the tissues ranging from a pinprick to a gunshot wound or from an abscess to a cancer). The only way to devise effective strategies for pertinent treatment or to prevent adverse progression is to appreciate, when investigating the pathogenesis, that it involves mechanisms at all levels of biological organization. For example, to understand gout it is important to know not only the molecular pathways of uric acid metabolism, but also the events leading to a painful big toe or a kidney stone. In some cases the causes of a condition are better known than the pathogenesis (e.g. tumors). See also Cause, Etiology, Lesions, Pathological scope of the lesion, Pathology.

Pathogenic mechanism Medically, it is the final common pathway of a series of events that has resulted from one or more causes. This pathway contains deviations from normal. See also Pathological scope of the lesion, Pathology.

Pathognomonic From the Greek *pathos*, meaning disease, plus *gnomonihos*, meaning skilled in a thing, it is a word used by Galen in the second century to denote the characteristics of a disease that distinguishes it from other diseases. It was believed that the uniqueness of a clinical manifestation was determined by the passions or feelings expressed by the person with the condition. The term was introduced into English language in the early seventeenth century. Today, it means that symptom or sign which is so distinctive or characteristic of a disease or pathological condition that a diagnosis can be made from it. See also Sign.

Pathological lesion event The result of an event on musculoskeletal structures. These can be anatomical and/or physiological disorders which involve losses, reduction, rearrangements, excesses and reversals (e.g. disappearing bone disease). See also Beginning, Process.

Pathological lying/pseudologia fantastica Differs from normal daydreaming in that the person believes in the reality of the fantasies intermittently and for sufficient periods of time to act on them. Pathological lying should be seen in the context of character disorders, particularly sociopaths and the 'hysterical character'. Many sociopaths use aliases, usually as understandable responses to social or legal difficulties they are in. However, sometimes there is no obvious need to avoid punishment or retaliation. Elaborate stories may be told to confuse or impress relatives and this may also involve extreme forms of behavior, such as masquerading as a physician, business man or military officer. These patients tend to outrage the moral sensibilities of their victims and commonly provoke punishment. When confronted with damaging evidence, they usually acknowledge their falsehoods readily. However, they have a compulsive need to act out their fantasies repeatedly. It is often difficult to ascertain whether the untruths are expressed with conscious or unconscious intent to deceive or are due, at least in part, to the delusion. Pathological liars can cause a great deal of problems in the medical-legal area. See also Conscious deceiver, Fantasies, Malingerers, Perjury.

Pathological scope of a lesion see Table 7

Pathological topographical effect Pathological events may: (1) occur systemically (e.g. a connective tissue disorder); (2) have distant causes (e.g. central nervous system lesions); (3) be regional (e.g. referred pain from neighbouring structures); or (4) have local effects (e.g. a fracture).

Table 7 The pathological scope of a lesion

(I) Origin: the study of what creates the lesion is called etiology
(A)   Immediate cause (the trigger factor that starts the lesion)
(B)   Precipitating cause (those allowing the trigger factor to act)
(C)   Predisposing cause (those paving the way for the trigger factor to act)

(II) Beginning : what went wrong with normal tissue
It is called pathogenesis or pathogenic mechanism and can involve cell or tissue abnormalities which are anatomical, physiological, and/or biochemical resulting in losses, reductions, excesses, mutations, rearrangements, substitutions, or reversals of a genetic or acquired nature

(III) Middle: the lesional manifestation characteristics
(A)   How does it show (the signs and symptoms)?
(B)   How bad is it (the grade)?
(C)   What is the extent of where it has gone (the stage)?
(D)   How is it moving on (the course)? Is it continuous, intermittent or periodic?
(E)   What does its pattern look like? Is it steady or are there remission? Do exacerbations occur at regular or irregular intervals?
(F)   What is its progression of the disease? Is it getting better, getting worse or staying the same? Is this a natural progression of disease or are there outside factors?

(IV) End: what the lesion itself did
Did the lesion heal, become chronic and passive, become chronic and active, or end with the patient's death

(V) Effects of the lesion: the result
(A)   Impairment (anatomical/functional abnormal deviation or loss that affects the patient's physical abilities and activities such as strength, motion and endurance)
(B)   Disability (the changes occurring in the patient regarding mental functions, finances, social life, quality of personal life or duration of life)

Pathology Is the scientific study of the disease as well as of the structural and functional alterations which result from the disease, including the natural history of these changes. Pathology determines what initiates the disease or injury (cause), why the disease arises (etiology) and what happens during the disease (clinical manifestations of signs and symptoms). As the number of new biochemical pathways or structures that occur in diseased tissue is few, it is primarily concerned with rearrangements, losses, reductions or accentuations of existing pathways and structures. In this sense, it is the study of deviations from normal in structure, physiology, biochemistry, as well as cellular and molecular biology. See also Lesion, Normal, Pathogenesis, Pathological scope of the lesion.

Patient/client/customer Are those who come to doctors for relief and treatment of pain and suffering. The term 'patient' literally means to suffer and is derived from the Latin word *pati*, meaning to 'bear up or carry on' in body, mind or spirit. That same patient, when referred by a non-medical person, is called a *client*. The original status of a client was rather lowly as they were at another's beck and call and dependent on them. In ancient Rome, the specific meaning of client was a plebeian under the protection of a nobleman who was always listening for orders since they were unable to take independent action. By the fifteenth century, a client was a person on whose behalf a lawyer acts and, in the seventeenth century, they became a customer. See also Pain, Suffer.

Patient abandonment A doctor/patient relationship can be terminated without liability if the patient is notified in writing by registered mail. In addition, a reasonable length of time must be allowed for the patient to obtain another doctor. If there is any question of terminating the patient's care, an attorney should be consulted. When the doctor/patient relationship is obviously strained or if the two are incompatible, it is wise to terminate the care of the patient before there is further adverse progression and possible litigation.

Patients cannot be abandoned without proper notification. See also Doctor/patient relationship, Negligence, Tort.

Patient's mass see Tumor

Pattern see Pathological scope of the lesion

Penal see Penalty

Penalize see Penalty

Penalty From the Latin *poena*, meaning punishment or fine, it has retained this original sense. Also deriving from a similar source are *penalize* (to punish or fine), *penal* (referring to jails as a place of punishment), and *penitentiary* (a state or federal prison), *punishment* (pain, literally torment or punishment, as is the phrase 'under the pain of death'), *punitive* (inflicting punishment or fine, or the usual consequences), *subpoena* (writ requiring a person to present evidence to a court or a penalty will be given), and the religious terms *penance* (undertaking penalties to atone for or receive absolution for a sin), *penitence* (the penalty or amends undertaken with accepting guilt) and *repent* (literally to be punished by feeling regret and remorse for sins and hence to reform). See also Pain, Punitive damages, Sanctions, Suffering.

Penance see Penalty

Pending Begun but unfinished. A *pending action* is one that has begun but has not been terminated by a final judgment.

Pending action see Pending

Penitence see Penalty

Penitentiary see Penalty

Percentage method of apportionment see Subtraction method

Percipient witness Those who relate facts they have observed without making interpretations on what they have seen. See also What is medical-legal.

Percussion see Physical examination

Peremptory Signifies something that is free from limitation by other authority; not subject to question, debate, delay or reconsideration; absolute, final. A *peremptory challenge* is used to reject a certain number of prospective jurors without giving a reason. See also *Voir dire.*

Peremptory challenge see Peremptory, *Voir dire*

Perfect moment see Risk

Performance see Condition

Perinatal The period shortly before, during and after birth. It is variously defined as beginning with completion of 20–28 weeks' gestation and ending 7–28 days after birth.

Periodic see Chronic

Perjury The action of swearing to a statement which is known to be false. In other words, it is willful utterance of a false statement, testimony or evidence while under oath. See also Oath, Pathological lying, Prevaricate.

Permanent and stationary (P&S) Results when further change, for better or worse, is not reasonably to be anticipated under usual medical standards, so the disability will remain without substantial change. In other words, patients are P&S when they have reached maximum improvement or their condition has plateaued for a reasonable period of time and their condition is as far restored as the permanent character of the injury will permit. When an injured workers does not return to their pre-injury level of function they get a permanent disability rating. See also Maximum medical improvement, Medical fiction, Permanent condition.

Permanent condition A condition which within reasonable probability will continue for an indefinite period of time without any present indication of recovery from the condition.

Permanent disability Is present after patients have reached maximum improvement or their condition has been stationary for a reasonable period of time. Permanent disability includes impairment of earning power, impairment of the normal use of a member, and/or represents a competitive handicap in the open labor market. As with temporary, permanent can be total (loss of all pre-injury work capacity and unable to compete in the open labor market) or partial (less than 100% loss of pre-injury capacity and with the ability to compete in the open labor market, even if this is only to a small degree). Loss of pre-injury capacity relates to *rehabilitation* and requires an assessment by a doctor. Inability to compete in the open labor market relates to the percent standard given by the rater assessing the loss of pre-injury capacity. Judges have jurisdiction over both. Refer to California Labor Code section 4452.5, 4661, and the Worker's Compensation Appeal Board Rules of Practice and Procedure in section 10900. See also Impairment, Open labor market, Pathological scope of the lesion.

Permanent disability rating factors These are subjective factors, objective findings, work restrictions and loss of pre-injury capacity. See also Interim permanent disability awards.

Permanent partial disability Means the worker has a reduced ability to compete in the open labor market. This should be compared with *permanent total disability*, which is the inability to compete for work in the open labor market, for any job or occupation. See also Interim permanent disability.

Personality, anti-social A personality disorder characterized by behavior that results in repeated conflicts with society and an incapacity to be loyal to individuals, groups or social codes. It is associated with low-tolerance to frustration, impulsiveness, destructive selfishness, inability to feel guilty and to learn from experience and punishment. They show an 'unfeelingness', callousness and a tendency to blame others for their inappropriate behavior or to offer rationalizations for it. Their irresponsibility is often particularly clearly seen in their work history. Synonyms include *sociopaths* and *psychopaths*. Such individuals are frequently classified into the 'conscious deceiver ' group of patients. See also Pathological lying.

Personality disorders see Psychogenic disease

Personality, passive/aggressive These individuals show aggression in passive ways (e.g. through stubbornness, pouting, procrastination, passive obstruction and passive revenge).

Personal service see Service

Perspiration see Sweat

Persuasion see Opinion

Pertinent see Red flag lesions

Pertinent evidence see Retroactive prophylactic restriction

Petition see Court of Chancery, Petitioner

Petition for appointment see Minors

Petitioner A petition is a written request to persons in authority. An example would be a petition to the legislature which asks the governor to pardon an offender. The person who makes the request and files an action in a court or original jurisdiction is the petitioner. Petitioners can also appeal the judgment of a lower court. The opposing party is called the *respondent*. See Applicant, Application, Complainant, Litigants, Plaintiff, Respondent.

Pharmacy see Illness

Phenotype The entire physical, physiological and biochemical make-up of an individual that is determined by both genetic and environmental factors. The phenotype is the individual's observed characteristics. See also Genotype, Syndrome.

Pheromones see Intangible, Sweat

Philosophical empathy see Empathy

Philosophical minds see Reasonable

Physical see Physical modalities

Physical examination Classically, this involves four procedures: (1) inspection (looking at the body): (2) palpation (feeling the various parts); (3) percussion (listening to the sounds of tapped body parts); and (4) auscultation (listening to sounds produced within the body by physiological or pathological processes). In addition, there are a multitude of diagnostic clues contained in the patient's clothing, jewelry, possessions, other extracorporeal attachments, as well as such factors as intonation and modulation of the patient's voice and the way patients relate their story. See also Examination, Muscle grading, Sensation grading, Signs.

Physical mobility aids Are devices used to help or assist a person's capacity for movement, some of which are designed specially for the purpose of compensating for a disability (e.g. canes, crutches, walkers, wheelchairs, cars and various adaptive devices for cars). They can be plaster or mechanical (e.g. continuous passive motion machines). Some involve the removal of some architectural barrier or include an animal (e.g. seeing dogs for the blind). In short, mobility aids are those that carry, support, protect, lead, follow or get things out of the way. See also Applications, Future medical treatment.

Physical modalities Physical (from the Greek *physis*, meaning nature) applies to material things considered as part of a system or organic whole. A modality is a therapeutic agent, especially in physical therapy. Physical modalities are used to treat disease and injury by physical means such as light, heat, cold, electricity, ultrasound, massage, hydrotherapy and exercise. A wide range of physical modalities have been used in mind and/or body therapies. See also Future medical treatment.

Physically challenged see Handicap

Physician assistant A person who has undergone 2 years of special study so he or she can aid a physician under his direction.

Physicians Are those whose basic training covers the handling of medical emergencies, as well as other types of disease diagnosis and treatment. It is the physician's training and the handling of emergency situations that distinguishes them from other doctors. See also Analogy reasoning.

Physiogenic signs and symptoms These have an organic, rather than a pyschogenic, basis.

Physiological overlay see Functional overlay

Pigeonholing see Abnormal, Classification, Normal

Pilot injury This is what caused the patient to enter the medical-legal arena and 'flies the plane'. It may relate to a physical or psychological problem, a disease, an injury, occupational exposure or the interference of some medically necessary appliances or aid. The case can be complicated by additional *passenger injuries*. When a second insurance company is covering a separate injury that has resulted from work exposure this is a co-pilot injury. See also Arising out of employment, Co-pilot injury, Manifestations of disability, Passenger injury.

Plaintiff The one who begins an action at law; the complaining party; the person trying recover money or other relief from a defendant. In a broad sense, the plaintiff can be said to be equivalent to the complainant, applicant, petitioner and litigant.

Plateaus/work preclusions/work restrictions Are those actual or prophylactic restrictions which allow an individual to readjust, to rehabilitate, to prevent or reduce pain, to prevent or reduce the adverse progression of lesions, and to prevent reoccurrances of lesions.

Plausible denial see Euphemisms

Plea The response of the accused to criminal charges.

Pleadings Are statements that constitute plaintiff's course of action and defendant's ground for defense. These are formal written statements of their contentions which are intended to describe to a court or jury the real matter in dispute. See also Answer, Complaint, Declaration, Reply.

Pleasure The mental state characterized by freedom from pain of the body and/or trouble in the mind, and the presence of a mood which has nice feelings. This is a state of increased aliveness as a result of stimulating the senses or in the mind by an agreeable activity. One way of reaching a pleasurable mood is by the fulfilling (can be giving or receiving) of a mental or physical desire that is craved. As it is an emotional state, pleasure is transient.

Polydrug Recently coined, it means two or more drugs used simultaneously (e.g. alcohol and marihuana).

Polygraph An instrument for simultaneously recording various physiological responses as represented by mechanical or electrical impulses. These include respiratory movements, blood pressure, pulse waves and the psychogalvanic reflex. Such phenomenon reflect emotional reactions and can be use in detection of deception (a *lie detector*). See also Pain test.

Polyneuropathy see Sensation classification

Positive abnormal see Abnormal, Adaptation

Positive abnormal people see Abnormal

Possibility see Medical possibility

Possible See Classifying information

Posterior/dorsal This is the back surface of a patient. Compare with Anterior.

Postmortem Composed of the Latin *post*, meaning after, and *mortem*, meaning death, it is the examination of the body after death in order to determine the cause of death. See also Autopsy, Coroner.

Postnatally acquired injuries/diseases In contrast to *self-deceivers* (who believe that they have a medical problem but do not) and *conscious deceivers* (who do not have a medical condition but try to make others believe they do) the postnatally acquired disease is physiological. This acquired condition may be an overt, tempered, masked or concealed organic problem. See also Acquired medical conditions.

Pound Equal in weight to 454 grams. One kilogram (kg) equals 2.2046 pounds (lb). See also kilogram.

Power of attorney This is a written instrument which allows a person to appoint another as his or her agent and confers upon the appointed person the authority to perform certain specified acts or kinds of acts on his or her behalf.

Practical/practice From the Greek *prattein*, meaning to do, doing, action, to be done. Even in early times, there was opposition between the trial and the study method of learning. Hence, the term *empiric* was applied to a trial-and-error doctor. Subsequently, the entire opposition was elevated into a philosophical attitude in *empiricism*. The person that actually has tried things out is called a *pragmatist*. A pragmatist does practical things that are workable and attainable and makes chaotic things manageable. They are not the theoretical and not scientific, but rather proceed by *rules of thumb*. Practical people are more left-brain oriented in that they tend to be more matter-of-fact, unimaginative, down to earth, unromantic, realistic, sensible and utilitarian. Practice is the utilization of a person's knowledge in a particular profession (e.g. the diagnosis and treatment of disease by a doctor). See also Skill.

Practitioner A physician or other person who is licensed, registered or otherwise permitted by the appropriate jurisdiction to distribute, dispense or administer a controlled substance in the course of professional practice.

Pragmatist see Practical/practice

Precedent A previously decided case which is recognized as an authority for future cases. In common law, precedence is regarded as the major source of law and may involve a novel question of common law or a new interpretation of a statute. Future cases use the precedent as a guide, highlighting either its similarities or differences. See also Case law, Common law, *Ratio decidendi*, *Stare decisis*.

Precipitated disease or injury One that arises *de novo*. Precipitate is from the Latin *prae*, meaning before, plus *cipito*, meaning head, and is to fall head long as if from a high place. It was a term used by Roman writers in referring to criminals executed by being cast from the Tarpeian rock in Rome or those who used it to commit suicide. A precipitated injury occurs when a cause(s) initiates a disease or injury. Precipitation is also important in the *lighting up* of pre-existing asymptomatic lesions (aggravation). Both precipitation and aggravation are different from *acceleration*. Precipitation is an important concept for the California worker's law as an employer takes an employee 'as he finds him' with respect to the physical condition at the time of his employment. See also Apportionment terms, Injury, Proximate cause.

Precipitating see Cause, Cause and effect, Proximate cause

Precipitating cause see Cause, Pathological scope of a lesion

Predisposing see Cause, Cause and effect, Pathological scope of the lesion

Predominant Ancient people believed humans were governed by the stars. Indeed, astrology's original purpose was to inform people of the course of their lives and to help them find their *lucky star*. Lucky stars, because they manifested the divine will, exerted controlling power; they were the brightest and the best. Subsequently, predominant came to mean, on a non-spiritual level, the prevailing authority — the strongest of the competitors. That which predominated held the advantage in number or quantity. Thus prevail, better and medical probability are conceptual synonyms for predominate. Compare this with the quantitative characterization of 'substantial', which is dependent upon authority or consensus determinations for its worth or value. See also Burden of proof, Medical probability, Prevailing party.

Pre-existing Something that exists before a certain point in time. In Californian law, as well in some other states, an employer must take an employee 'as he finds him'. At a later date, during litigation for a pilot injury, it may become clear that the employee also had a problem which pre-dated that particular employments' injury. In this situation, if medical evidence proves that there was a ratable disability progression of the pre-existing disease, independent of and uninfluenced by the industrial pilot injury, then it will be included in the apportionment. The pre-existing disease need not be symptomatic and disabling at the time of industrial injury so long as it has manifested itself by the time the patient's permanent disability has reached a stationary ratable stage. A *pre-existing condition is one that exist prior to the pilot injury*. See also Apportionment terms, Co-pilot injury, Causation issues, Dormant, Manifestations of disability, Passenger Injuries, Pilot Injuries.

Pre-injury capacity It is the most the worker could do just prior to the date of injury. It involves a range of factors such as power, fitness and potential, etc. This is estimated and judged by a doctor. Unless otherwise stated by the doctor, the injured worker is considered to be 'normal' just prior to the date of the injury and with no prior limited work capacity. This means that there is no subjective disability, no objective impairment and no use of appliances. The basic and difficult question is how to translate 'normal' into numbers. Unless otherwise stated, it is assumed that the average patient can lift 100 pounds (man or women) although, as a general rule, the average women can only lift 65 pounds. The judgment becomes very complex when cumulative trauma is involved. Most agree that for cumulative trauma, pre-injury loss begins at the point of discovery. California worker's compensation law tends to favor an evaluation that uses a percentage reduction of pre-injury capacity (i.e. 'avoids very heavy lifting' would be stated as a 25% loss of lifting capacity). Compare with Job standard requirements, Repeated. See also Adverse, Educated estimate, Estimate, Normal.

Prejudicial see Harmless error

Prejudiced people see Analogy reasoning

Preliminary charge see Complaint

Preliminary hearing/arraignment A hearing before indictment to determine whether probable cause for the arrest of a person existed and/or if there is sufficient evidence to hold the accused for trial.

Premeditation Prior consideration of an act with intent and deliberateness for whatever period (no matter how short) and the determination to carry the act out. See also Intent, Murder.

Preponderance see Clear and convincing evidence

Preponderance of evidence This is roughly equivalent to medical probability, where there is greater weight of the evidence presented by one side than the other. This is determined by value, not amount. See also Beyond a shadow of doubt, Beyond reasonable doubt, Burden of proof, Clear and convincing evidence, Evidence, Medical probability, Predominate, Reasonable doubt.

Pre-rating report see Report

Prerogative see Privilege

Prescribed, prescription From the Latin *prae*, meaning before, plus *scribo*, meaning to write, it is to command. It originally meant an introduction or set of rules or commands which were 'written down before hand' and which were to be followed explicitly. From here it became the orders for a regimen or a medicine written by a physician which are to be followed by the patient. A prescription consists of: (1) the heading or *superscription* with the symbol Rx of the word recipe, meaning take; (2) the *inscription*, which contains the names and quantities of the ingredients; (3) the *subscription* or directions for compounding; and (4) the *signature*, usually introduced by the sign 'S' for signa, meaning 'mark'. The signature gives the directions for the patient which are to be marked on the receptacle. The *receptacle* contains compounded or filled prescriptions which bear a label showing the prescription number, the name of the person actually and personally filling, compounding or dispensing the prescription, the direction for its use internally or externally, as specified by the prescriber, the date of its compounding or filling, the name of the store or its proprietor.

Prescribed drugs Any simple or compound substance, or mixture of substances, prescribed as such or in other acceptable dosage forms. They are designed for the cure, mitigation or prevention of disease, or for health maintenance by physicians or other licensed practitioners of the healing arts within the scope of their professional practice.

Presence see Intangible, Manifestations, Measurements

Present complaints These are what the patient has now or within an arbitrary period of 3 weeks. This term is used when gathering information on the characteristics of any lesional manifestations. However, to fully understand the disease, it is important to know all of the complaints (even those that ceased some time ago) in order to be aware of the full picture. See also Chief complaint, Pathological scope of the lesion.

Presume The term originally arose from the word *prompt* (from the Latin *emere*, meaning to take) and it is to take something for granted ahead of time. It is one of a group of similar terms which includes *assume* (to take upon oneself) and *presumptuous* (to assume an unwarranted, unauthorized responsibility). Legally, the word presume (and also the word speculate) has to be used very carefully by witnesses. The witness can use presume in the sense that he or she believes something to be a fact, affirms as true without actual proof to the contrary or deduces from known facts without direct evidence. However, unless the witness relates this definition, the opposing counsel will tell the jury that presume means to go too far in acting boldly or taking liberties; to undertake something without right or permission. See also *Prima facie*.

Presumption An inference based on the rule of law that judges are compelled to draw a particular inference from a particular fact or particular evidence, unless (or until) contrary evidence is offered that disproves the truths of the inference. This is called *presumption of law*. Californian legislation has defined certain conditions (e.g. cancer, hernias, heart disease and tuberculosis) as job-related injuries when they effect certain employees (e.g. peace officers, fire fighters, forestry officers and correctional personnel). These presumptions shift the burden of proof onto the opposing party. Heart problems in an active duty police office are, for example, presumed to be compensable under the California worker's compensation law unless there is substantial evidence to the contrary (called *rebuttable presumption*). To contest the police officer's claim, the employer has the burden of proof to show that the heart problem is not industrially related. To overcome a presumption requires a high standard of proof, almost beyond 'a reasonable doubt'. See also Burden of proof, *Res ipsa loguitur*.

Presumption of fact An inference that affirms or denies the existence of some unknown fact, based on the existence of some fact that is already known or that has already been proved.

Presumption of innocence The prevailing assumption that the accused is innocent until proven guilty.

Presumption of law see Presumption

Presumption, rebuttal see Presumption

Pre-trial conference In order to reduce and focus the issues in a lawsuit, the judge and lawyers meet in order to agree on what will be presented at the trial and make a final effort to settle the case without a trial. Frequently, however, the opposing counsels will have already communicated in order to negotiate a settlement. This is also the term used for the meeting, if a case is going to trial, when the friendly counsel will meet his or her witnesses to discuss pertinent information.

Pre-trial hearing The judge tries to reduce and focus the issues and controversy in a lawsuit.

Pre-trial motion These are made by attorneys at a pre-trial hearing. For example, since a jury trial is required only when there are disputes as to matter of fact, the court may be asked to make a decision on those cases that can be decided purely on legal matters. Alternatively, there may be a request for a *summary judgment* because the issues of the fact raised in the pleading do not really exist. The sole function of the judge is to determine, from all the available evidence, if there exists a material issue of fact that is honestly disputed. If so, the judge denies the motion and sets the case down for a future trial. If not, he or she may grant a final and binding summary judgment.

Prevail see Evidence

Prevailing party see Court cost, Predominant

Prevalence Regarding a disease, it is the frequency (usually given as a percentage) the disease occurs among a representative sample of population. See also Incidents.

Prevaricate To be evasive for the purpose of deceiving. In its widest sense, it means *lying*, although this is not entirely accurate. If 'cowboys' had existed in the streets of ancient Rome at the time of Caesar, spectators would have pointed to their bowed legs and told others to look at the 'prevaricator.' Then it would be noted that this 'cowboy' could not walk in a straight line. This concept extended into the Roman law courts where it was applied to a prosecutor who was supposed to represent one party, but made a secret arrangement with the opposite party and betrayed his client. He did not walk straight; he straddled the issue. Prevaricate was, therefore, a false defense or accusation; it was also the type of crookedness and falsehood that marked a prevaricator, which is what it still means today. See also Dishonest, Pathological liar, Perjury.

Prima facie This is Latin for 'at first view, on its face', and is something that does not require further support to establish existence, validity or credibility. It is presumed to be true unless proved otherwise. A 'prima facie *case*' has the minimum amount of evidence necessary to allow it to continue in the judicial process. 'Prima facie *evidence*' is evidence that, if unexplained or not contradicted, would establish the fact alleged. See also Evidence, Res ipsa loquitur.

Prima facie case see *Prima facie*

Prima facie evidence see *Prima facie*

Primary cause see Cause

Primary evidence see Evidence

Primary gain This face-saving mechanism designed to preserve self-esteem is *the reduction of tension and conflict through the various neurotic defense mechanisms*. For example, patients with malignant emotional distress may unconsciously repress their conflict in such a way that it shows itself as a conversion reaction. Thus, they obtain a satisfactory symbolic expression for the repressed conflict. Success is measured by the degree to which the conversion mechanism appears to be protecting the patient from the emotional distress that accompanied (or would accompany) an open conflict. Thus, the primary gain may be considered maximal when the patient is free from anxiety or depression or has little or no concern about the symptom. The serene woman with conversion paralysis, who is 'resigned to God's will', and who tells her doctor that she only came because of the insistence of the family, has a highly effective conversion mechanism. Primary gain usually far outweighs the secondary gain in terms of its overall importance and is usually the justification for functional pain. However, they are usually associated in some way. For example, the depressed patient uses *chronic* (i.e.

over 6 months) non-organic pain at an unconscious level to legitimize his dependency (primary gain) and to secure caretaking (*secondary gain*). The pain is an early manifestation of an unrecognised or so-called *masked depression* that is smoldering beneath the surface. See also Masked depression, Saving face, Secondary gain, Tertiary gain.

Primary treating doctor The one primarily responsible for managing the care of the patient. They submit *treating reports* that provide information on the patient's complaints, progress and other pertinent factors.

Primitive magic see Treatment

Prisoner at the bar see Bar

Private law Also called *civil law*, it regulates relationships among people and does not involve the government directly. See also Bailiff, Classification of law, Court of Chancery.

Privilege It is something that is special, exceptional and artificial. It is something not enjoyed by all or only to be enjoyed on certain special conditions; a peculiar benefit, favor or advantage, etc. It may involve doing or avoiding. A *prerogative* is an exclusive and peculiar privilege which a person possesses simply because of their status or position (e.g. reason is the prerogative of man). Kings and nobles have often claimed prerogatives and privileges opposed to the inherent rights of the people. See also Reasonable.

Privileged communication Occurs in a setting of legal or other recognized professional confidentiality. It allows people to resist a legal demand to disclose some information. Included are conversations between attorney and client, doctor and patient (especially in mental health and AIDS situations), husband and wife, priest and penitent, and often journalists and their referral sources. A breach of such privileged communication by one party can result in a civil suit in tort by the other party. See Attorney/client privilege, *Ex parte*.

Privileged information The information that transpires from privileged communication.

Probability of an event Example: the probability of picking red marbles from a bag of mixed colors, is the number of red marbles divided by the total number of marbles. See Risk.

Probable see Classifying information, Medical probability, Risk

Probable cause Sufficient legal reasons either to allow the arrest of the person or to undertake a search and seizure.

Probation A convicted individual who is released by the court without imprisonment but is subject to court imposed conditions.

Probity see Fair play, Honesty, Professionalism

Pro bono The taking of a case by an attorney without a fee.

Procedural law The legal rules designed to ensure the enforcement of rights through the courts. Different procedural laws are used depending on the type of court in which the case is heard (e.g. criminal or civil) and the type of law (e.g. common law or equity jurisprudence). The type used in Anglo-American common law procedure is adversarial, with the lawsuit essentially being concern of the parties and their attorneys. Unless a procedural problem arises, the judge simply listens to the presentation. Each side is allowed to state its own case in its own way (within the rules) and to have a chance to answer the arguments put forward by the other side. This assures that both sides are treated fairly and meet on equal terms. See also Classification of law.

Procedure The legal method for carrying on a lawsuit, including pleading, process, evidence and practice. This is apart from the substance and content of the law itself.

Proceeding The succession of events in the legal process, the form in which actions are to be brought and defended, the manner of intervening in suits, of conducting lawsuits, and the method of deciding the outcome, of opposing and of executing judgment. See also *Ex parte*.

Process From the Latin *procedere*, meaning to go forward, it moved into the English language via old French and described something that advances over a period of time. In the seventeenth century its meaning extended to its main modern sense, 'a set of operations for doing something'. For abstract thinking, a process is something that occurs and is marked by gradual changes, either as a continuous series or a spiral. It is fundamentally important to understand that *no word*

can adequately describe a process. The best that can be done is to arbitrarily partition the process and give each partition a name. Thus, there are names for the partitions and an umbrella name for the process. One of the major reasons that medical and legal terminology is so confusing is that the umbrella name can be used for any one partition, a partition name can be used for the umbrella term and one partition name can be used for another partition. The untangling of *informational mess* is greatly assisted by partitioning a process into its origin, beginning, middle, end, result (i.e. effect) components. Each of those terms have been discussed separately. In law, the process is a formal writing (writ) issued by authority of law. For example, it is a formal legal documents used to compel attendance of a defendant in court regarding a civil law suit to answer a complaint. See also Beginning, Disease, End, Middle, Origin, Umbrella term.

Prodrome/prodromal From the Latin term *pro*, meaning before, plus *dromos*, meaning a running, it is literally a 'running before'. A prodrome designates the pre-symptomatic or early manifestations of a disease (e.g. a transient ischemic attack may herald a cerebral stroke).

Profess see Professional

Profession see Professional

Professional From the Latin term *profiteri*, meaning to declare publicly, derives *profess* (to declare openly before others), *professor* (one who makes a public claim to knowledge in a particular field and declares publicly, as in a lecture hall) and *profession* (the area of activity in which one professes a skill or competence). A profession can be any occupation (e.g. dancers, athletes, teachers, architects, engineers), so that even a tramp who scorns work and lives by begging or petty theft has a profession. However, the term *professional* usually applies to scholarship and, although in this sense it originally only related to religion (prior to 1500), it now refers to many specific fields, especially those that recognized professors (e.g. medicine and law, etc.). See also Informed consent, Probity.

Professionalism Usually applies to professionals whose occupations or vocations require probity as demanded by society. *Probity* (from the Latin *probus*, meaning morally good, scrupulous, honesty) is used especially in people's relationships with each other. Probity is honesty tried and proved, particularly in those things that are beyond the reach of legal requirement and concern commercial dealings. *Integrity* is moral wholeness without a flaw. When used in relation to contracts and dealings, integrity has reference to inherent character and principle and denotes much more than superficial or conventional honesty. In medicine, the *hippocratic oath* sets forth a code of ethics similar to the United States Constitution in which state and local governments must conform. There are various types of organizations and committees who set out rules of ethics and then act as judge and jury to determine how well those rules are carried out. Professionalism is conformity to those rules — the living up to the highest principles and ideals as determined by ethical and skillful standards of that professional community. See also Honesty, Informed consent, Integrity, Normal, Oath, Probity, Reasonable.

Professor see Professional

Prognosis From the Greek *pro*, meaning before, plus *gnosis*, meaning knowledge, it is foreknowledge and is used medically to indicate a reasoned forecast concerning the course, pattern, progression, appearance, duration and end of a disease. An expert prediction of outcome is based upon an accurate diagnosis, knowledge of the natural history of the disease, the disease's response to treatment and the natural progression of disease regarding the patient in question. Important considerations include the patient's personality, if the patient is in harmony with his or her body and with the external environment, whether non-vital or vital structures are involved, the nature and severity of the disease and the stage of development of the person at the time the disease or injury occurs (e.g. a fetus is particularly susceptible to an adverse outcome from German measles). See also Disease, Natural history, Natural progression of disease, Pathological scope of the lesion

Prognosis, guarded This is a term used frequently in medicine but rarely defined. In general, it seems to mean that the long-term prognosis is unpredictable.

Progression see Pathological scope of the lesion

Projected orthopaedic expenses form Having a 'ball park' figure for the cost of a possible/probable need for surgery is often needed to settle a case. See also Costs, Future medical, Medical-legal expense.

Prolonged In Latin the prefix *pro* extends the word long in time, place, position or space. 'Longs' (from old

English word *lang*) is an extension beyond a standard, beyond what is known or easily verified. This makes 'long' a unit of time measurement which can either be arbitrary or, as in the medical-legal arena, have a specific quantity assigned (25% more time than some standard). To engage in something that is to be partially avoided is to reduce by 25% that thing below the standard. In the California Workers' Compensation Scheme prolong is a work preclusion modifier. In saying 'avoid prolonged standing', the doctor means the patient can stand 80% of the time, 6 hours of an 8 hour day, or should sit 15 minutes per 8 hour work day. See also Vocational rehabilitation terms.

Prompt see Presume

Pronate This is anatomical reference which indicates that the front of the body is facing. It means to bend, turn or incline forward, as in turning the palm of the hand to face the floor.

Pronation see Anatomical references, Figure 1 (page 7)

Proof In general is the meeting of a standard. On a personal level it is that which you believe to be genuine and true. Legally, proof is the establishment of a fact by evidence as determined by the court or the trier of fact. The burden of proof may require a party to raise a reasonable doubt concerning the existence or non-existence of a fact, with or without a predominance of the evidence, by clear and convincing proof or by proof that is beyond a reasonable doubt. Doctors involved in the worker's compensation system would do well to use these concepts as part of a well-reasoned report. Medical-legal proof need not be certain, but it must be close enough so that a prudent person would reasonably act on the information. See also Beyond reasonable doubt, Certainty, Evidence, Legal fact, Normal, Reasonable, Standard of proof in burden of proof, Valid.

Prophylactic From the Greek *pro*, meaning before, plus *phulasso*, meaning to preserve or guard, it is literally to guard before, or simply to guard or preserve. Medically, prophylactic is a defensive or preventive measure against the possibility of a disease. When considering disability restrictions, it is what a doctor advises a patient to avoid in order to prevent or minimize accelerated pain that might otherwise lead to a period of partial or temporary disability, need for medical care or increased permanent disability (e.g. a patient with a successful hernia repair may need to avoid heavy lifting). See also Work restrictions.

Prophylactic restriction Is a defensive or preventive measure which reduces the possibility of a disease or injury. Since the sixteenth century, prophylactic has been used in the context of guarding against the potential for aggravation of an impairment and the possibility of changing the worker's job responsibilities. If the restrictions were exceeded the patient would be at a significant 'risk' for further damage. See also Acceleration, Aggravation, Injury.

Pro rata According to a given proportion, rate or percentage.

Pro re nata (PRN) A Latin term meaning 'according to circumstances' or as needed, as necessary.

Pro se Persons acting as their own attorney, whether or not they are an attorney.

Prosecute see Sue

Prosecution If you prosecute someone, etymologically you 'pursue' them. The legal application of 'prosecutes' emerged in the late sixteenth century. It is when a person is *indicted* or charged, by the grand jury, and *arraigned* (formally called) before the appropriate court where the *indictment* or charge (a formal written statement charging a person with an offense) is read and he or she pleads guilty or not guilty. Arraign and indict apply strictly to criminal proceedings. See also Malicious, Sue.

Prosecutor A public official who prepares and conducts the prosecution of persons accused of a crime (e.g. a district attorney).

Prosthesis From the Greek *pro*, meaning before, plus *thesis*, meaning a placing or putting, it is literally 'a placing to or an increase'. In surgery the term came to denote the supply or replacement of any defect or part loss (e.g. false teeth or an artificial limb). Generally, a prosthesis is an artificial substitute for a missing body part for functional and/or cosmetic reasons (e.g. an artificial leg or a total joint replacement device).

Protective custody The imprisonment of an individual for his or her own protection.

Pro tem Abbreviation for *pro tempore*, which means for the time being. An attorney who acts for a substitute judge on a temporary basis is said to serve *pro tem*.

Protocol From the Greek *protos*, meaning first, plus *kolla* meaning glue, it originally referred to a label or sheet that was glued to the papyrus roll to show its contents. The Greek word *protokollon*, designated the first leaf of a papyrus. Later it came to denote the original notes or records of an experiment, autopsy or clinical examination. There are now many types of protocols, including a plan for the investigation of a new drug, a manual for nurses and a treatment plan.

Prototype patients The three types of patient are: (1) *textbook patients* who have significant organic lesions, are straightforward in their presentation, honest and completely or partially accurate in discussion about the problem; (2) *self-deceivers* who do not have organic lesions, but are honest in their erroneous belief that they do have one; and (3) *conscious deceivers* who have no organic lesions and are consciously dishonest because they attempt to deceive others into believing that they have a health problem. See also Secondary gain.

Providence see Jurisprudence, Reasonable

Provisional remedies Court actions that 'freeze' activities of the plaintiff and defendant before the trial starts. They can become operational from the time that both sides are present at a hearing or during a proceeding in which the defendant is not initially heard (i.e. *ex parte*). Some remedies serve to prevent the disappearance either of funds required for the payment of the eventual judgment or of specific property involved in the litigation. See also *Ex parte*.

Proviso It is the stipulation that limits, modifies or renders conditional the operation of a statute or contract.

Provocation A person's actions or behaviors which incite another to do a particular deed.

Proximal An anatomical reference term used to designate nearness to a source or beginning of a body part. For instance, the human upper limb consists of an *arm* (between the shoulder and elbow) and a *forearm* (between the elbow and the wrist). The arm is proximal to the forearm. See also Anatomical references, Figure 1 (on page 7).

Proximate cause A cause that initiates an effect. Medically, before a cause initiates the effect (e.g. an impairment), there are several intervening stages that include pathogenic mechanisms, lesional manifestations and an end result of what happened to the lesion (see Table 7 on page 98). As discussed under the term cause, a precipitating cause is that factor which permits the immediate cause to act. For example, a car accident (precipitating cause) resulted in a blow to the patient's head (immediate cause). The car accident is the proximate cause to the blow on the head because it is the nearest, most direct and immediate event which lead to the injury. The legal definition of proximate cause is that which in natural and continuous sequence, unbroken by any new independent cause, produces an event, without which the injury would not have occurred. A blow to the head would not have occurred without the car accident (i.e. it is the proximate cause of the blow to the head). It is that which gives a direct effect that is foreseeable, which implies that there is nothing intervening between the cause and the effect and it must follow the natural course of events. See also Causes, Condition, Horse play, Origin, Pathological scope of the lesion, Substance.

Proximate injury see Horse play

Proximate result see Substance

Prud see Jurisprudence

Prudence see Jurisprudence

Prudent person see Facts, Fair play, Foreseeable risk, Jurisprudence, Negligence, Normal, Rage, Reasonable person

Pseudologia fantastica See Pathological lying

Psychiatric injury Is a diagnosed mental disorder that caused a disability or need for medical treatment. Disability is an *effect* that restricts a worker's ability either to get or to perform any job. In other words, disability is the inability or reduced ability to compete in the open labor market.

Psychic distress amplification Exaggerated complaints in the form of vague, elaborate and vivid similes. For example, instead of the crisp, economical and relatively uncomplicated pain descriptions given by normal patients, *self-deceivers* sensationalize the effects (e.g. 'burning like a red-hot coal'). See also Overlay.

Psychic scar see Emotional wounds, Trauma, Trauma — psychic.

Psychogalvanic reflex see Pain measurement test

Psychogenic see Physiogenic signs and symptoms

Psychogenic disease Imagine a horizontal line which shows range of behavior and has *neurosis* at the left end and *psychosis* at the right. These two extremes can be easily differentiated. In between these extremes neurosis and psychosis share many features, although they can be viewed as a continuum in the spectrum of mental disease. Now, consider that this horizontal line is crossed by a vertical line which has *character disorders* at the top and *sex deviants* at the bottom. All psychogenic disease is a combination of these four factors. An example, *neurotic (psychoneurotic)* behavior, is a 'normal variant' between normal and psychologically abnormal people. They have an emotional disorder due to unresolved conflicts, with anxiety as the chief characteristic. Anxiety may be expressed directly or indirectly (e.g. by conversion, disassociation or displacement, etc.). In contrast to the *psychotic*, the psychoneurotics do not have a gross distortion of external reality or disorganisation of personality. Character disorders (are also called *personality disorders*) have a deeply engraved, long-enduring, poorly adaptive and inflexible pattern of thinking, feeling and behaving. Examples include paranoid, histrionic and anti-social (sociopath or psychopathic) disorders. See also Clinical manifestations, Test.

Psychogenic overlay see Functional overlay

Psychoneurotic see Psychogenic disease

Psychopaths see Anti-social, Personality

Psychophsiological disorder see Psychosomatic

Psychosis see Psychogenic disease

Psychosomatic From the Greek *psyche*, meaning mind, and *soma*, meaning body, it is the branch of medicine which treats physical ailments caused by mental illness. It has always been known that illness can make us unhappy, but it now widely believed reverse is also true (that unhappiness can actually make us ill). Bodily symptoms of a psychic, emotional or mental origin are also called a *psychophysiological disorder*.

Psychotic see Psychogenic disease

Public defender   A lawyer whose duty is to defend accused persons unable to pay for legal assistance.

Public law   see Classifying law

Public offense   An act or omission forbidden by law. It used to describe a crime rather than violation of private rights by *infringement* (through the deeds of others) or *infraction* (pertains to laws, rights, agreements, acts or treaties). A public offense, the commission of which authorizes the citizen's arrest, includes *misdemeanors*. See also Classifying crime, Crime.

Punishment   The infliction of pain or loss as a penalty for ego, social, moral or legal disobedience, it is the 'payback'. Punishment for *negative pleasure* are those of 'like kind' and for the purpose of self-protection (although, hopefully, it will also prove corrective). For *sick pleasures* it involves personal and destructive loss without regard to 'like kind' in extent or severity.

Punishment is to be distinguished from *malice* which, in the legal sense, is an intent to injure even though there is no personal ill-will. For example, if a policeman attacks an unknown traveller he is showing malice. See also Malice, Pain, Penalty, Suffering.

Punitive   see Penalty

Punitive damages   Are extra (monetary) awards made by the court when a defendant's conduct has involved fraud, maliciousness or violence, etc. The extra award is part of the punishment and is used to make an example of the defendant in order to deter others from acting in a similar way. See also Costs, Damages, Pain, Penalty.

Purpose   see Intent

Pyramidal tracks   see Extrapyramidal, Motor neuron disease, System

Q

Qualified individual with a disability (QID) see Americans with Disabilities Act

Qualified injured worker Relates to rehabilitation. Doctors decide if the industrial injury precludes patients from performing their usual and customary occupations. See also Vocational rehabilitation.

Qualities see Attachment, Magnitude, *Sine qu non,* Test

Quantity Those things with presence that can be measured. See also Manifestations, Test.

Qua'ter in di'e (QID) Four times per day.

Quash It originally derived from the Latin *quatere*, meaning to shake, and is to 'shake off, drive away'. Legally, it is to vacate or void a summons, subpoena or indictment, etc.

Quasi in rem A judgment that affects the interest of one particular party rather than all parties.

Query Is to inquire into with an implication of doubt.

Questions of fact Evidence decided by a jury. See also Trial components.

Questions of law Rules of human conduct determined by the judge. See also Trial components.

Quid pro quo This is Latin for 'something for something'. It is the exchange of one thing of value for another thing of value.

R

Radial side see Anatomical references, Figure 1 (page 7), Lateral.

Rage From the Latin *rabies*, meaning madness. Rage suggests a sudden outburst of temper that may manifest itself irresponsibly. A state of 'frenzied ferocity' is a natural way to react in a life- or limb-threatening struggle for survival. Rage drives a person beyond the bounds of prudence or discretion. The term *Fury* denotes even stronger emotion, which sweeps the individual into uncontrollable violence. Instinctual rage brain cell impulses work through the autonomic nervous system where they have their clearest and most uncomplicated expression. As a result, rage affects not only the body parts, but also parts of the brain, particularly the limbic portion. See also Anger, Paroxysm.

Raison d'etre see Primary gain

Rapacious see Greedy

Rapid eye movement (REM) see Nocturnal penile tumescent test

Rapport Establishing a sympathetic, understanding relationship for another person which involves caring about his or her health and feelings, mutual trust and respect. See also Doctor/patient relationship.

Rare see Vocational rehabilitation terms

Ratable report see Report

Rating report see Report

Rating report generic topics see Table 8

Ratio decidendi The grounds on which a judge decides a case. In the common law system of the United States,

Table 8 The generic topics used in a rating report.

(I)	**Routine section**
(A)	Chief complaint
(B)	Medical history
(C)	Physical examination
(D)	Pain diagram
(E)	Laboratory tests
(F)	Review of records
(G)	Review of radiographs
(H)	Subrosa films
(II)	**Comments and recommendation section**
(A)	Diagnosis
(B)	Discussion of injury (research)
(C)	Temporary disability (when, how long)
(D)	Permanent disability (subjectives, objectives, work restrictions, pre-injury capacity loss)
(E)	Causation
(F)	Apportionment (specific injury(ies) and/or cumulative trauma)
(G)	Future medical treatment
(H)	Vocational rehabilitation

(III) Addressing questions of the referral source

it forms a *precedent* which is often binding on judges trying similar cases in the future. This is called *case law*.

Rational empathy see Empathy

Real see Certainty, Metaphysical systems

Real evidence see Demonstrative or objective evidence

Reality see Facts

Reason The process used to obtain new knowledge from old knowledge, which involves: (1) drawing logical inferences; (2) uses a step-by-step process; (3) contains non-feeling thoughts; (4) it is performed for a specific purpose; and (5) follows a set of rules. Reason is the opposite of sensation, perception, feeling, desire, opinion, memory or imagination. Reasons are supports for conclusions. See also Analogy reasoning, Deduction, Dialectical method, Induction, Opinion, Syllogism.

Reasonable Has its origin in the concept of *divine providence*. Divine care of humans and the universe required rational forethought plus foresight to 'fit things together'. Such intellectual powers were considered to derive from the soul. Being made in the image of God meant that the rational soul was given to each person. *Sages* were people aligned with the divine in ways of thinking, forethought, foresight and benevolence. As a result, sages had spiritual morals, wisdom, prudence and reasonableness (from the Latin *raison*, to make good judgments). The four cardinal virtues are courage, justice, temperance and prudence, and these are embodied in a common-sense, reasonable character. In this context, *common sense* is practical understanding and good judgment when dealing with life's problems. A *prudent person* was therefore considered to have *discretion* (good judgment, caution, self-control), *foresight* (the ability to prepare for what is going to happen), *forethought* (doing unpleasant things now for the sake of pleasant things in the future) and similar traits of good character and integrity. When applied to action or conduct, reasonableness is that which shows attentiveness, precaution, practicality and staying within the rules. *Reasonable prudence* is the degree of care which a person of ordinary prudence would exercise in the same or similar circumstances (e.g. in professionalism). Particular groups do, however, have their own standards. For example, *scientific minds* seek answers to questions in the external, exoteric, visible and physical world. For scientists it is reasonable that their propositions and conclusions remain open to rational dispute. In the case of *occult minds*, the search for answers is esoteric, unseen, inside the head, by using introspection, inner observation and inward-pointedness (as in meditation). Such a person would consider it reasonable not to get sidetracked in their path of contemplation. Finally, *philosophical (abstract) minds* use critical reflection by argumentation to find meaning, compatibility and differences for abstract questions. It is reasonable for them to use logic and speculation as basic tools. In short, reasonableness centers around suitability in a particular set of circumstances. This is usually determined on a case-by-case basis. 'Reasonable' does not have quite the same degree of absolute correctness that is related to 'certain'. See also Adaption, Doctor/patient relationship, Due care, Foreseeable risk, Normal, Oath, Patient relationship, Privilege, Prudent person.

Reasonable doubt A degree of doubt causing a prudent person to have some concern about accepting the truth of a charge. Jurors in a criminal trial are instructed that innocence is to be presumed unless the jury can see no reasonable doubt to the guilt of the person charged. This does not require positive proof and some error can exist; it means that the evidence must be sufficiently conclusive to satisfy the judgment and conscious of the jury as to the guilt of the accused. Compare with Predominance of evidence.

Reasonable man see Due care, Negligence, Prudent person, Reasonable

Reasonable medical probability see Burden of proof, Framing medical-legal conclusions, Future medical treatment

Reasonable person A hypothetical person who exercises qualities of attention, knowledge, intelligence, discretion, foresight, forethought and judgment that society requires of its members for the protection of their own interest and the interest of others. Reasonable persons choose a sensible course, especially in managing their practical affairs. Thus, the test of *negligence* is based on either a failure to do something that a reasonable person would do or the doing of something that a reasonable person would not. See also Negligence, Prudent person, Rage, Reasonable.

Reasonable probability method see Framing conclusions

Reasonable prudence see Reasonable

Reasoning principles see Opinions

Rebuttal The disproving of other evidence or re-establishing the credibility of challenged evidence by offering counterarguments. See also Answer.

Rebuttal presumption see Presumption

Receptacle see Prescribed/prescription

Reckless disregard   To be careless or heedless in regards to conduct, reputation or the consequences of actions. That is, to lack prudence or caution and as a consequence be careless in respect of some duty or task, or to be negligent. See also Reasonable person.

Recompense   see Compensation

Record   This applies to any writing or mark, etc., that serves as a memorial giving enduring attestation of an event or fact. Legally, it includes all documents that give a precise history of a suit from beginning to end. Record also means the total of a person's known actions or inactions that substantially express his or her character. See also Documents, Medical report, Report.

Recurrence   see Reoccurrence of an injury

Recurring   see Chronic

Red flag lesions   Are those that require further medical investigation and, perhaps, treatment. Throughout history the 'red flag' has been associated with blood. Indeed, by the seventeenth century it was a signal for battle and warned of a danger in which blood could be shed. A doctor's judgments should be made on on red flag (pertinent) lesions and not 'red herrings'. Compare with Red herring pathological lesions.

Red herring pathological lesions   Originally, the term derived from the practice of trailing red herrings over the ground when training a dog to follow scent. However, the dogs, on smelling the red herrings, would loose any other scent it had been following. This diverted the dog onto a false trail. Thus, red herring lesions confuse or divert attention by presenting something irrelevant or *non pertinent*. It is important that any doctor involved in a legal case knows what is, and what is not, a red herring. He or she will probably have to explain to lay people what these red herring are and why, for instance, no action was taken. Compare with Red flag lesions. See also Art of medicine, Cause, Objective minus, Superimposed condition.

Re-direct examination   Is an opportunity to present rebuttal evidence after the original evidence has been subjected to cross-examination. See also Direct examination.

Referee   An 'arm of the court' who takes testimony relative to a case, investigates it and reports it to the court, but does not make the final ruling in the case. Agreed Medical Examiners are medical referees.

References for legal knowledge   This depends upon a person's level of expertise. At an appropriate level, legal books written for laymen '101' courses in school, legal libraries and the 'bar hotlines' can be useful. For a more advanced student, there are law schools, legal texts and law journals. Still higher are constitutions, statutes and other coded laws, common-law documents and appeal court decisions. The latter are particularly good because they carefully explain the rationale behind the decisions.

Reformation   Rewriting a contract to conform with the actual intent of the parties. See also Court of Equity.

Regular hands   see Casual worker

Rehabilitated   see Self-rehabilitation

Rehabilitation   The process of rendering a physically or mentally disabled person fit to engage in a remunerative occupation. Rehabilitation is from the Latin *re*, meaning again or back, plus *habilitas*, meaning ability, and is literally to 'again have the ability' to work or do something. Here, *ability* is power to perform with competence. Once injured workers are qualified injured workers (QIWs), they are entitled to rehabilitation benefits provided they can be reasonably expected to benefit from such a program (i.e. have the ability).

Re-hearing   The same court hears a civil or criminal case again.

Relationship empathy   see Empathy

Relative end   see End/ending

Relative facts   see Evidence, Facts

Relative rest   Is a medical concept implying that a body part (e.g. the elbow joint) should be used but in a different stress pattern so as to reduce adverse stress. See also Ergonomics, Job trials, Rest.

Relevant   see Answer, Irrelevant

Relevant answer   see Answer

Relevant evidence Is *pertinent evidence* that relates to, or has a bearing on, a question of fact in dispute during a trial. See also Evidence.

Reliability Consistency over time.

Religion see Bad faith

Remand To send back for further deliberation. See also Deliberation, Jury.

Remuneration see Compensation

Reoccurrence of an injury Must be distinguished from *recurrence*, which literally means 'running back', and is used in anatomy to designate structures that turn or run back on their course (e.g. recurrent laryngeal nerve). *Occurrence* is something that takes place, especially unexpectedly and without design. Reoccurrence is an additional occurrence. Thus, with a reoccurrent injury there must be a pre-existing lesion. Agents causing reoccurrences can either *light up* a dormant condition, *aggravate* a lesion or *accelerate* a lesion. Any of these three may or may not be apportionable depending upon the subsequent lesional course and its *staging* at the time of the reoccurrence. Reoccurrence must also be distinguished from *exacerbation* where the subsequent clinical manifestations are not caused by an independent intervening agent in exacerbations but result solely as a delayed consequence of the prior injury. See also Accelerate, Aggravate, Apportionment terms, Exacerbate, Light up, Pathology scope.

Repeated This is a term used in the worker's compensation system in the United States but does not have a generally accepted definition. It derives from old French *repeter*, meaning to go back to, and relates to the quantity of a certain type of physical activity required by the job. Thus, the point of reference standard for repeated is the *job requirement* for a given activity. To establish a job-reference standard, it is important to know how many times the worker is required to do an activity of the same type on a regular basis. If the he or she is doing the activity that meets job requirements, then the worker is doing the job continuously. Here, *continuous* is synonymous with 'repeated', however this applies to the actual job. A job-reference standard would be determined by a legally accepted job analysis. Avoiding a repetitive activity is a 50% reduction. See also Vocational rehabilitation terms.

Repent see Penalty

Repetitive trauma see Continuing trauma

Replevin An action to recover property.

Reply The response by a party (e.g. the plaintiff) to charges raised in an original plea or response of the other party (e.g. the defense). See also Affirmative, Answer, Declaration.

Report Etymologically, to report something is to 'carry it back'. The word was borrowed from old French term, *reporter*. The metaphorical application 'to bring back news' originally developed in Latin. Legally, it is a record of a court's proceedings or a judge's decisions, etc. In the medical-legal arena, it is classified as a pre-rating type of report (often loosely called a *treating report*) which contains a record of a patient's complaints, progress, treatment and/or the discussion of the of case-specific or special interest issues. See also Rating report, Report comments, Treating report.

Report comments This is the bringing together of all the information. It starts by blending information obtained from the history and physical examination as well as in the records, radiographs and other sources. It is helpful to point out and explain inconsistencies in the history(ies), physical examination(s) and test(s). Mention should be made of any further 'work-up' that is needed, such as tests, records, consultations or research. Ensure that there are no *informational gaps* where the reader would have to make major assumptions in interpreting the report. Keep in mind that just because the patient has a lesion, this does not necessarily mean it is the cause of the patient's impairment. Furthermore, just because a problem occurred on the job does not necessarily make the job responsible; it could have been a coincidence. Under all circumstances it is necessary to give supporting reasons for you opinion. See also Americans with Disabilities Act, Causation, Causation diagnostic impression, Causation issues, Cause and effect, Disputed medical fact, Examination report format, Extent of disability questions, Framing medical-legal conclusions, Functional limitations, Great probative value, Maximum medical improvement, Medical information, Medical issues, Medical-legal report, Permanent disability factors, Rating report comments, Treating report issues, Well-reasoned reports, Work restrictions.

Repressed Thoughts and feelings are driven into ones subconscious to affect reactions one is helpless to account for and sometimes exploding into neurotic symptoms. See also Concealed, Concealment in medicine, Suppress.

Reputation How a person is judged by others. See also Genotype, Report, Syndromes.

Res Is Latin for a thing, object or status, and is the subject matter of actions that are primarily *in rem* (i.e. actions that establish rights in relation to an object as opposed to a person).

Res ipsa loquitur This is Latin for 'the thing speaks for itself' and refers to a doctrine under which negligence is inferred. It is a form of presumption and to avoid liability the defendant must prove he was not negligent. See also Negligence, Presumption, Tort.

Res judicata Is Latin for 'a matter decided' and means that a previously decided issue can now be considered conclusive.

Research Derives from the Italian word *cercare*, to seek, and Spanish term *cercar*, to surround. It is a systematic search for facts that includes study, examination, investigation and checks, etc. Its sense, particularly in scientific investigation, derives from the nineteenth century and indicates scholarly or scientific inquiry. *Medical-legal research* is special because it requires knowledge of pathology and psychology. However, case-specific information is extremely hard to find and a large amount of time is needed to search through books and journals in order to find two or three pertinent pieces of information. *Medical-legal directives* must then correlate this information with other medical data, the 'facts' of the case at hand, pertinent legal language, theories, concepts, definitions and laws. See also Bench, Jurist, Medlars.

Respect Is the value you place on something outside of you, such as people, animals, plants, things and places. Respect comes from Latin *respicere*, meaning to look back at and hence look at, regard or consider. The key modern meaning 'deference esteem' developed toward the end of the sixteenth century. At that time, noble character was honored and respected. Respect in the fullest sense is given to that which is lofty, worthy, honorable or to a person with such qualities. We also pay an external respect to one of lofty station, regardless of personal qualities, showing respect for the office (e.g. the court). See also Bench, Values.

Respondent The party who answers a pleading in equity or on appeal. Compare with Petitioner. See also Appeal, Litigants.

Rest Denotes freedom from toil or effort. It is a cessation of activity and, while it does not suggest any special way of passing time, it always implies recuperation from mental or physical fatigue as its aim or result. In law, a party *rests its case* when all of the evidence has been presented. See also Relative rest.

Restrain see Suppress

Restriction Is holding within a prescribed limit or boundary. Work restrictions, also called *work preclusions* or *work plateaus,* are limits that doctors place on the injured's physical activities at work, on the working conditions, or away from work to prevent or minimize temporary disability or increased permanent disability. Those that are temporary relate to the worker's present place of employment and may or may not resolve. Those that are permanent relate to the worker's ability to compete in the open labor market. See also Report comments.

Rests its case See Rest

Result While *end* stops an action, result is the *consequence of that action.* For example, the end of the war is reached when a treaty of peace is signed, but the result of war is victory or defeat. A *work product* is an event, a result of prior action. The results of medical treatment may be a cure or an impairment, which may or may not be permanent. When the term *end result* is used, end is an intensifier which suggests finality of the result. See also Effect, Sequela.

Resuscitation see Death

Retaliation see Negative pleasures

Retribution see Punishment

Retroactive law Is one that relates to, and affects, actions which occurred before the law came into effect. See also Justice, Law.

Retroactive prophylactic restriction Is an attempt on the part of the doctor to relate work restrictions to be applicable just before the pilot injury occurred when, in fact none existed. This is considered *legal fiction* and is not acceptable legally.

Revenge This is one of the most important words in the medical-legal arena, and it refers to the determination to repay real or supposed offense with injury. Revenge may also involve the retaliatory act. Deceptive patients seeking revenge want to inflict harm or suffering upon another as a result of personal anger and resentment for something done to them. Revenge is also associated with the concept of *enemy*. See also Emotional distress, Equality, Sabotage, Vengeance.

Reversal Means to abolish, repeal, nullify, revoke or set aside a judgment or decree. For example, an appellate court may reverse or set aside the decision of an inferior court.

Review of records Some prefer to give an attached one- or two-paragraph summary of events related to the injury(ies) involved in a chronological order. This would include: (1) the patient's age at the time of injury; (2) the patient's occupation at that time; (3) a description of the injury event; (4) all pertinent medical intervention; and (5) the source of the information. Personally, I like to extract the pertinent information and identify it for the records. Then I collate the information from the records and my history taking in chronological order.

Right see Lawful

Right of action see Causation

Risk The taking of chances where there is the element of uncertainty, and the possibility or probability of loss or failure. The origins of the word have never been satisfactorily explained. One persistent theory is that its ancestral meaning comes from a Greek habit of sailing dangerously close to the underwater 'hills', cliffs or rocks. Another suggests that it comes from Latin *resegare*, meaning cut off short, and derived from the notion of coastal rocks being cut off sharply or sheered. The English language acquired 'risk' from the French in the nineteenth century. The degree of risk can vary from a probable chance of success to completely unknown chance, and so the word is often supported to clarify this point. For example, a *calculated risk* is one that has a probable or high possibility of success. Before taking a risk it is wise 'to look before you leap' and consider the following points: (1) the number of favorable outcomes; (2) the total number of possible outcomes (and when this is divided into the number of favourable outcomes one gets the *probability of an event*); (3) the magnitude of possible outcomes (e.g. the worst consequence), no matter

how remote; (4) the tactics available to get a favorable outcome; and (5) how long will it take to get the result; etc. Much of the advantages and disadvantage associated with medicine, especially surgery, are associated with the frequency and magnitude of risks that have to be taken. At the moment of crisis, physicians must consider the chance of failure from their decision, both as it relates to the patient as well as the ramifications of that failure from a personal and legal perspective. 'After the fact' it is extremely hard or impossible for physicians to remember all of the factors being considered at the moment of crisis. The failure to remember is generally far more costly than crisis decisions made by non-medical persons. It takes great courage for a physician to disregard potential personal losses in the face of a life- and limb-threatening situation. To be successful is to have experienced a *perfect moment*, to be a hero. The chance of experiencing a perfect moment is what drives most daredevils. In law, an assumption of risk occurs when a person knowingly moves forward in the face of danger. Often, this knowledge prevents compensation for injuries a person suffered. See also Assumption of risk, Incidence, Probability of an event.

Risk factors see Arise out of employment

Roots, nerve A series of nerve 'pairs' (bundles) exit at each side of the spinal cord. They have a dorsal (or posterior) as well as ventral (or anterior) component. In total, there are 31 pairs of nerve roots: eight cervical, 12 thoracic, five lumbar, five sacral and one coccygeal. When planning surgery, it is important to be aware of any vertebral anomalies, particularly if there are four or six lumbar vertebra; if there are four, the L4 nerve root comes off the top of the sacrum; if five, the L5 nerve root comes off on top of the sacrum; if six, the S1 nerve root comes off the top of the sacrum. Such knowledge avoids operating at the wrong level.

Rule of thumb A rough estimate or guess based more upon experience and practical common sense rather than precise and accurate technical theory, knowledge or measurement. One theory concerning its origin suggests that it derives from brewers testing the temperature of fermenting beer by dipping a thumb into it. From the brewer's considerable experience, this thumb test would be sufficient to show him how the brewing was getting on. A more logical theory is the frequent use of the lower part of the thumb (roughly equal to one inch in the average adult male) as a crude measuring device. Although rules of thumb are a standard measurement for non-medical people dealing with medical problems, it is very important that they are not used by medical professionals. See also Hypersensitivity, Medical fiction, Practical.

Rules From the Latin *regula*, it is a statement of a prescribed course of action to obtain a result.

Rules of evidence The word rule comes from Latin *regere*, to govern, direct. In law, rule means a regulation governing court procedure in association with the potential for exercising power in enforcing obedience. Thus, there are detailed laws governing human conduct. Rules of evidence are standards governing whether evidence in a criminal case is admissible. See also Evidence.

S

Sabotage Etymologically, it derives from the idea of 'clattering along in noisy shoes'; hence the notion of 'clumsiness,' 'to do work badly' and, finally, 'destroy tools, machines or work time deliberately.' When acquired into English language around 1910, sabotage gradually broadened to include any deliberate disruptive destruction which interfered with, or halted, industrial production. See also Revenge.

Sadness Derives from the same Indo-European base that produced satisfy and saturate. Indeed, sad originally meant to have enough of something, in which case the person was *sated,* i.e. a bit sad. However, by the time it had reached English through pre-historic Germanic *sathaz,* sufficient or enough had already extended to *weary.* It was in the fourteenth century that the modern sense 'unhappy' emerged. The original notion of 'sufficiency' no longer exists for the word.

Sadism see Suffer

Safety In prehistoric Indo-European, *solwos* meant whole, and it shares this origin with the words *uninjured* and *health* — what made you safe also made you whole or healthy. Safety causes right to occur where wrong existed. Nowadays, safe implies that a danger has passed or is no longer to be feared (e.g. a safe place). Safety is freedom from danger, injury or damage. See also Due care, Sanity, Secure.

Sage see Reasonable

Sagittal plane This divides the body into a right and left half. See also Anatomical references, Figure I (page 7), Lateral.

Salvage procedure A descriptive term for any operation, or operations, to save a body part from disaster.

Sanctions Penalties imposed for violating a law. See also Penalty.

Sanity The word literally means sound or whole. Originally, it meant 'sound or hold in body and mind', but later this became restricted to soundness of mind. In criminal law, sanity means the ability to distinguish right from wrong. Compare with Insanity.

Sated see Sadness

Saving face An internal mechanism to preserve self-esteem. This is termed *primary gain* and is something that everyone does but is particularly prominent in children and childish adults (i.e. blaming others, denying responsibility, lying, etc.). Patients with *chronic pain syndrome* legitimize the curtailment of their activity by their pain. They can then become passive and less dependent without losing face. See also Primary gain.

Say what you believe see Opinion

Schadenfreude Pleasure derived from misfortune of others. See also Sick pleasures.

Schizoid personality see Jekyll and Hyde

Schizophrenic see Jekyll and Hyde

Science From the Latin *socio,* meaning to know, it is to co-ordinate, to arrange and to systematize knowledge.

Scientific certainty see Biological law, Facts, Medical certainty

Scientific conjecture see Facts, Scientific method, formal type

Scientific facts see Facts, Medical certainty, Scientific method — formal type

Scientific law see Facts, Medical certainty, Scientific method — formal type

Scientific method, formal type This is one of the three major groups of scientific method, the others being the informal and fun types. It has been very important in the progress of science and proceeds through a rationalized order using an educated guess, conjecture, hypothesis, theory and actuality. This *process* starts with an *origin*, which is the predisposing, precipitating and immediate factors that result in the *beginning* of an investigation. The essence of the beginning is an educated guess (a *conjecture*). This conjecture is an inference, presumption or judgment that is based on incomplete or insufficient data or evidence. It is not a *surmise*, which contains a greater feeling of imagination and distrust. The educated guess gives rise to a *working hypothesis* (a conjecture assumed to be true until proved otherwise, and is used as a basis of discussion, reasoning and, perhaps, action). A working hypothesis is the best available explanation but cannot, or at least has not yet, accounted for all the phenomena which are involved. At this stage testing has to be carried out and if the best explanation survives this testing it becomes a *diagnostic impression hypothesis*. When the diagnostic hypothesis accounts for 'cause and effect', it becomes a *tentative hypothesis*, and when other researchers agree on the tentative hypothesis, it reaches the next stage, a *verified hypothesis*. What has occurred is a progression from low level of possibility to high level of possibility. When researchers do a great deal of testing and the verified hypothesis is never rejected, the level of a scientific theory is reached. This means that the theory makes a satisfactory account for all the phenomena with which it is involved. When a theory has stood the test of time and been internationally verified due to reproducible results, it becomes a *biological law*. Thus, in summary, the formal scientific process involves going through a series of *possibilities* (hypotheses) and a *probability* (a theory), to finally become a *medical certainty* (a biological law). Compare with Scientific method — fun type, Scientific method — informal type. See also Conjecture, Facts, Hypothesis, Guess, Inductive reasoning, Theory.

Scientific method, fun type This is one of the three major groups of scientific method, the others being the formal and informal types. The objective here is to find something that works, even if it is not true or, at least, you were not able to prove it is true. The process includes the following in the order that they are shown: free thinking, imaginative reasoning, creativity and making it work. Unlike the fun method, in the formal scientific method the process is always self-correcting and always seeking further information through experimentation. If knowledge is acquired, then the scientist will be in a situation where he or she can consider a number of new options which will expand on the truth. In contrast, the fun method involves unrestrained thinking and does not give a final answer. The answer exists because it works. Many great discoveries involved the fun method (e.g. Einstein used it to ride a beam of light into infinity in order to formulate his Theory of Relativity). Compare with Scientific method — formal type, Scientific method — informal type. See also Preface.

Scientific method, informal type This is one of the three major groups of scientific method, the others being the formal and fun types. In contrast to the formal scientific method, the informal type may use anecdotal material. The process includes the following in the order that they are shown: *purpose* (what do you want to learn?), *research* (find out as much about your topic as you can), *hypothesis* (predict the answer to the problem), *experiment* (design a test to prove or disprove your hypothesis), *analysis* (record of what happened to the experiment) and *conclusion* (was your hypothesis correct?). Compare with Scientific method — formal type, Scientific method — fun type.

Scientific mind see Reasonable, Scientific method, all types

Scientific theory see Scientific method — formal type

Search warrant see *Ex parte*

Sebaceous glands see Sweat

Second degree murder see Murder

Secondary evidence see Evidence

Secondary gain This should be distinguished from primary gain. In psychoanalytic theory, *primary gain* is reduction of tension and conflict through the various neurotic defense mechanisms. The author uses the term primary gain for *textbook patients* who seek to be cured or relieved of their impairment/disability. Secondary gain is of two types: tangible and intangible. *Tangible secondary gain* is a conscious desire to acquire certain *things*, such as money or drugs. *Intangible secondary gain* pertains to the patient's *feelings* that need to be cared for or expressed. Such motivations might include vindictiveness towards a boss, partner or doctor; a desire for support and reassurance from someone in order to feel better; a need to feel recognised, important or loved; and the need for sympathy or support. Ways of attaining secondary gain are most commonly by controlling or manipulating behaviors. With deceptive patients, secondary gain refers to the advantages conferred on the patient by being ill. In contrast to the *malingerer* who is quite deliberate in his objectives, self-deceivers are largely unaware of how they use symptoms and illnesses to affect others. See also Malingerers, Primary gain, Saving face, Tertiary gain.

Security   Etymologically, something that is secure is 'carefree'. The metaphorical extension from 'free from care' to 'free from danger, safe' occurred while still in post-Augustan Latin. What makes you secure protects you from danger so that you are guarded against and not likely to be exposed to danger. See also Safe.

Seddon classification of nerve injuries see Table 9

Seldom see Vocational rehabilitation terms

Selective abstraction   Focusing on destructive aspects of an experience on the one end while focusing on the constructive and good; 'the lily' in the swamp, on the other end. For example, the power of positive thinking.

Self-deceivers see Classification of patients, Concealment in medicine, Postnatal acquired injuries, Prototype patients. Compare with Malingerers, Normal patients

Self-defense   A plea used to justify the use of force to ward off an attack if the attack was unprovoked, retreat was impossible or there was an imminent threat of harm to the person concerned or his or her family or property.

Self-discipline   Systematic and rigorous training, where *training* is active mental or physical exercising in order to form habits. Self-discipline is used to get rid of *childishness* and enhance *child-like* traits which include liveliness, increased curiosity and a greater desire to explore. This leads an individual into the unknown, which requires the evolution of decision-making and problem solving. As more problems are conquered, the person's intellect grows and the evolution toward maturity occurs. Maturity is about beneficial self-discipline. See also Childish, Child-like.

Self-incrimination   Occurs when a person says or does something that might charge or involve themselves in a crime or fault. Under the Fifth Amendment to the Constitution of the United States, which states that 'no person ... shall be compelled in any criminal case to be a witness against himself...', a person cannot be forced to make such a statement.

Self-procured care   Is when one party (e.g. the employee) obtains medical treatment independently of the other party (e.g. employer or insurer). In this situation, doctors providing medical services do it on a lien basis. See also Lien.

Table 9 The Seddon classification of nerve injuries.

Name of injury	Type of injury
Neuropraxia	A localized conduction block, with preservation of function distal to the lesion. Signs of denervation do not develop and full recovery occurs within days or weeks
Axonotmesis	Lesions which give rise to axonal interruption, but with preservation of the connective tissue framework of the nerve. Wallerian degeneration occurs distal to the lesion and signs of denervation develop. Recovery takes place by axonal regeneration, in which the axons regain their former peripheral connections and is, therefore, satisfactory
Neurotmesis	Lesions in which the axons are interrupted and additionally the connective tissue components of the nerve are damaged or the nerve is completely transected. Recovery has to take place by axonal regeneration, but is always incomplete because the fibers may not take the correct route at the site of injury

Self-rehabilitated This may be total or partial. A patient who has been *totally rehabilitated* is one who has, during the interval between the time the patient was considered permanent and stationary from an old injury and the time of occurrence of the 'pilot' date of injury, no manifestations of disability. In other words, the patient had complete physical and/or mental restoration as it related to the prior pertinent injury so there is no impairment of earning capacity, no impairment of normal use of a member and no competitive handicap in the open labor market. The patient is considered to have undergone *partial rehabilitation* if there are residuals of permanent disability, but with some improvement. If there was no lessening of permanent disability, then the patient has not been rehabilitated.

Sensation An impression made upon the mind through the medium of the nervous system, usually through one of the sense organs. When the stimulation of a sensory nerve is transmitted to the brain, so as to affect consciousness, the result is a sensation. Sensations can be either painful or non-painful. *Non-painful sensations* are called paresthesias or, a more inclusive term, dysaesthesias. *Painful sensations* result from nerve root or peripheral nerve lesions. See also Dysaesthesia, Seddon's classification of nerve injuries, Sensation classification — painful type, Sensation grading, Sunderland classification of nerve injuries.

Sensation classification, painful type This is a confusing topic in the literature with a staggering array of diagnostic labels. As a clinical tool, this author reduced the numerous terms for nerve lesions in medical dictionaries to the four shown in Table 10. A further reduction in confusion can be made by knowing that: (1) the four types of pathological lesions can affect either the nerve root of the peripheral nerve, which is apart form the central nervous system; (2) one, two or multiple nerves may be involved. Thus, there are different names applied depending upon the cause of the lesion, its location and the number of nerves involved. Concerning the terminology: (1) the prefix *poly-* (e.g. polyneuropathy) means that many nerves are affected simultaneously; (2) the prefix *mono-* (e.g. mononeuropathy) means an affection of one nerve; (3) multiple mononeuropathy suggests that either (a) several individual nerves are damaged at various points along their course, (b) dysfunction of several large nerves has

Table 10 The author's classification for painful types of sensation.

Name	Type of pain sensation
Neuritis	Inflammation of a nerve from inflammatory agents, toxic conditions, chemical or immunological irritants
Neuralgias	Mechanical nerve disturbances from crush, stretch, foreign bodies, punctures or lacerations
Neuropathies	Degeneration of nerves which give rise to peripheral, proximal, symmetrical or asymmetrical patterns
Causalgia	A broad term which encompasses disorders of the sympathetic nervous system, the blood supply to nerves (*vasa nervorum*) and the nerve supply to the nerves (*nervi nervorum*). In causalgia, pain spreads beyond the territory supplied by the nerve involved

Table 11 Pain complaints graded according to their severity.

Grade	Degree of pain sensation
1	No loss of sensation or no spontaneous abnormal sensations
2	Decreased sensation with or without pain, which is forgotten during activity
3	Decreased sensation with or without pain, which interferes with activity
4	Decreased sensation with or without pain, which may prevent some activities
5	Decreased sensation with severe pain, which may cause outcries as well as prevent most activity
6	Decreased sensation with severe pain, which may prevent all activity

occurred asymmetrically at slightly different times, or (c) multiple isolated lesions in a single large nerve trunk; and (4) the prefix *radiculo-* (e.g. radiculopathy) suggests nerve root involvement. Obviously, there are different degrees of severity, different courses, different patterns and different effects. Most of these lesions cause pain, but some can also cause paresthesias (an abnormal tickling, prickling or burning sensation) or dysaesthesias (simple, or more often combinations of, pain from thermal or tactile disturbances and non-pain sensations). See also Dysaesthesia, Parethesia.

Sensation grading see Table 11

Sense of loss see Suffer

Sensitivity In evaluating the reliability of a test or criterion, sensitivity is the proportion whose result is positive among those who truly have the condition. This should be compared with *specificity,* which is the proportion of negative results among those who truly do not have the condition. With rare diseases, high specificity is desired in order to reduce the 'false positive' results (those that do not have the condition, but the test is positive). However, in the common disorders, high sensitivity may be more important in order to detect all cases of the condition. See also False positives, Incidents, Prevalence, Specificity.

Sentiment see Opinion

Separate wheat from chaff see Decision

Sequela Is whatever happens after the termination of a medical lesion process. Examples might be adhesions, deformities or infections, etc. See also Result.

Serious and wilful misconduct benefits The law wants a safe and healthy work place. Employers and employees are encouraged to exercise due care. If one or both parties, by omission or commission, cause an injury to result, then monetary penalties can be applied. This is particularly true when the conduct is of a semi-criminal nature. An employer may not insure against this liability. See also Condonation exception, Horseplay.

Serious injury Is that which results in more than 24 hours of hospitalization for anything other than observation, it is the loss of a body part or any serious degree of disfigurement. See also Injury.

Seroma see Hematoma

Serum see Hematoma

Service The delivery of a legal document which notifies a person of a lawsuit. This can be either *personal service,* when copy of the process is personally delivered to the man or women concerned, or *constructive service,* when the delivery occurs through the mail, via an authorized representative or by publishing it in a newspaper. See also Notice.

Settlement This is when opposing parties end a lawsuit by making an agreement between themselves and thus eliminating the necessity of judicial resolution to the controversy. See also Compromise and release, Compromise settlement, Conclusion.

Seven factors of function see Aging

Severe pain see Pain grading

Shall Means *must.* See Should

Shamans see Treatment

Shifting the burden of proof This is when the defense, having the original burden of proof, has presented a *prima facie* case for the defense so that the plaintiff must rebut it with contrary evidence (or vice versa). See also Burden of proof, Prima facie.

'Shotgun' treatment see Manipulation

Should/shall/must In law, the word 'should' means that the provision is not mandatory, but 'shall' or 'must' are mandatory.

Show cause order A court order, issued at the request of one party, requiring a second party to convince the court that a specific act should not be carried out or allowed.

Sick pleasures Also called *vicious pleasures* or *vicious delights,* they are totally personal, selfish and destructive. The emotion of hate and the thought of revenge are at its core. See also Masochism, Negative pleasures, Punishment, Schadenfreude.

Sign Form the Latin *signum,* meaning a distinguishing mark, a signal, it is loosely synonymous with physical findings and the term 'objective'. It derives from the

'X' people used in bygone days when signing their letters instead of writing their names. *Pathognomonic signs* are specific and characteristic objectives of a given disease or condition (e.g. Aschoff bodies seen in rheumatic carditis). Signs are not to be confused with symptoms. Compare with Subjective, Symptoms. See also Lesions, Objective, Objective/Subjective scale, Pathognomonic, Pathology scope.

Signature see Prescription, Prescribed

Simile see Metaphor, Risk

Simplicity/simplification From the Latin *sem*, meaning one, plus *plico*, meaning fold, it is to open up unfolded; lay out flat. Simplification is a process that naturally becomes less complicated.

Sine qua non This is Latin for 'without which not', meaning that without which the thing cannot be; an absolutely essential and necessary thing. For example, if a couple built a swimming pool without a surrounding fence and a neighbour's child fell in the pool, then the *sine qua non* is the original couple's failure to place a fence around the swimming pool. The swimming pool would be considered an *attractive nuisance*. Philosophically, *sine qua non* relates qualities which are the power that objects have to cause ideas as to what something is — what makes that object an individual as a separate category in a big picture outline. A quality of a thing is that which makes it fundamentally unlike anything that is similar or different and the requirements for patents, trademarks, copyrights and personal styles.

Six common clinical styles of worker's compensation patients These are: (1) malingerers; (2) deliberate deceitful exaggerators who consciously magnify a minor lesion; (3) self-deceiving exaggerators; (4) attention-seeking exaggerators who magnify a real problem so it is believed; (5) normal textbook patients; and (6) stoic patients who have more of a problem than they present. See also Classification of medical patients, Stoic.

Skill The ability of a person to use his or her own knowledge effectively or to do something well, especially as a result of practical experience over a long time. It can also refer to a practical technique. See also Practical.

Skylarking see Horseplay

Slander The damaging, or *defamation*, of another person's reputation through the the the written word (*libel*) or a speech (slander). See also Libel.

Sliding impairment see Impairment

Slight pain see Pain grading

Smoke screen In life generally, and the medical-legal arena in particular, smoke screens are pervasive. It encompasses such terms as hiding, secrets, mysteriousness, obscure and unintelligible. A *smoke screen hides by diversion* in the sense it deflects, deviates or turns aside. It is a deliberately fashioned red herring, or a topic designed to be inflammatory, which switches a person's focus from the pertinent to the non-pertinent. For example, a conscious deceiver may loudly claim harassment to divert attention from embezzlement. Smoke screens are used for all types of strategy, tactics, logistics and actions, such as: (1) those used for *a person's own benefit* to survive, thrive or save face (e.g. to hide that fact that the person was responsible); (2) those used for the *benefit of others* (also called white lies); (3) those used to the *detriment of others* (e.g. a dishonorable person who says his actions are in the best interest of my client, patient or customer); (4) the unintentional conveying of a misperception (e.g. in very complex subjects that do not lend themselves to easy explanation); and (5) to avoid giving an answer, etc. In legal proceedings it is important to be aware of the smoke screens that we use on others and keep alert for those others use on us. See also Con-artist, Concealed, Concealment in medicine, Deception.

Social security confidentiality The United States Federal Privacy Act of 1974 states that upon request, a claimant may have access to his/her social security claim file. The medical reports in the file will be reviewed prior to their release. If this is deemed not to be in the best interests of the claimant, the file will be released only to an authorised representative. Release of reports by the social security administration to other agencies is restricted by applicable federal and state laws.

Social Security Federal Guidelines The Disability Evaluation Division assesses the medical and vocational aspects of claims for social security benefits. The judgment is made by a staff physician and a disability evaluation analyst. *Social security disability* is defined as the inability to engage in any substantial gainful activity by reason of a medically determinable physical or mental impairment which can be expected to result in death or has lasted or can be expected to last for a continuous period of not less than 12 months. Information needed includes objective evidence from the claimants records regarding a history, physical, and laboratory findings, clinical course, therapy and response, and the results of any special tests (e.g. electrocardiography, psychological tests and consultative reports, etc.)

Social Security Guidelines For Physicians A narrative report, copies of the doctor's records, or completion of any of the appropriate forms are equally satisfactory. Doctors may respond by using their remote telephone dictation system. A reasonable fee, as determined by the agency, will be paid upon request. The payment request must be in writing on a separate form and it must be attached to the report (or included in the doctor's dictation). Social security regulations prohibit payment for reports from federal agencies

Sociopaths see Pathological lying

Sodomy Variously defined by law to include sexual contact between humans and animals, and oral-genital or anal contact between humans. Medically, sodomy refers to human/animal sexual contact and anal intercourse.

Somatization The expression in physical terms of emotional pain. A *somatist* can deny and repress a problems (e.g. physical/sexual abuse or other psychological traumas) which becomes apparent from physical manifestations.

Somatization disorder see Conversion reaction, Functional overlay

Somatoform disorders A group of disorders with symptoms which suggest a physical disorder but without demonstrable organic findings to explain the symptoms. There is positive evidence, or a strong presumption, that the symptoms are linked to psychological factors or conflicts, categories include somatization disorder, conversion disorder, hypochondriasis, body dysmorphic disorder and pain disorder.

Spacial intelligence Also called *visual intelligence*, it is the ability to create, hold and manipulate images in a the mind in order to accomplish a task effectively (e.g. to fit a set of suitcases into the car trunk). See also Associational intelligence, Disorientation, Intuitional intelligence.

Spacial orientation See Disorientation

Specific injury Occurs as a result of one incident or exposure which causes disability or need for medical treatment. A definable injury, for example, is immediately known to the patient and causes the patient to do something (e.g. report the injury, apply home remedies, take time away from work or seek medical treatment) for that specific lesion. Compare with Cumulative trauma. See also Date of injury, Injury, Serious specific injury, Trauma.

Specificity It is the number of people who have a disease who test positively for that condition. See also Incidents, Sensitivity.

Specific traumatic injuries see Injury

Specific performance see Court of Equity

Speculate In an abstract rational sense, it means to have pondered the different aspects of a subject and evolve ideas or theories by mental re-examination of the subject; it is *a priori* reasoning (i.e. knowledge from reflection). However, caution is required, because a speculation is also a theoretical scheme that has not been sufficiently checked or tested by practice. This could be presented to a jury as as mere guess and not of serious thought. See also A priori, Presume, Theory.

Spirit of the law The essential character of the lawmaker's intent. Equity is the spirit of all law and is that which is equally right or just to all concerned. It contains the ideas of 'fairness' and 'impartiality'. See also Court of Equity, Equity.

Spiritual pain see Suffer

Spiritual suffering see Suffer

Sprain According the ancient lexicographers, a 'sprain' literally means to 'press out' of place the ligaments and muscles around a joint. Today, a sprain is a joint injury in which some of the fibers of a supporting ligament are ruptured, but the continuity of the ligament remains intact. It is *ligaments that are sprained*, not muscles (which are strained).

Staging A way of classifying malignant neoplasms for treatment, prognostic and research purposes. Groupings are based on physical examination, radiographs and biopsy. For musculoskeletal tumors, the Ennekings Staging System is commonly used (e.g. IA lesions are those that are low-grade and intracompartmental, IB are low-grade extracompartmental, IIA are high grade intracompartmental, IIB are high-grade extracompartmental, while stage III lesion are high or low grade, either extra- or intracompartmental, with either regional or distal metastasis). See Pathology scope, Subclinical disease.

Standard age Arbitrarily, it is considered to be 38–39 years of age.

Standard of proof see Beyond reasonable doubt, Burden of proof, Facts, Guilt, Predominance of evidence, Proof

Standing The legal right to bring a lawsuit. Only a person with something at stake has standing to bring a lawsuit.

Standing before the court A party must have the capacity to sue and be a 'proper' party. To have standing before the court, parties must present facts sufficient to show their individual needs require the remedy which is being sought. See also Causation, Cause of action.

Stare decisis In Latin, this is 'to stand by that which was decided', and represents a doctrine that directs courts to follow principles of law laid down in previous cases when based on substantially similar facts, in a similar manner to precedent. See also Precedence.

State courts At state level, litigation starts with the trial courts, which include: (1) district, county or municipal courts that have general jurisdiction over civil or criminal cases; (2) juvenile or family courts that hear domestic, juvenile delinquency, and youthful offender cases; (3) criminal courts; and (4) probate court for wills and claims against estates. The judgments of these trial courts can be appealed by the state supreme court, with or without going through the intermediate appellate courts. No two states have identical court systems.

Stationary Not subject to variations or to changes of place. See also Maximum medical improvement, Permanent and stationary.

Status quo Is Latin for 'state in which', and is the state in which something is; the existing state of affairs as in political or social relationships at the time in question; the existing situation at any given time. See also Homeostasis.

Statute From the Latin statua, meaning erected, set up, caused to stand, establish, it is a written laws of state or federal legislatures expressed in the form necessary to make it the law of the government unit concerned. See Classification of law.

Statute of limitations A law that limits the time during which a particular legal action may be brought.

Statutory law Laws enacted by legislatures. These are different to 'case law' or 'common law'. See also Civil law, Classification of law.

Stipulated award see Conclusion

Stipulation An agreement between opposing parties in a lawsuit about some aspect of the case. For example, certain facts may be accepted as true by both sides. See also Admission, Compromise.

Stocking-glove anesthesia/hypesthesia/hypoesthesia In this, sleeve anesthesia, and regional psychogenic pain there is either a diffuse decrease or absence of sensation. In the psychogenic type, a hand or foot shows a uniform loss of all sensory faculties such as to touch, temperature and pain. Furthermore, the loss of sensation is sharply demarcated at an anatomical landmark rather than according to dermatomes. Whether of the hypesthesia or anesthesia type, both may be seen as much in organic conditions as in psychogenic conditions. Organically, this is particularly true of the neuropathies whereby there is degeneration involving nerves — diabetes, heavy metal toxicity, diptheria, pernicious anemia. These should always be ruled out in conversion reactions of 'self-deceivers' and 'faking' of conscious deceivers. Three key points of the psychogenic type are: (1) there is an abrupt change from normal sensation to the part complained of; (2) there are associated inconsistencies on the evaluation, and (3) the patients are either conscious deceivers or self-deceivers. In organic conditions, at the site of sensory loss, there is a gradual return of sensation to (almost) normal over a few inches adjacent to the original area of sensory loss — called 'feathering' of sensation.

Stoic In 308 BC in Athens the philosopher Zeno founded the stoicism school of philosophy. It acquired its name form the adjacent market place, called Stoa Poikile (meaning painted portico), where Zeno gave public lectures. His philosophy was that happiness and wellbeing were not dependent upon material things or on a person's situation in life, but on his or her reasoning faculty. Through reasoning, a person could emulate the calm and order on the universe by learning to accept events with a stern and tranquil mind. His followers were called stoics. Today, a stoic is a person who controls his emotions under stress, who endures the hardships of life without complaining and who otherwise intentionally suppresses feelings so that a deadening of sensibilities results. See also Impassivity, Six common clinical styles of worker's compensation patients.

Strain An overstretching or overexertion of a muscle. Compare with Sprain.

Stress Is an engineering, physics and psychological term applied to physical and emotional aspects of the human body. In a psychological sense, stress is an internal reaction which results from internal triggers in response to internal or external stressors. In other words, emotional stress is a reaction to a problem. Note that stressful mental or physical activities are not synonymous with cumulative trauma. A certain amount of stress is needed to survive and thrive. It takes mind control and mental toughness to have just the right amount of beneficial stress without tipping over into stress overload where *cumulative trauma* results. See also Emotional distress.

Strict liability When it pertains to products, it is the legal doctrine under which manufacturers and middle men who make or sell products that are defective and consequently cause injury, are liable to victims regardless of lack of negligence or intent.

Subacute That arbitrary time between acute and chronic. For example, a subacute disease is one that has existed for more than 6 weeks but less than 12 weeks. See also Acute, Chronic.

Subclinical disease Is without clinical manifestations (i.e. no signs or symptoms). Generally, a disease is capable of being detected or inferred by appropriate investigation (e.g. laboratory studies, bone scans, radiographs or magnetic resonance imaging). However, the disease may not be diagnosable at all, despite being advanced, because of the absence, or limitations, of the examining methods used. For example in a generic *staging* (i.e. a hierarchy of distinct phases or stepping stones in any process) subclinical would be stage 0, minimal manifestations (e.g. pain only) would be stage I, slight pain would be stage II; moderate pain stage III and, finally extreme or destruction pain stage

IV (it is important to realise that different diseases have unique staging techniques that use different parameters). Subclinical diseases may fluctuate between none and a few signs and symptoms. It is here that patients often need more than the usual number of laboratory and test procedures. That a disease is subclinical in no way implies that those affects are without consequences to human health. If nothing else, the condition uses up body reserves or actually disrupts function. Actual functional disturbances, although not detectable by routine physical examination, can sometimes be demonstrated by special testing. A subclinical illness is one that has not shown its presence. See also Concealment in medicine, Pathology scope.

Subjective This has been the subject of a large amount of philosophical debate throughout the centuries. Some say *objective* is based upon perception of an object others can see, while subjective is based on sensations, ideas, attitudes, feelings, emotions and beliefs that exist in a person's mind, i.e. the absence of measurable presence. Medically, subjective designates those psychological processes that are dependent on the experience of an individual and are not directly observable by others. Complaints that a doctor is not able to confirm include those that involve the senses, emotions and feelings of the patient (e.g. pain, numbness, dizziness, nausea and weakness). These impressions may become indirectly accessible for appraisal through the patient's reactions to a physical investigation or via the patient's verbal report.

There are two special categories of subjective factors: (1) *subjective plus* (those 'invisible' features that can be substantiated by associated objective signs and true patterns of defined disease or injury such as rigidity of muscles, swelling or inflammation); and (2) *subjective minus* (complaints of conscious deceivers that are knowingly untrue and not there). However, in medicine, the situation is never just what a doctor is told (subjective factors) and can see (objective factors), the situation is usually far more complex. Indeed, in law, subjective ratings are based on the doctor's *interpretation* of subjectives. See also Intangible, Objective/subjective scales.

Subjective appraisal See Estimation, Educated estimate

Subjective fair play see Fair play

Subjective minus The patient is lying (i.e. it is untrue or not there). See also objective/subjective scale, Pathological lying, Prevaricate, Subjective.

Subjective non-pain disability   see Dysaesthesia, Function, Functional overlay, Functional prolongation, Paresthesia, Seven factors in aging, Sensation.

Subjective pain disability   see Pain grading, Pain frequency rating, Pain measurement test

Subjective plus   These are reproducible subjective complaints by a patient (i.e because it 'fits' or 'works,' the truth seems valid in advance of proof). See also Certainty, Objective/subjective scale.

Subjective vertigo   see Vertigo

Subjective/intangible   see Intangible

Subluxion   see Dislocation

Subnormal   see Anatomical abnormality

Subpoena   From the Latin *sub*, meaning under, plus *poena*, meaning punishment/fine, it refers to a judicial writ (writing) requiring a person to appear in or present evidence to a court 'under penalty' for refusing to do so. Disobedience may be punishable as contempt of court. See also Discovery, *Duces tecum*.

Subpoena *duces tecum*   A court order commanding a witness to bring certain documents or records to court. However, the wording may be such that the witness does not have to attend or certain documents need not be present. See Discovery, *Duces tecum*.

Sub rosa   Is Latin for 'under the rose'. Its legal meaning developed initially from the Roman myth that Cupid gave Harpocrates, the God of science, a rose in exchange for his promise to keep the Venus' secrets. This led to the Roman custom of hanging a rose as an emblem of secrecy over a secret meeting. It is still used in reference to secretive activities.

Sub rosa films   Surveillance films that are made secretly behind the scenes; on the sly. See also *Sub rosa*.

Sub rosa observations   These are secretive observations used to distinguish between a malingerer involved in a conscious deception and a patient with somatization disorder. During observation the patient is unaware that he or she is being observed. See also *Sub rosa*.

Sub rosa palpation   This is a technique used to detect conscious deceivers who show withdrawal from the slightest touch to a part of the body (e.g. to the back). This involves a doctor examining a part known not to be painful (e.g. on the back of their legs) with one hand, while the other rests on the exquisitely tender part of the back. If there is no reaction to the hand on the back the patient may be a conscious deceiver. At least it represents a 'straw' for a positive inconsistency. See also *Sub rosa*.

Subscription   see Prescribed, Prescription

Substance   The material constituting an objective thing (e.g. an organ or body). A hazardous substance is that which is toxic, corrosive, an irritant, a strong sensitizer, flammable or combustible, or generates pressure through decomposition, heat or other means. They can cause significant personal injury or illness during, or as a *proximate result* of, any customary or reasonably foreseeable handling or use. Examples of a 'proximate result' are the foreseeable problems that children would have from ingesting a hazardous substance. Compare with Proximate cause.

Substantial   Originally from the Latin *sub*, meaning under, plus *sto*, meaning to stand, it was the underlying matter of which a thing consists. The use of the word expanded in sixteenth century English to include 'standing under,' from which our word *understand* derives, and pertained to standing under a tree in a rain storm. It then became to know something as a consequence of standing underneath it, or from seeing a situation from the lowest level upwards. The concept further expanded and included standing before, upon and among. Looking at something from these different angles gave a more comprehensive knowledge of the underlying essence. Once a person had the essence, he or she could resist, persist and subsist. Such an essence was considered real, of great value and relatively great in size and did not contain the trivial, unimportant, poor, weak and unsound. Substantial eventually came to mean enough of the essence of something to make it self-consistent, solid, true, of real worth and authoritative. Nowadays it usually refers to information that lies between scientific facts and valuative judgments (i.e. preference determinations about the worth of qualities and\or quantities as in art, music and poetry.) Considered opinions about what is substantial involves separating the wheat from the the the chaff and then applying common sense determinations regarding how well another thinks, feels, says, and does things as it conforms to a reasonable standard. As a qualitative application, *substantive law* involves principles and detailed rules that define legal rights and duties (contrasted to procedural or adjective law). As a quantitative application, a *substantive cause* is defined as that in the 35–40% range of *substantial limitation*. See also Burden of proof, Common sense, Predominant, Reasonable, Substantial limitation.

Substantial evidence see Burden of proof

Substantive cause see Substantial

Substantive law The body of principles and detailed rules defining the nature and extent of legal rights and duties. Compare with Objective law, Procedural law. See also Classification of law, Substantial.

Substantial limitation is defined by the Equal Employment Opportunities Commission in the United States as an impairment that restricts the individual's ability to perform either a class of jobs or a broad range of jobs in various classes, as compared to the average person having comparable training, skills and abilities. An inability to perform a single, particular job does not constitute a substantial limitation. See also Americans with Disabilities Act, Substantial.

Subtraction method of apportionment This is one of several methods which are used to express opinions about apportionment. It is particularly useful when there is naturally progressing disease process (California Labor Code Section 4663), pre-existing disability (California Labor Code Section 4750) or disability occurring after an industrial injury (California Labor Code Section 4750.5). When permanent disability exists, the medical expert witness should give the factors of all impairments and then describe factors of impairment for each injury or condition that causes a rateable disability. For example, the injured worker's overall work preclusion is a limitation to light work. Now, absent the industrial injury, as a result of the natural progression of the pre-existing disease process, the injured worker would have a restriction precluding very heavy work. As an alternative, the doctor could use the *percentage method of apportionment*. Once all of the criteria for legal apportionment has been satisfied, the doctor could state, 'I apportion 75% of the disability to industrial causes and 25% of the disability to the natural progression of the underlying condition.'

Success see Viable

Sue From the common Latin term *sequere*, meaning to follow, its legal use emerged in the fourteenth century

and was based on the notion of 'following' up a matter in court. It is to initiate proceedings and is similar to *prosecute*. See also Causation, Summons.

Suffer It originally derived from the common Latin term *sufferire*, meaning to hold it up from underneath, to sustain. Its modern sense evolved from 'sustain' via 'to undergo something unpleasant, to endure'. The cause of suffering was believed to be either of a spiritual or of a worldly nature. Spiritual suffering centered around a lack of love fulfilment, while worldly suffering included disturbances of basic natural feelings associated with a person's connection with other forms of life and/or the emotional, rational or somatic pain derivatives of basic feelings. Characteristic of suffering is an enduring quality and quantity of *destructive inner manifestations* (e.g. helplessness, emptiness and despair) which would be more than normal unhappinesses of daily living. Typically, these manifestations are so great that they are projected externally so others can observe them. Suffering is a important medical-legal term and in this arena the psychological components of an emotion have been considered to be feeling tone plus a thought, with the type of thought determining whether feeling tone is pleasant or unpleasant and the intent good or bad. Destructive thoughts in emotional distress have a *sense of loss* at their core: (1) *anger* (the thought of being violated which results in the feelings of revenge); (2) *anxiety* (a loss of control over a person's own thoughts about people, things or oneself which leads to feelings of uncertainty); (3) *depression* (the thought that a person has lost control over him or herself which leads to feeling of worthlessness and hopelessness); and (4) *emotional pain* (the thought of loss of things, people or oneself). *Suffering is particularly associated with depression and emotional pain.* In both cases there is loss of love, in the case of depression it is self-love and in emotional pain it is the loss of love for and from things outside oneself. This should be compared with *spiritual pain*, which is the experience of love being prevented because there is nobody available to accept it or the designated receiver fails to accept it. Some individuals derive pleasure from suffering, either from inflicting it on themselves (*masochism*) or other people (*sadism*). See also Anxiety, Pain, Pain and suffering, Penalty, Sick pleasures, Tolerance, Tort.

Suicide This is the self-inflicted destruction of a person's own interests (e.g. when a person intentionally takes his or her own life).

Sui juris Having the legal capacity to act for yourself. See also Competence, Sanity.

Suit To engage in a legal prosecution or lawsuit; to take legal action against. See also Litigation.

Summary judgment An order by a judge which decides a case in favor of one side on the basis of the pleading, which occurs before the trial, or before or after a hearing. It can be issued once a judge determines that no genuine factual dispute exists but one party is entitled to a judgment. See also Judgment.

Summary proceeding In law, this is applied to proceedings in a court of law which are carried out rapidly due to the omission of certain formalities which are generally required by common law. See also Common law.

Summons A notice to defendants that they are being sued and are required to appear in court. A *jury summons* requires one to report for possible jury duty.

Sunderland classification of nerve injuries This has five categories (degrees) of nerve injury and is related to the Seddon classification. First degree injuries correspond to neuapraxia, second degree injuries to neurotmesis and the third and fourth degrees are subdivisions of neurotmesis. The fifth degree consists of complete severance of the nerve trunk. See also Seddon classification of nerve injuries (Table 9 on page 123).

Superimposed conditions Are not the same as concurrent (running along side; existing or happening together). Concurrent conditions can mask each other's natural history manifestations. Superimposed means to lay something on top of something else. If disease B was laid on top of disease A, the clinical manifestations would get worse because a new lesion has been placed on an old lesion of like kind. Failure to see the difference between superimposed and concurrent injuries clouds diagnosis, treatment, and prognosis. Suppose, in the low back, the patient had L5 facet arthritis and then sustained a fracture of the L5 facets. Pain coming from the L5 facets would be worse as a result of the superimposed fracture on a pre-existing arthritic facet. As an illustration of concurrent injury, suppose a patient with an asymptomatic L5-S1 spondylolisthesis had an injury involving the overlying musculature. A doctor would be following the 'red herring' path if he was to treat the spondylolisthesis and not the myofascial pain. See Apportionment terms, Concurrent, Pathology scope, Red Herring.

Superimposed pre-existing lesion see Injury

Superior part of the body The upper, cephalad portion (the head end) of the body. See also Anatomical references, Figure 1 (page 7).

Supernormal see Anatomical abnormality

Superscription see Prescribe, Prescription

Supinate The act of turning the upper limbs so that the palms are upwards in the direction of the face, in a similar manner to somebody cupping their hands when asking for a drink. See also Anatomical references, Figure 7 page 59.

Supplementary proceedings see Application

Supposition An almost exact synonym of *hypothesis* (see entry for definition). See also Scientific method.

Suppress To finally and effectively put something down; prevent something occurring. It is a much stronger word than *restrain*. Legally, it is to forbid the use of evidence in a trial because it is improper or was improperly obtained. In psychology, it is a conscious, deliberate, non-evasive expelling of certain thoughts or feelings from focal awareness, in order to turn ones attention elsewhere. It can relate to mental problems. See also Evidence, Repression.

Surgeon From the Greek *cheir*, meaning the hand, plus *ergon*, meaning work, it is literally those who work with their hands inside a patient's body. See also Operation.

Surgical operation Any act performed with instruments or by the hands of a surgeon. Also called a *surgical procedure*, it is performed for the purpose of curing or benefiting a person by altering an existing undesirable state. The boundaries defining an operation are sometimes indistinct. See also Treatment.

Surgical placebo Operating on asymptomatic pathological lesions.

Surgical planning see Future medical, Nerve, Projected Orthopaedic expenses, Roots, Salvage procedure

Surgical procedure see Surgical operation

Surmise see Conjecture

Survival see Viable

Suspending part see Traction

Sustained   A court order allowing an objection or motion to prevail and become effective. Compare with Overruled. See also Directed verdict.

Sweat   The fact that moisture appeared on the skin in hot weather was noted by ancient people. However, it was not until 1722 that the Dutch anatomist, Hermann Boerhaarve, noted sweat glands, and 1834 before they were fully described by Breschet, a French anatomist. It has subsequently been determined that the skin contains two types of sweat glands; *eccrine* (small sweat glands) and *apocrine* (large sweat glands). Eccrine sweat is clear with a faint odor. Its composition varies with fluid intake, external temperature and humidity, and some hormonal activity. The apocrine glands are almost rudimentary structures which are formed from follicular epithelium in a similar manner to *sebaceous glands*. The major development of these glands, which is greater in women, occurs during puberty in response to the autonomic nervous system rather than thermal stimulation. Their distribution is limited to the areolae of the breast, the pubic and perineal regions and probably the axillae. The organic material of the apocrine glands undergoes bacterial decomposition to produce an odor which some species use as recognition signals and sex attractants (*pheromones*). Sweat is the substance formed in sweat glands before it appears on the surface of the skin. *Perspiration* means any secretion passing through the skin and includes secretions which passed through at places where there are no sweat glands. When apocrine glands become infected, they are called *furuncles* (i.e. a boil) and *carbuncles*. Persistent abscess formation of apocrine gland regions is known as *hydradenitis suppurativea*.

Sworn inquest see Beyond reasonable doubt

Syllogism method see Deductive reasoning

Sympathy   Originally, it derived from the Greek *sumpatheia*, meaning to share feelings with, or feel similarly to, someone else, whether this is sorrow or joy. From this it was associated with *humane*, or what is expected of mankind at its best in the treatment of sentient beings in order to prevent or relieve suffering. Nowadays, sympathy implies some degree of equality, a kindred or union, so that a person can have a sympathy for the struggles of a giant or the triumphs of a conqueror. As this sense of the word developed, it did suggest shared emotions, but essentially little or no deep feeling connection. By the time *empathy* was introduced, sympathy meant caring without the state of a deep fundamental feeling connection (this is *love*). Empathy is not necessarily a sign of love, but rather one simply gets into the feeling flow of someone or something. See also Empathy.

Symptoms   Although symptom is often considered synonymous with subjective, this is not entirely the case. In fact, it is only one type of subjective. From the Greek *sun*, meaning together, plus *ptoma*, meaning a fall (as in collapse or casualty), it is literally a 'falling together' or something that happens in connection with another thing. This developed because it was believed that a fall-off in bodily functions was associated with a collapse of the patient's physical integrity. As a result of both falling together, this indicted the presence of a disease. The word appeared in the English language in the fourteenth century and is now used to indicate any manifest departure from the normal which is considered indicative of disease. Symptoms are the patient's complaints. Compare with Objective, Signs. See also Objective/subjective scale, Pathology scope, Subjective lesions.

Syndromes   From the Greek *sun*, meaning together, plus *dramein*, meaning run, it originally referred to a running course or passageway similar to those between rows of columns where camels would race. The concept of this 'passageway' was carried over into medicine to describe a concurrence of collective pathological lesions whose manifestations, when combined together, constituted the picture of disease. That is, several related signs and symptoms, each originating from different causes, become part of a syndrome. Typically, the complex of clinical manifestations are *phenotypic* (capable of being observed). However, they may be many steps removed from the *genotype* (the genetic constitution of the individual). In genetics, a syndrome is a combination of phenotypic manifestations. See also Disease, Pathology scope.

Synovium see Mobilization

System   From the Greek *sun*, meaning together, plus *histemi*, meaning to place or set, it is literally to set or place together. In ancient Greece, it was an assemblage of things in a regular order so as to form a plan or scheme. A system is an organized whole — a set or series of interconnected or interdependent parts that function together in a common purpose. The teamwork produces results that would have been impossible to achieve by any one part acting or operating alone. In medicine, it designates a combination of parts (e.g. the digestive or nervous system).

System, extrapyramidal The main motor pathways of the central nervous system are called the *pyramidal tracks*. They were named in the seventeenth century by Duverney from the pyramids of the medulla oblongata which are composed of similar nerve tracks. The extrapyramidal system is a functional rather than an anatomical unit. It comprises the nuclei and fibers (excluding those of the pyramidal track) which control and co-ordinate motor activities, especially those related to the postural, static, supporting and locomotive mechanisms. Included in the extrapyramidal system is the corpus striatum, subthalamic nucleus, substantia nigra and the red nucleus, as well as their interconnections with the reticular formation, cerebellum and cerebrum. Some authorities include the cerebellum and the vestibular nuclei. It is also called the *extracorticospinal tract*.

System review see Past medical history

T

Take nothing see Non-suit, Judgments *in personam*

Talipes varus see Varus

Tangible see Intangible

Tangible physical evidence See Demonstrative evidence

Tarda Delayed in appearance. For example, genetic congenital/development lesions which are genetic problems present before birth due to, for example, a mutation, but not manifest until sometime after birth. See also Acquired medical conditions.

Target date for work An estimated date of return to work.

Tempered From the Latin *temperare*, it was originally to mix or to blend in due proportions. It now means to restrain oneself.

Temporary disability (TD) Is legally defined as physical incapacity reasonably expected to be completely cured or materially improved with proper medical treatment. Temporary disability is, therefore, a favorable prognosis and permanent disability an unfavorable one. Since the relevant factor in TD is actual wage loss, a patient is entitled to TD indemnity when a compensable injury has resulted in an impediment of earning capacity. Temporary disability wages are paid until injured workers reach the maximum level of recovery from their injury. *Total temporary disability* means that the patient is unable to earn any income during the period when she or he is recovering from the effect of their injury. *Partial temporary disability* means that the worker cannot perform one of the many essential aspects of his or her job, but could return to modified work if it were available. With either temporary or total TD, the purpose is to enable the injured person to recuperate from that injury while providing financial support until he or she is either permanent and stationary or able to return to work (i.e. at whatever level the person is capable). See also Permanent disability.

Temporary injunction These command the parties to do, or not to do, certain acts that may cause irreparable harm to the other side while the suit is pending. An example is a *temporary restraining order* given *ex parte*. See also Ex parte.

Temporary restraining order see Temporary injunction

Tentative diagnosis see Diagnostic impression

Tentative hypothesis see Scientific method

Term From the Greek *terma*, meaning end, boundary, it is a fixed or definite period of time. In human pregnancy the term (gestation) is between 38 and 42 weeks from the first day of the last menstrual period. See also End.

Tertiary gain It suggests that a person other than the plaintiff is seeking to make a gain from the plaintiff's problem. Such people could include family members or care givers. See also Primary gain, Secondary gain.

Test It originally derived from Latin *testum*, meaning a pot or earthen vessel, because the alchemists tried or 'tested' things by heating them in a pot or 'testum'. By the fourteenth century the word 'test' then transferred to the procedure, as seen in one of Chaucer's books. Today, a test is a procedure to detect or measure the concentration of a substance, especially by specific chemical, enzymatic or immunological reaction, or by its biological effect on man or animals. Test may be qualitative (to indicate the presence or absence of something) or quantitative (used to measure the sum degree of precision how much of that substance is present).

Test for malingering see Faker test

Test, nocturnal penile tumescent Designed to distinguish organic impotence from psychogenic impotence. Since males tend to have six to eight erections per night during the rapid eye movement (REM) cycle of sleep, pressure inducers can be applied to the penis to indicate whether the male is physically able to achieve an erection. If he has erections, this tends to rule out an organic basis for impotence. See also Classification of medical patients, Psychogenic disease.

Testimony Evidence given by a witness under oath. This should be distinguished from evidence derived from written material, physical objects or other sources. See also Oath.

Textbook patients Are those psychiatrically uncomplicated cases with organic lesions presenting as overt, tempered, masked or subclinical. See also Classification of medical patients, Prototype patients.

The bench see Bench

The court see Bench

The thing speaks for itself see Res ipsa loquitur

Theorem see Theory

Theory From the Greek theoria, meaning contemplation or speculation, theory (which itself had derived from theoros, meaning spectator), in its initial sense was 'looking'. Thus, a theorem or theory was something to be examined. Its ancient usage was revived with the medieval translation of Aristotle, at which stage theory referred to the viewing or contemplation of the abstract principles, whether in science or art. From here it became a doctrine covering all the known facts but for which absolute proof is lacking (similar to probability). It is when a hypothesis, a comprehensive guess which explains all the facts, is regarded as verified by the scientific community. However, the lay public also use theory to mean 'your opinion'. See also Evidence, Hypothesis, Probability, Speculate, Scientific method, Speculate, Valid.

Therapeutically beneficial Are those things that aid self-rehabilitation. An example would be to stretch an uncomplicated stiff shoulder as this is likely to loosen it. See also Treatment.

Therapies of medicine Are those non-operative, semi-invasive, operative, situational adjustments required, for example, to get the patient into the right job with appropriate ergonomic modifications, and the cessation of medical activity (watchful waiting). See also Treatment.

Third party A person, government agency or business not actively involved in a legal proceeding, agreement or transaction but having influence on it. A third party claim is an action by a defendant that brings a third party into a lawsuit. See also Defendants, Litigants.

Third party claim see Third party

Third-party defendants These are other parties implicated by a defendant who has said that a complete determination of a controversy cannot be made without the presence of these other parties. See also Defendants.

Thoughts see Emotional distress

Thumb From an ancient root which meant a mass, heat or swelling, it initially referred to a short, thick or swollen finger (thumb) or toe (big toe). Later it come to be restricted to the first digit (in Latin the pollex or pollux).

Time of injury see Cumulative exposure

Tinnitus From the Latin tinnio, meaning to ring, it is a ringing, buzzing, roaring, clicking or other noise in the ears. See also Vertigo.

Tissue This originally applied to a particular kind of rich, delicately woven fabric. However, in 1800, the French physiologist Bichat, who studied the structures of the body, likened the substance of the body to a woven fabric and described 21 kinds (e.g. fibrous, granulation, fat and bone).

To address the court Is to formally speak to the court (greet the court) for some special purpose.

Tolerance From the Latin tolerare, meaning to 'bear it', 'lift it' or 'carry it', it is metaphorically to hold up and keep up a burden of care, pain, grief, annoyance, etc., without sinking, lamenting or repining. Originally, tolerance referred to long-continued suffering, where to suffer (as it was used in the Bible and by Shakespeare) referred to concession. This meaning has became rare and instead it referred to allow, permit or tolerate. Nowadays, this has extended to the notion of patient endurance and is used more expressively to denote charitable leniency toward opinions or practices which are not shared by that person. Colloquially, tolerable signifies something that is moderately good or agreeable (i.e. just endurable) and the term *zero tolerance* means that no leniency or endurance is shown. A warning, in court, where legal professionals manipulate the meanings of words, it can be defined as forced acceptance without a viable choice. See also Anxiety, Pain, Pain and suffering, Tort.

Torment see Pain, Tort

Tort From the Latin *tormentum*, meaning an instrument of torture worked by twisting. *Torture* and *torment* are intense and terrible sufferings. Tort, an almost exclusively legal term, is any private or civil wrong or injury, except for breech of contract. Torts can occur by omission or commission. Although some torts can be crimes, a tort is generally thought of as an infringement on the rights of an individual. The most common tort action is a suit for damages sustained in an car accident. See also Classification of law, Due care, Libel, Malpractice, Pain, Patient abandonment, Penalty, *Res ipsa loquitur*, Slander, Suffer.

Tort feasor A wrong-doer who commits a private injury to another person from breach of duty recognized by law. See also Lawful, Liability, Malfeasance, Misfeasance, Non-feasance.

Torture see Pain, Tort,

Total rehabilitation see Self-rehabilitated

Total temporary disability see Temporary disability

Toxin In ancient Greece, as *toxon* meant a bow for shooting arrows and the word *toxeuma* referred to an arrow, *toxikos* came to mean a poison which was smeared on arrows to render them more deadly. Hence, toxin literally means a poison. Its bacteriological sense was established by Brieger, in 1888, to designate the poisonous substances elaborated by growing pathogenic organisms. Today, it is applied to any poisonous substance encountered in the practice of medicine, whether from a bacterial or chemical origin. Both can produce personal injury or illness through ingestion, inhalation or absorption through any body surface.

Traction The act of drawing or exerting a pulling force, along the axis of a structure. Practically all tractions can be analyzed into four components: (1) a *suspending part* (e.g. a Thomas splint and a Pearson attachment); (2) the *balancing force* (e.g. ropes attached to the splint); (3) the *traction force* (e.g. coming by way of a soft wrap or through a pin in the bone); and (4) the *counter-traction* or pull in the opposite direction to the traction force. With the advancement of surgical procedures, the use of traction devices has reduced, but there are certain instances when it is needed. For example, when using a full or half thigh/groin ring, particularly in women using the bed pan, the author designed a ringless traction-suspension splint for the lower limb (Bailey 1967*; 1969†). In addition, soft wrap tractions continue to be used very frequently for children (e.g. Bryant's, Russell's and halo pelvic traction, etc.).

Training see Self-discipline

Transduction see Mutation

Transference The unconscious assignment to others of feelings and attitudes that were originally associated with important figures (parents, siblings, etc.) in a person's early life. The transference relationship follows the pattern of its prototype and thus the transfer of, for example, hostile or affectionate emotional tones by the patient to the analyst based upon the unconscious identification.

Translocation see Mutation

Transmission see Inherited

Transverse (coronal) plane of the body Divides the body into front and back. See also Anatomical references, Figure 1 (page 7).

Trauma Is a Greek word for a wound which resulted from sudden physical injury or violence. Subsequently, this also included emotional wounds such as any

* Bailey, J. II (1967) Balanced traction-suspension for a fractured femur in a thrashing patient. *Clinical Orthopaedics* 51, 123-125.
† Bailey, J. II (1969) A ringless traction-suspension splint for the lower limb. *The Journal of Bone and Joint Surgery* 51A, 1012-1014.

scarring emotional experience. A traumatic injury is a wound caused by external force, including stress or strain, emotion or a physical occurrence. They can be identified as to time and place of occurrence and member or function of the body affected plus can be identified by a specific event or series of events within a single day or work shift. Traumatic injuries also include damage or destruction to prosthetic devices or appliances. See also Apportionment terms, Pathology Scope, Specific Injury.

Trauma, psychic A bad emotional shock that creates a *psychic scar* and therefore makes a lasting impression. An example would be sexual abuse during childhood. See also Hurt, Trauma.

Traumatic injuries see Trauma

Treasury bench see Bench

Treating report issues In worker's compensation cases there is an initial comprehensive report which includes treating report issues listed in Table 12. See also Report comments.

Treating reports see Report

Table 12 The issues discussed in the treating report.

(I) Core issues
(A) Causation (e.g. arising out of employment or in the course of employment)
(B) Treatment
    (1) The plan (e.g. is it operative? Is hospitalization required?)
    (2) The anticipated duration
(C) Work status (e.g. can the patient work in a regular or modified capacity and, if so, when?)
(D) Anticipated permanent and stationary date
(E) Estimates of permanent disability, if any
(F) Prediction of qualified injured worker status if any

(II) Specific case issues
(A) Medical history
(B) Physical findings
(C) Further work-up needed (e.g. tests, records, consultations and prognosis)

(III) Special interest issues
(A) Defense advocacy questions (e.g. 'Was the patient compliant?)
(B) Applicant advocacy questions (e.g. 'Explain why the patient was non-compliant')

Treatment From the Latin *trahere*, meaning to draw away, drag, handle, it is an ancient action or program of action directed at patients to restore their health or improve or stabilize function by counteracting disease and/or stimulating healing. Shamans did both by marking a magical pattern on the ground and summoning those spirits producing the disease in order to work their primitive magic on the spirits. See also Differential diagnosis, Doctor-patient relationship, Future medical treatment, Manipulation, Maximum medical improvement, Operative procedures, Surgical operation, Surgical placebo, Therapeutically beneficial, Therapies of medicine, Watchful waiting.

Trial A contest between two parties, only one of whom can win. Trials are the ultimate test and expressions of the law and there are two main types: (1) criminal trials which involve a prosecutor who acts on behalf of the community and is in opposition to the alleged offender who will be punished if found guilty; and (2) civil trials between two private persons, in which the plaintiff claims compensation for some injury said to have been caused by the defendant. Each case is peculiar in facts and circumstances.

Trial by ordeal see Anxiety, Beyond reasonable doubt, Common law, Oath

Trial components Every trial has two essential elements: (1) the court has to establish the facts of the case; and (2) it then finds the legal rule that applies. If the court consists of a jury as well as a judge, the *jury decides questions of fact* and the *judge decides questions of law*. The most difficult problem is to establish *the facts* (what actually occurred or what should have been done). For facts, the court depends upon the procedural law that includes evidence.

Trial court judges These judges have direct contact with the litigation and the litigants.

Trial de novo see De novo

Trophic changes The Greek word *trophon*, meaning food, was used to denote a relationship to nutrition or nourishment. Disturbances in the nutrition to skin, nails, subcutaneous tissues, muscles, bones and joints are called trophic changes. For example, trophic changes in the skin and nails includes glossy, smooth skin; hyperhidrosis (excessive sweating); hypohidrosis or anhidrosis (reduced or absent sweating); white, leathery skin in caucasians; cyanosis or discoloration; hypertrichosis (excess of hair), hypotrichosis (loss of hair); edema of the skin; brittle, ridged nails; and atrophic ulcers, etc. In the musculoskeletal system there may be Charcot joints, bone atrophy or osteoporosis (from paralysis or disuse) and muscle atrophy. A major cause of trophic changes is that of physical inactivity, ischemia and denervated tissues. This knowledge is very helpful in distinguishing between psychogenic and organic paralysis (i.e. prototype I and VI patients). See also Classification of medical patients.

True crimes see Felony

True medical-legal facts see Anatomical losses, Facts, Functional losses, Trust

Trust Is a practical and tranquil resting of the mind concerning the integrity, kindness, friendship or promises of a person. We have trust in parents, for example, because we believe that they will act morally in accordance with our highest standards and values, and we believe they will *act ethically* and in a socially correct manner. *Trustworthy* is applied to persons and denotes moral integrity and truthfulness. In law, trust is a fiduciary relationship whereby a *trustee* holds legal title for the benefit of another (the *beneficiary*). There is confidence placed in the trustee that he or she will take care of the property for the benefit of the beneficiary. *Confidence* is a belief, based on your experience of a person's judgments and actions, that he or she is honest and reliable. However, a trustworthy person is not necessarily a good witness because he or she may have unconscious sympathy for one party. Trust was probably borrowed from old Norse *traust*, to help, confidence, firmness. This, together with its modern German and Dutch relatives *trost* and *troost*, derive from the same ancient Germanic base that produced the English true and truth. See also Attachment, Bad faith, Doctor/patient relationship, Guardian, Empathy, Ethics, Prudence, Reasonable, Reasonable man.

Trustee see Trust

Trustworthy see Trust

Truths see Facts, Real, Trust

Tumor The Latin word *tumor* means a swelling and was applied by the ancients to any swelling of unknown

Table 13 Twelve step program to dependency rehabilitation.

Step number	What step involves
1	Admit that we are powerless over alcohol and that our lives have become unmanageable
2	Come to believe that a power greater than ourselves could restore us to sanity
3	Make a decision to turn our will and our lives over to the care of God as we understand Him to be
4	Make a searching, fearless moral inventory of ourselves
5	Admit to God, to ourselves, and to another human being the exact nature of our wrongdoing
6	We are entirely ready to have God remove all these defects of character
7	Humbly ask God to remove our shortcomings
8	Make a list of all persons I have harmed, and become willing to make amends to all of them
9	Make direct amends to such people wherever possible except when to do so would injure them or others
10	Continue to take personal inventory and when I go wrong promptly admit it
11	Sort through prayer and meditation to improve our conscious contact with God as we understand Him, praying only for knowledge of His will for us and the power to carry that out
12	Having the spiritual awakening as the result of these steps, we try to carry the message to other alcoholics and to practice these principles in all our affairs

cause and origin. Its use has continued until the present time, although meaning is now restricted to new growths such as cancers, sarcomas and other malignancies. It is wise, when talking to a patient about a tumor, to use the less frightening term 'mass'. It would require a biopsy to determine whether it is malignant. See also Dwarfs.

Turpitude Behavior that is contrary to justice, morality and honesty. See also Bad faith, Unlawful.

Twelve step program This is Alcoholics Anonymous program to rehabilitate people dependent on drugs and as taken from Alcoholics Anonymous. See Table 13 (page 139). See also Narcotic.

U

Ulnar (medial) side of the body   Describes parts nearest to the centre of the body when the little finger is next to the thigh. See also Anatomical references, Figure I (page 7), Medial, Mesial.

Umbrella term   The word given to connect several entities. See also Conversion reaction, Dwarfs, Facts, Greedy, Process.

Uncertainty see Risk

Underlying disease (or pathology)   The 'pathological scope' of a disease includes an origin, beginning, middle and end (OBME). It is this OMBE that the law calls the underlying pathology and is not ratable or apportionable, unless it becomes a rateable impairment.

Understand see Substantial

Undue influence   Somebody who subtly abuses his or her trust by overpowering a person's will and inducing the person to perform an action he or she would not freely have performed or cause him to not perform an action he would otherwise freely have performed. See also Fiduciary, Trust.

Undue stress   Is that which is greater than ordinary stress.

Unhealthy   See also Classification of medical patients, Illness and sickness, Psychogenic disease.

Uninjured see Safety

Universal witness   One who is an agreed medical examiner and a witness for both sides. See also Witness.

Universe centered   Having a goal of harmony outside oneself.

Unrelated injuries   This means that other injuries (second, third, etc.) are not directly caused by the original pilot injury. This is to be distinguished from *derivative injuries* which cause a disability to another part of the body as a direct result of the single 'pilot' injury. An example would be the patient who injured his right ankle at work and, as a result of an altered gait, started having low back pain. See also Apportionment, Pilot injury.

Unwritten law (common law)   These are laws that are enforced by courts and found in their written opinions but that are not found in statutes or ordinances.

Upper motor neuron disease   see Motor neuron disease

Usual and customary occupation   Is another legal term eluding definition or characterization. In general, it is that work which the employee has customarily performed on a regular basis over a reasonable period of time just prior to the time of injury. It is not necessarily the work which the employee last performed prior to filing a claim nor is it necessarily work in the highest skill which the worker possesses. Patient's usual and customary occupation is generally indicated on a job analysis and should be distinguished from any job or that job on a particular day. Raters generally determine these issues. See also American Disabilities Act.

V

Valgus body position Valgus is a Latin word which originally meant awry or bowlegged. In the nineteenth century, sense of the term seems to have become reversed and *genu valgus* now means *knock-kneed*. Valgus refers to the distal portion of a limb deviating away from the midline of the body. See Anatomical references, Figure 5 (page 57).

Valid From the Latin *validus*, meaning strong, effective. After observation, hypothesis and testing, the determination of validity (or verification) is the final step in reasoning by induction when using the *scientific method*. The hypothesis is verified when it accounts for all the related facts. There must be an agreement between the observed facts and the logical conclusions in the case (i.e. the hypothesis must fit the facts and the facts must fit the hypothesis). Of two 'possible' hypotheses, that one that best accounts for the greatest number of facts under consideration is preferred. In law, to *validate* or *authenticate* is to establish something as true or genuine by the testimony of an expert or authority. Official documents (e.g. passports and birth certificates, etc.) are validated and are legally binding because they are sound in form and substance. The opposite of valid is *invalid*. See also Proof, Scientific method.

Validate see Valid

Valleix phenomenon Proximal radiation of pain as a result of a hypersensitive nerve track.

Values The measure of how strongly something is, or is not, desired. This is similar to worth, which is the esteem in which qualities or quantities are, or are not, held. Values and worth may be mild, slight, moderate or extreme, whether on the positive/negative, constructive/destructive, or appropriate/inappropriate scales. *Emotions* are like/dislike opinions about value and worth judgments one makes. Medically, *normal values* are the range in concentration of specific substances found in normal healthy tissues, secretions, etc. The *liminal value* is the stimulus intensity required to just produce a noticeable impression. See also Respect.

Variance The fact or state of undergoing change or alteration; the tendency to vary or become different.

Varus A word donating position. It can relate to the foot (*talipes varus*), when it refers to inversion; to the big toe (*hallux varus*), when it means the toe is turned away from the others; and to the legs (*genu varum*), when it relates to an outward bowing in which the knee (genu) points away from the body but the legs point towards it (the person is *bowlegged*). This is determined by the most distal part of the limb. See also Anatomical references, Figure 5 (page 57).

Vasa nervorum Blood supply to nerves. See also Table 10, page 124.

Vegetative functions Autonomic nervous system activities related to growth, nutrition or homeostasis.

Vegetative signs Refer to disturbances of sleep, loss of appetite, weight loss, constipation and loss of sexual interest.

Vengeance Although it originally meant the indignant vindication of justice, today it signifies the most furious and unsparing revenge. Vengeance is often incorrectly referred to as the *avenging* of wrong by inflicting wrong equal to the injury. However, avenge is actually the unselfish settlement of a wrong, or redress for an injustice. Vengeance relates to revenge, the selfish infliction of harm because of personal anger. It is important that the doctor appreciates the difference so he or she is more tolerant of deceptive patients with avenging intents. See also Negative pleasures, Revenge, Sick pleasures.

Ventral see Anterior, Figure 1 (page 7)

Venue The place where the legal case should be heard. This is usually determined by where the plaintiff or defendant lives, where the cause of action arose or where the real property is situated. The venue can be changed. See also Change of venue, Jurisdiction.

Verbal histrionics see Histrionics

Verdict From the Latin *vere*, meaning truly, plus *dictum*, meaning saying, it is an expression of any important decision by, for example, a jury on a case in court. The truth which, as Pontius Pilate knew, is something no one can determine, is nowadays left to the finding of the 12 men or women of the jury who deliver their verdict.

Verdict, general A decision stating in general terms the ultimate conclusion that has been reached. For example, an award of $6.00 has been made to the plaintiff.

Verdict, special The jury answers a series of specific factual questions proposed by the judge, who will then determine the verdict, based on the jury's responses. This can be complicated and so does not occur often.

Verification see Hypothesis, Inductive reasoning, Prolonged, Hypothesis, Theory, Valid

Verified see Theory

Verified hypothesis see Scientific method

Vertigo Is an ancient word, which literally meant swirling or turning around, that moved into English language in the sixteenth century. Today it is considered an illusion of movement, whether this is the sensation of the external world revolving around the patient (*objective vertigo*), or the person revolving in space (*subjective vertigo*). It may result from diseases of the inner ear or may be due to disturbances of the vestibular centers or pathways in the central nervous system. Vertigo may cause dizziness, but not all dizziness is vertigo. *Dizzy* originally meant foolish and then extended to apply to a giddy, swimming or whirling sensation in the head. Nowadays, dizziness is considered a sensation of lightness in the head, of being dazed or giddy, as in the moments before fainting. Medical-legally, it is important to distinguish between dizzy and vertigo. See also Tinnitus.

Viable, viability This originally referred only to the chances of an organism's *survival*. However, it is now frequently used as a synonym for *durability* and even *success*.

Vicious delights see Revenge, Sick pleasures

Vicious pleasures see Revenge, Sick pleasures

View see Opinion

Vocational rehabilitation The provision of services that are reasonably necessary to restore a *qualified injured worker* to suitable gainful employment. Such services may include, but are not limited to, medical care, vocational evaluation, counselling, retraining, job placement assistance and job trials. Their use is an administrative decision.

Vocational rehabilitation terms See Table 14

Table 14 Terms used in vocational rehabilitation

Term	Definition
Rare	0–10% or not exceeding $\frac{1}{8}$ of a work day.
Occasionally	11–33% or between $\frac{1}{8}$ and $\frac{1}{3}$ of a work day
Frequently	34–55% or between to $\frac{1}{3}$ and $\frac{2}{3}$ of a work day
Continuously	67–100% or $\frac{2}{3}$ or more of the day
Never	It is not necessary to perform job duties
Seldom	It is performed only few times a day and then for only a short duration or not every day
Repeated	It is performed more than once every 15 minutes
Prolonged	It is performed for more than 30 minutes at each occurrence
Continuous	It involves more than 1 hour of steady work, without interruption
Excessive	The worker experiences discomfort sufficient to discontinue the activity
Repetitively	It occurs again and again, without altering action or position over a set period of time
Intermittently	Periodically occurs after an interruption

Voir dire It is literally to speak the truth and refers to the preliminary examination which the court and attorneys make of perspective jurors to determine their qualifications and suitability to serve as jurors. *Peremptory challenges* or challenges for cause may result from such examination. See also Peremptory.

Voluntary arbitration see Arbitration

Voluntary manslaughter see Manslaughter

Waffling Being uncertain in report conclusions; providing superfluous information; evasive use of language. See also Decision.

Waiting periods Remaining stationary or quiescent in expectation of something.

Waiver An intentional and voluntary surrender of some known right.

Watchful waiting/ masterful neglect/ not providing treatment see Masterful neglect

Weary see Sadness

Weighing evidence see Examination

Well-being see Health, Stoic

Whirlpool see Wordings of law

White lies see Smoke screen

WHO see impairment

Will power see Desire, Emotions

With prejudice A term applied to orders of judgments dismissing a case. It means that the plaintiff is forever prevented from bringing a lawsuit on the same claim or cause.

Without prejudice Here, the plaintiff can bring a lawsuit again on the same action.

Witnesses Persons who testify to what they have seen, heard or otherwise experienced. This is done under oath. See Also Affiant, Beyond reasonable doubt, Charge, Evidence, Eyewitness, Facts, Hearsay evidence, Hostile witness, Impeach, Oath, Material witness, Presume, Professionalism, Speculate, Trust, Universal witness, Valid.

Woolsack see Bench

Wordings of law These are often intentionally ambiguous in meaning in order to permit the infusion of new ideas. This is even true concerning the legislation or constitution of the United States of America, because the words must be adaptable. Thus, laws come to express the ideas of community. In this way, laws are like whirlpools, maintaining the same configuration while the elements and the direction change.

Words of art The vocabulary or terminology of a particular act, science or profession for which there is a particular meaning. In medicine and law there are certain expressions which are idiosyncratic or peculiar to each. In law, *last clear chance, promissory estoppel, reliance* are all words of art because they have either no or different meanings outside of the legal context. In medicine, there are terms that encompass clinical findings so that those terms convey a certain meaning or a specific concept in an abbreviated form. Examples are subjective plus and subjective minus. The worker's compensation system uses certain terms to descriptively define certain disabilities (e.g. a frozen shoulder, a frail arm and a stiff neck). Use of these terms typically results in a very high rating. In certain cases, raters tend to use 'words of art' rather than objective factors.

Words of focus see Abnormal

Work hardening programs Trained personnel show recovering patients how to do their job better and at a progressively harder pace compatible with their medical condition.

Work people People employed in manual or industrial labor for a wage — commonly called workers.

Work preclusions see Plateaus, Restrictions

Work product That work done by an attorney in the process of representing his client which is ordinarily not subject to discovery. Work product can generally be defined to encompass writings, statements, or testimony which would substantially reflect or invade an attorney's legal impressions or legal theories as to a pending or reasonably anticipated litigation. An attorney's legal impressions and theories include his/her tactics, strategy, opinions and thoughts. See also End.

Work restrictions see Plateaus, Restrictions

Working class The grade of society comprising those who are employed to work for wages in manual or industrial occupations.

Working hypothesis   see Scientific method, Hypothesis

World Health Organization, disability   see Disability, Impairment

World Health Organization, impairment   see Impairment

Worldly see Origin

Worldly morals see Reasonable

Worry see Anxiety

Wrist see Figure 6, page 59

Writ A formal legal writing; a judicial order directing a person to do something. See also Process.

Writ Of Ceriorari A discretionary proceeding by which an appellate court may review the rulings of a subordinate tribunal. See also Appeal.

Written law Rules of court enacted by the legislative branch. See also Civil law, Classification of law.

Wrongful death Death resulting from those who committed wrongs or injustices to another.

X

Xeroradiography A relatively new process whereby X-ray images may be obtained through the electrostatic process without the use of films, darkrooms or chemicals.

X-ray and work sheet This is the booking form for new patients.

Xystus This is derived from the ancient Greek verb *xystos*, to scrape or polish. It referred to a long covered portico that was used by Greek athletes for exercising in bad weather or during the winter. The Romans applied xystus to any open colonnade or tree-planted walk. Nowadays it refers to a surgical instrument for scraping bones.

Y

Yes but see Affirmative defense

Yelp Pride, boasting; also a quick sharp cry.

Yin and yang The symbol central to the ancient Chinese philosophy of Taoism, is an excellent teaching example to show balance and harmony involving differences. The black yin represents the female, darkness, inwardness, yielding and the unknown, while the white yang symbolizes the male, light, protrusion, aggressiveness and the overt. Interlocking to create a whole, one appears to fall to earth, the other rising heavenward. Both fit snugly together to form a circle, perhaps as parts turning around one another, or holding forever fast. In either case, the entire figure has no beginning or end. Yin and yang can function as a graph in which complementary relationships are described. Both represent nature's ability to keep things in balance in a constantly shifting process of give and take in the medical-legal arena or elsewhere.

Youthful offender A youth varying in age from 16–19 who has committed a crime not punishable by death or life imprisonment and has not previously been convicted of a felony.

Z

Zeal Consuming earnestness, always tending to vigorous action, though often without the hopefulness of enthusiasm. Unreasoning zeal, especially if excessive is fanaticism.

Zealous Meaning fervent plus earnest, it comes from the Greek *zelos* meaning emulation or rivalry, and still contains the idea of persistence in pursuit.

Zeitgeist A German word meaning the spirit of the age; the typical attitude of the times; the characteristic moral or intellectual feeling of a particular era; the trend of culture and taste of a period in history. The zeitgeist of the Periclean Age (461–431 BC) of ancient Greece was the attainment of greatness in the arts (i.e. architecture, sculpture, music and drama). The zeitgeist of the middle ages operated against scientific investigation.

Zenith The point in the sky straight above ones head. Figuratively it is the 'nothing-beyond-which-point'. Its antonym is nadir.

Zero mode see Abnormal

Zero tolerance see Tolerance

Zolaism Means calling 'a spade a spade'. It is based upon the name of Emile Zola, a French novelist, known for his bald and detailed realism and absence of reserve.

Zygote From the Greek *zygosis*, meaning a yoking or joining together, it is the cell resulting from union of a male (sperm) and female (ovum) gamete, until it divides. More precisely, the cell after synapsis at the completion of fertilization until first cleavage. See also Heritable.